The Roman Frontier with Persia in North-Eastern Mesopotamia

The Roman Frontier with Persia in North-Eastern Mesopotamia

Fortresses and roads around Singara

Anthony Comfort

Archaeopress Roman Archaeology 96

ARCHAEOPRESS PUBLISHING LTD
Summertown Pavilion
18-24 Middle Way
Summertown
Oxford OX2 7LG
www.archaeopress.com

ISBN 978-1-80327-342-6
ISBN 978-1-80327-343-3 (e-Pdf)

Cover: walls of Singara, a photo taken by Aurel Stein in 1938. Courtesy British Academy and APAAME. For some other photos of Singara in this series see https://www.flickr.com/photos/apaame/17424160461/in/photostream/

This book is available direct from Archaeopress or from our website www.archaeopress.com

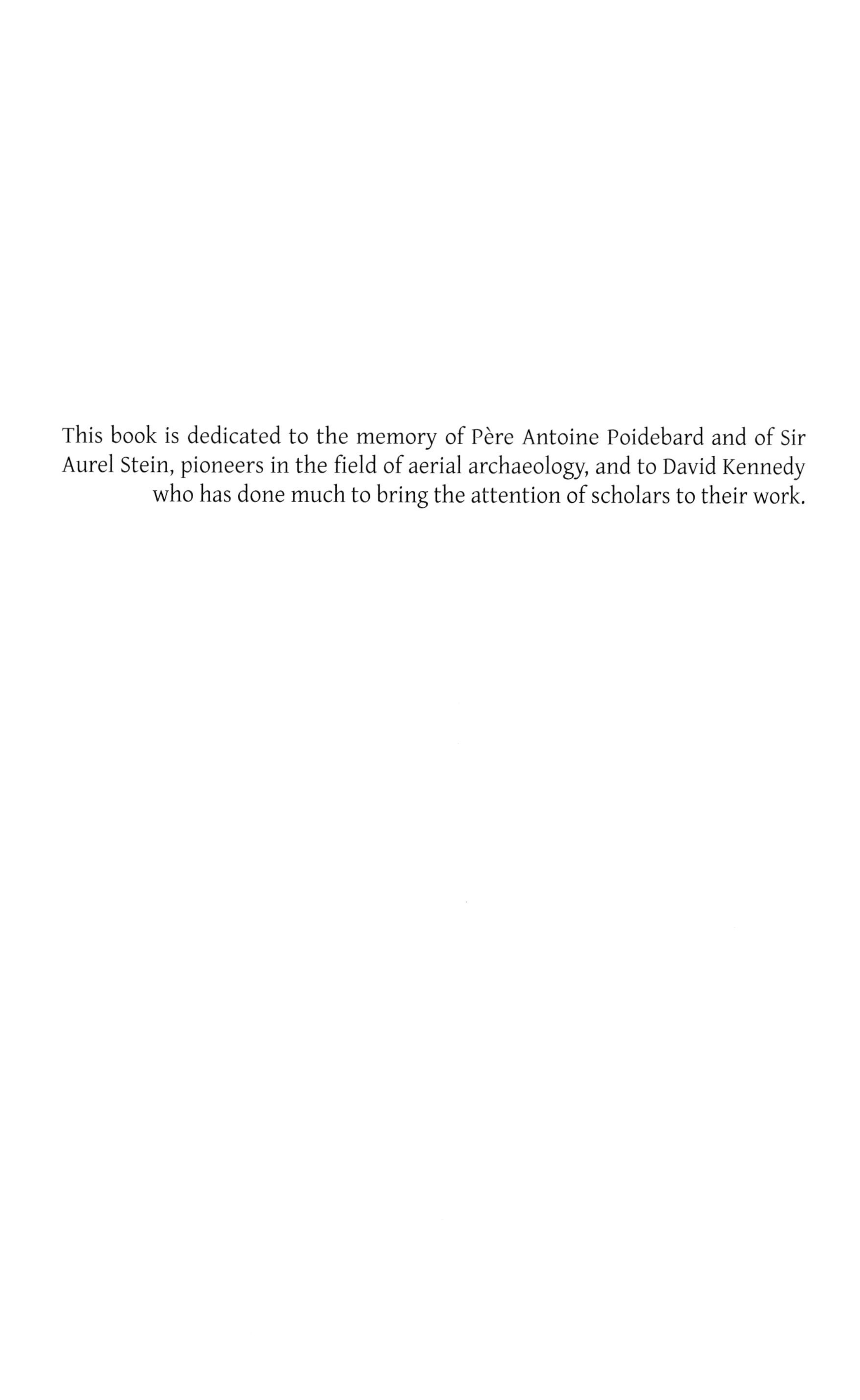

This book is dedicated to the memory of Père Antoine Poidebard and of Sir Aurel Stein, pioneers in the field of aerial archaeology, and to David Kennedy who has done much to bring the attention of scholars to their work.

Contents

List of Figures and Tables

Chapter 1

Introduction

This book is a study of the historical geography of north-east Mesopotamia during the period when it was a centre of conflict between the Roman empire and its only true rivals in Late Antiquity: the Parthians and then the Sasanian Persians. It is the outcome of a personal interest in Rome's eastern frontier dating back many years. In 1995 the writer began visiting and working with a Franco-Turkish archaeological team around Zeugma, firstly a large Hellenistic and then a Roman city on the Euphrates, which became the main crossing point of the river for the Seleucid kingdom (from 312 to 63 BCE) and then an important link between Rome and Parthia. He conducted a broad one-person survey of the areas to be inundated by the dams at Birecik and Carchemish (completed in 2000), as a member of the team then excavating the sites of Zeugma on both banks of the river.[1] David Kennedy was a mentor and inspiration for this work which made use of Russian satellite photography, then easily available.

Because of the recent impossibility of visiting south-east Turkey, north-east Syria and much of northern Iraq as an archaeologist – and even of obtaining recent aerial photographs – for the moment the study of the historical geography of these areas has to rely on satellite imagery. Archaeologists are fortunate now to have easy free access to the satellite photos on Google Earth but especially to the Corona series of black and white photos taken from space in 1967 and 1968 (see box at end of this chapter).

The Birecik dam inundated much of the ruins of the city of Zeugma itself (which was preceded by the twin Hellenistic cities of Seleuceia and Apamea, located respectively on the east and west banks of the river), but also many other remains from antiquity, including several other crossing points of the river Euphrates and especially that at Ayni. The latter had probably once been known as 'Capersana' during the Roman period and is located some 30 kilometres north of Zeugma.[2]

The results of the author's work on the Euphrates were published in *Anatolian Studies* (2000; Comfort and Ergeç 2001) and led to a strong personal interest in the ancient roads and fortresses of the region, especially to the east of the river Euphrates. When he later conducted research for a doctorate at Exeter University, supervised by Stephen Mitchell (Comfort 2009[3]), it was natural that these would be the focus of the thesis. To collect material for this he was at that time able to travel widely in south-east Turkey, especially the upper Tigris valley, and also visited Cyrrhus and the northern sections of the Euphrates valley in Syria. These visits made possible a series of articles on fortresses of the Tur Abdin and on roads and bridges of the region, which built on research conducted on the ground for the doctoral thesis.[4] Very regrettably the completion in 2020 of the Ilısu dam on the Tigris, near the point at which

[1] See Zeugma 1 to V, Istanbul and Lyons. Also Wagner 1976, Kennedy 1998, Aylward 2013.
[2] Following Dussaud 1927: 459-460
[3] The date of this thesis has been referred to by other scholars as 2008 but it was not in fact approved until 2009.
[4] Comfort 2011, 2017, 2018, 2021

Map 1. Setting, showing area of concern

Turkey's frontier joins those of Syria and Iraq, has now inundated much of the upper Tigris valley too.

After his work in south-east Turkey, in 2016 the writer participated in the 'Eastern Habur Archaeological Survey' conducted by the University of Tübingen.[5] This provided an opportunity to investigate remains from classical antiquity in the Kurdish region of northern Iraq. A book, co-authored with Michal Marciak, discusses the remains along the Tigris valley

[5] The eastern Habur is a tributary river of the Tigris whose lower reaches form the current border between Turkey and Iraq. It has to be distinguished from the western Habur – or Khabur – which is the river that is central to much of this book and joins the Euphrates at Circesium (Busairah).

north of Mosul, including the sections of the valley in south-east Turkey around Diyarbakir and up to its source in Lake Hazar (Comfort and Marciak 2018).

These visits to the region did not include tours of the sites in northern Mesopotamia south of the Syria/Turkey frontier, that is, on the west bank of the Tigris in eastern Syria and in northern Iraq. The security conditions in these regions still make travel very hazardous and even in south-east Turkey the security situation has made it difficult for archaeologists to visit and obtain permits.

Nevertheless, in recent years this part of the eastern frontier of the Roman Empire has begun to attract the attention which it deserves. Mitford recently published the results of a lifetime studying the frontier in eastern Turkey (2018). Various studies of the region to the south, especially in eastern Syria and northern Iraq, had already made use initially of aerial photographs - and more recently of satellite imagery. The collection of aerial photographs taken by Poidebard in the 1930s,[6] and also those used by Van Liere and Lauffray, are no longer accessible, although a large number of Stein's aerial photographs stored at the British Academy have recently been made available online by APAAME.[7] Further aerial surveys have not been possible in the wider region of the Near East, except to a limited extent in Jordan.[8] However, satellite photography available from Google Earth, but especially the Corona imagery of the 1960s (now made easily accessible via the website of the University of Arkansas[9]), have compensated to some extent for the impossibility of obtaining more aerial photos.

Most archaeological studies of this region of north-eastern Mesopotamia have been concerned primarily with sites of the Bronze Age, but some general studies have recently been published which have elucidated the history of the region in the later Roman empire, up to the military expansion of the Arabs following their unification by the prophet Muhammad. The battles of the Yarmuk and Qadisiyya (both in 636 CE) put an end to the Roman presence in Syria and Mesopotamia, as well as entirely eliminating the Persian Empire of the Sasanians. The Arab invasions thus constitute a simple way of bringing the study of Roman Mesopotamia and the frontier with Persia to an end.

This book addresses the most eastern parts of the Roman empire south of Armenia and in particular those bordering the frontier with Persia. It concentrates on the area around Singara, a military outpost on or near this frontier which became a small city and a Roman colony under the emperor Septimius Severus - or possibly as early as the emperor Marcus Aurelius. Singara is now situated in northern Iraq; this book thus complements the study of those roads and fortresses along the Romano-Persian frontier in south-east Turkey, which were the main object of the writer's doctoral thesis (Comfort 2009).

The fortress-city of Singara was surrendered to the Persians by Jovian, following the disastrous outcome of the emperor Julian's expedition to Ctesiphon, capital of the Sasanian empire, in

[6] The photographic plates published in the second volume of this work (but not yet the text in the first volume) may be consulted at http://digital.library.stonybrook.edu/cdm/ref/collection/amar/id/155083 .

[7] www.apaame.org and https://www.flickr.com/photos/apaame/albums/72157652009016911 - accessed 31/01/2022

[8] Poidebard 1934, Gregory and Kennedy 1985, Riley 1986, Kennedy and Bewley 2004. Some of Stein's photos are included in an archive of Stein material at the British Academy. These have been scanned by APAAME and are available on-line.

[9] https://corona.cast.uark.edu/. It should be noted however that the resolution of some Corona imagery is poor.

363 CE. It was again captured by the general Maurice in 578 CE shortly before he became emperor,[10] but after 363 it had lost its significance as a crucial element of the Roman frontier.

Thus, the book concerns principally the period from Trajan's invasion of Persia in 115 to 363 CE, although the subsequent years up to the Arab conquest of Syria and Mesopotamia are also part of the story. It seeks to review existing studies of the frontier but also to provide some new information about the roads and fortresses of the area. Because of the difficulties associated with travel in the region it too relies on the aerial photographs of Poidebard and Stein and on satellite imagery to illustrate the places discussed. The Peutinger Table is also used extensively to situate routes and various places of importance during the conflict between Rome and Persia in this region of northern Mesopotamia.

Although travel has become difficult or impossible in recent years various early writers in Arabic have described north-east Mesopotamia, known to them as the Jazira, in summary fashion; these include Ibn Shaddad, Ibn Hawqal (born in Nisibis), al-Maqdisi, al-Qazwini and Ibn Battuta. Yaqut states that it was the birthplace in around 1086 CE of Sultan Sinjar (or Sanjar), son of Malik Shah and one of the greatest Seljuks.[11] (This writer does not speak Arabic and has relied for the most part on Le Strange's summary of 1905). European travellers did visit the region in the nineteenth and early twentieth centuries and in some cases their accounts are of value for understanding its ancient history and geography. In particular, Forbes (1839); Layard (1853); Sachau (1883); Von Oppenheim (1899, 1900: Vol II); Sarre and Herzfeld (1911-1920). In the mid-twentieth century visitors specifically interested in the region's archaeology included Mallowan (1936a, b), Lloyd (1938), Oates (1956, 1968, Oates and Oates 1959) and Ibrahim (1986). Hauser has recently discussed the road network around Hatra (1995, Hauser and Tucker 2009) and for this reason this paper treats Hatra only briefly. (Its relationship with Rome in the years before its destruction by Shapur I in 240/241 CE remains obscure.)

Other writers on the historical geography of the region whose work has been important in the preparation of this book include Chapot (1907), Dussaud (1927), Dillemann (1962) and, for later periods, Honigmann (1935). Recent works include Wheeler (2007), Edwell (2008), Cameron (2018) and Palermo (2019 – especially Chapter 3). '*Roman Military Architecture on the Eastern Frontier*', Shelagh Gregory's doctoral thesis, published by Hakkert (1995), together with her article in 'The Roman Army in the East' (1996), have also been an important source of information for some of the fortresses of the region as have both the text and the photos published in 'Rome's Desert frontier from the air' (Kennedy and Riley 1990). Harrel's recent study entitled 'The Nisibis War; the defence of the Roman East AD 337-363' is a valuable addition to the material available for that period (2016) although there is room for doubt about several events which he portrays as certainties.

Earlier studies of roads in northern Mesopotamia have concerned the region of Hatra, 110km to the south-east of Nisibis (Altaweel and Hauser 2004, also using Corona satellite imagery) and the Jaghjagh valley, 80kms to the north-west (Palermo 2015). This book concerns only

[10] Theophylact Simocatta iii.16.1

[11] However the Jazira was defined in the 13th century CE by Izz ad Din ibn Chaddad (or Shaddad) as a wide region including the Diyar Modar (Harran and Rakka), the Diyar Rabi'a (Nisibis, Ras el- Ain, Cizre and Sinjat), as well as the Diyar Bakr (Amid/Diyarbakır, Mayarfarqin/Silvan, Hisn Keyf, Arzan and Mardin (Cahen 1937). In this book it is thus only the Diyar Rabi'a which is concerned.

north-eastern Mesopotamia as far north as the Tur Abdin whose escarpment runs east-west some 4 to 30km north of the Berlin to Bagdad railway (which constitutes the current border between Turkey and Syria for over 300km). It seeks to offer a new approach to studies of Rome's eastern frontier by presenting and illustrating the known sites, some of which have already been discussed in Kennedy and Riley 1990, a book which includes many interesting reproductions of photos taken especially by Poidebard and Stein.

The author thanks in particular Eberhard Sauer for his invaluable comments and support and also Chris Lightfoot and Peter Edwell for their observations on an early version of this book, which was more especially directed to the study of the road network. There will certainly remain errors and omissions for which of course the author is solely responsible.

Aerial photography, satellite imagery and maps

Although aerial photographs taken for purposes of mapping are known to exist for Syria and Iraq, as well as for south-east Turkey, these are not available to archaeologists. Apart from the photos taken by Poidebard in 1929 and subsequent years for Syria and in the late 1930s by Aurel Stein for northern Iraq, which are discussed below, such photos were available for study by some earlier writers, but have not been seen for decades.

In the 1960s the United States began a series of space flights by satellites for reconnaissance purposes. In view of their great scientific interest, President Clinton made these publicly available from 1995. The University of Arkansas has mounted a website for the Middle East which allows easy access to the best of these black and white Corona photos. In many cases several photos of the same area can be seen and compared, with recent satellite images such as those from Google providing a backdrop to allow easy identification of sites' location. Apart from the physical evidence of ancient sites provided by such imagery, the names of many - essentially pre-historic – sites are also provided on this Corona website of Arkansas University (https://corona.cast.uark.edu/).

Although the quality and resolution of these photos can vary substantially, they are of immense importance to archaeologists because they show the landscape of the 1960s, in many areas unchanged since the Roman period. Since then, modern agriculture and the construction of housing and infrastructure have severely modified this landscape. The CAST site of Arkansas has the additional advantage that it allows images to be copied with a scale bar in place. Data from more recent US satellite missions are now also available (in particular, see U2 Aerial Photography | Jason Ur (harvard.edu), but these are much more difficult to consult.

Now almost everyone with access to the internet may also visit the satellite imagery made available for the whole world by Google Earth. Here too the quality of the available imagery is varied. In some cases, archived images can show detail not available in the most recent imagery. The images freely available from the website 'Zoom Earth' also used to show features not visible on Google Earth but have recently become less useful. Other high-resolution imagery is available for purchase. Unfortunately, the cost is usually prohibitive for a study involving a wide area such as this.

One evident advantage of the location of a site on modern satellite imagery is the immediate availability of coordinates. In this book these co-ordinates are provided as degrees, minutes and seconds to allow for easy verification and checks on the ground.

All satellite images reproduced below are shown with north at the top. Occasionally this is not the case for the aerial photographs of Poidebard and Stein which may be oriented differently. All Corona images are credited hereby to the 'Center for Advanced Spatial Technologies, University of Arkansas/U.S. Geological Survey'. Only the date is provided in the text below for such images since the other data specific to each image is readily available from the CAST site of the University of Arkansas. The credits for other satellite imagery are indicated with the image.

Maps 2, 3 and 4 were drawn by the author using an extract of Tactical Pilotage Chart G-4B as a base and the programme MapMaker Pro. The constraints of the base-map precluded extension to the south to include Circesium and Hatra and the coordinates in latitude and longitude meant that scalebars could only be approximate.

Chapter 2

Geographical and historical background

This section of the book seeks to provide readers with a short geographic and historical context for the roads and fortresses described later. North-east Mesopotamia - and Singara in particular - lies just to the north of the 250mm isohyet line, below which rain-fed agriculture is no longer possible. The line of the Sinjar hills, clearly visible from Mardin, 135kms to the north-west, creates a visual barrier separating the rich agricultural plains below the southern escarpment of the Tur Abdin from the much dryer regions to the south. Most of these plains constitute the area of eastern Syria now occupied by Kurds and known as Rojava.

Descending south from the Tur Abdin are several water courses, especially the Western Khabur river which originates in deep springs at Resaina and then travels eastwards to the current major town of Haseke before turning south to the Euphrates, which it joins near the Roman fortress of Circesium. This place remained an essential anchor-point of the frontier for several hundred years and is discussed below in Chapter 3. Other rivers leading south include the Jaghjagh (sometimes spelt 'Djaghdjagh'), known to the Greeks as the *Mygdonius*. This descends from the Tur Abdin past the ancient city of Nisibis to join the Khabur near Hasaké and the two rivers together constitute a north-south line to the Euphrates which appears to have been the frontier in Mesopotamia between Roma and Persia from 363 CE until the seventh century.

The book examines the frontier in Mesopotamia from the time of Trajan through to the Arab conquests but especially the period 115 to 363 CE when this frontier was extended eastwards from Nisibis and the Jaghjagh/Khabur line to the Tigris. At some point the river Tigris did in fact constitute the frontier but it is uncertain how far south Roman control extended and for how long. It is possible that for a period the eastern-most extent of the empire reached what is now the city of Mosul on the west bank of the Tigris, opposite the ancient Assyrian city of Nineveh which was still in existence on the east bank during the Sasanian period.

The line of the frontier between Rome and the Parthians and then the Sasanians appears to have changed on many occasions and these changes are discussed in Chapter 5 below. But after the loss of Singara in 363 to Shapur II the frontier north from Circesium (at the confluence of the Euphrates with the western Khabur river) remained rather stable as far as the Tur Abdin (which it probably circumvented in an eastwards bulge to the Tigris river). After 363 it went north from the Euphrates to a point near the fortress of Thannouris, described below, and the modern city of Hasaké, and then continued north along the line of the Jaghjagh river to a point west of Nisibis. It then probably followed the eastern and northern edge of the Tur Abdin along the river Tigris to its junction with the river Batman before crossing the Taurus mountains.[1] The changes in the frontier are also discussed by Frézouls (1981).

Singara (modern Sinjar) was a Roman city and fortress near the most easterly point of the frontier of the Roman empire in Mesopotamia; the city and its region are likely to have been

[1] For a discussion of the line of the frontier in this region see Comfort 2009: 229-244.

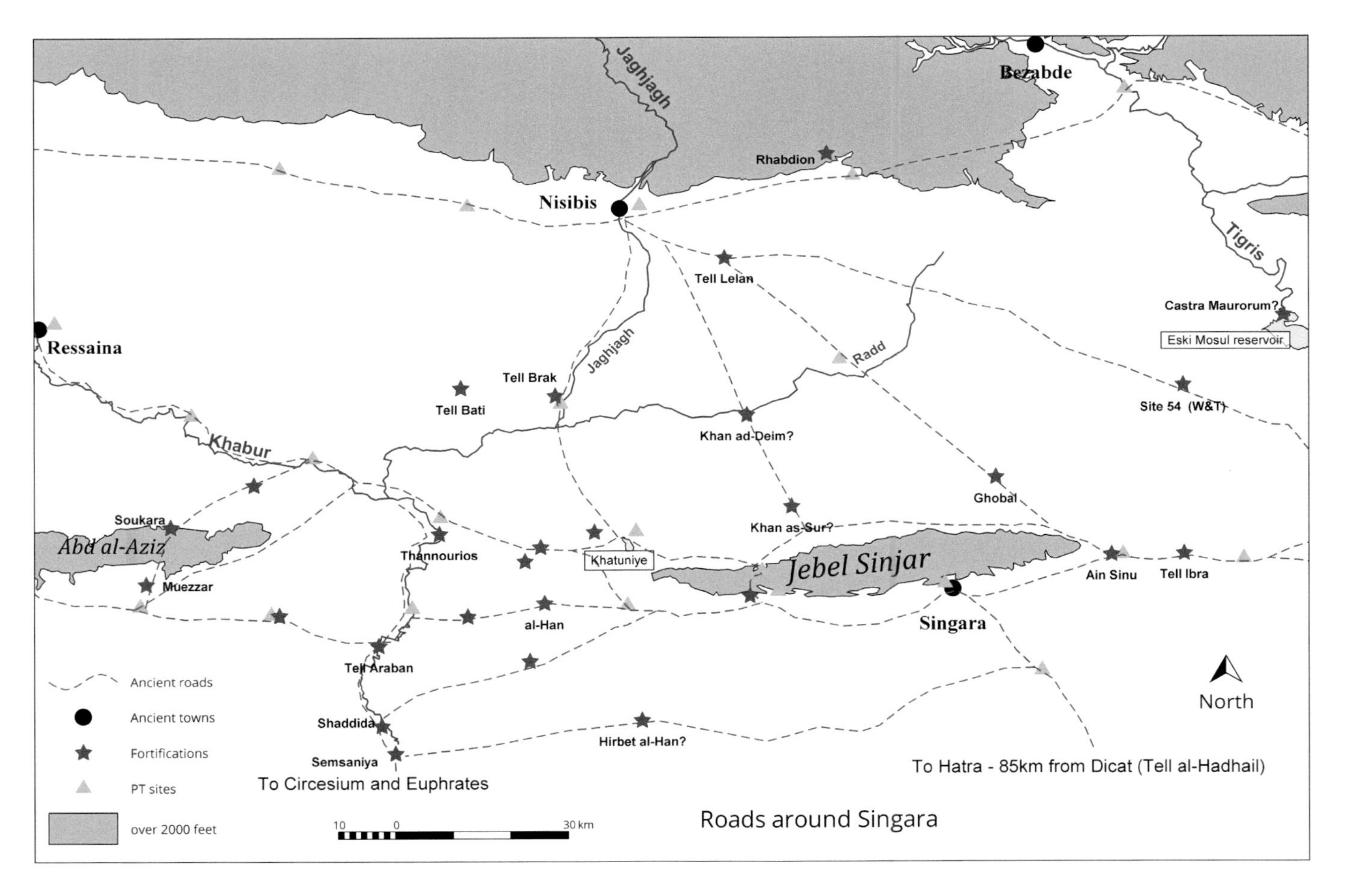

Map 2. Fortresses and roads

controlled by Rome for much of the nearly 200 years between 167 and 363 CE,[2] when the city is known to have been formally surrendered to the Persians by the emperor Jovian after the death of his predecessor, Julian. It is situated at the southern foot of a large mountain chain (Jebel Sinjar, maximum elevation 1463m) and lies 115 km due west of Nineveh. It is uncertain whether the Roman frontier ever reached Mosul/Nineveh on the west bank of the Tigris. More probably at its maximum extent the junction of the Roman frontier with the river Tigris was at Eski Mosul, known as Shahrabadh in Sasanian Persia but Balad in the early Islamic period. This ancient city has been partially excavated, but the excavation reports are still not available.[3] It lies 49km north-west of Mosul itself.

In regard to Mosul in Late Antiquity, a Sasanian fort at the site of the modern city protected the bank opposite Nineveh and there was probably also a small settlement with a bridge across the river (Morony 1982: 7;[4] the role of Nineveh as a Sasanian stronghold on the Tigris is discussed in Simpson 1996: 95-98; for the archaeological evidence of Roman activity across the river at Nineveh see also Eiland 1998).[5]

The importance of the Sasanian presence in north-east Mesopotamia has been more recognised since publication of work on the Gorgan Wall at the south-east corner of the Caspian (Sauer, Rekavandi et al. 2013); in the latter work reference is made also to the fortifications of north-east Mesopotamia. The book on Sasanian Persia edited by Sauer (2017) has done much to bring the period to the attention of scholars and in particular its chapter on Sasanian cities by St John Simpson which firmly places Sasanian Persia as an urban civilisation fully comparable to the later Roman empire (2017).

The study of the historical geography of northern Mesopotamia must inevitably involve a large number of place-names - ancient, early modern and actual. In many cases, the modern identification of ancient names is difficult if not impossible. The reader's forbearance is requested since the text risks becoming indigestible, but various maps are provided which should aid comprehension.

Roman occupation of much of the more western parts of the region continued until the reign of Phocas and control was only lost definitively at the time of the Arab invasions. But for north-eastern Mesopotamia CE 363 is the crucial year: following the death of the emperor Julian, his successor Jovian surrendered to the Persians Nisibis, Singara and Castra Maurorum. Singara had in fact already fallen after a lengthy siege to the Persians in 360, despite the presence of two legions, I Parthica and I Flavia.[6] In 363 its loss became definitive.

[2] According to Chapot (1907: 300), the status of colonia had already been awarded to Singara by Marcus Aurelius. Chapot cites as a source Joseph Eckhel (Doctrina numorum veterum, 8 vol., Vienne, 1792-1798, III.519).

[3] Seton Lloyd 1938 only lists this site (his site 1), mentioning s 'Ruins of a very considerable Islamic town, lying on the west bank of the Tigris. At the northern end, a rectangular fortified khan3 stands upon a mound dating from a much earlier period.' There was apparently an important ford here; See Comfort and Marciak 2018: 65-68.

[4] Morony cites (n71) Baladhuri, Tabari and Ya'qubi. See also Comfort and Marciak 2018: 62. No archaeological remains are known of this fort.

[5] For the possibility if a Roman outpost south of Mosul and not proven archaeologically, see Kennedy, 1988.

[6] Ammianus Marcellinus XX, 6.7 and XXV, 7.9.

For much of the period 100 to 640 Northern Mesopotamia was the principal battleground in the struggle for supremacy between Roma and Persia, although Armenia to the north was frequently also a bone of contention.

Like Armenia, the area which is now eastern Syria and northern Iraq was converted to Christianity rather early. Edessa, in north-western Mesopotamia, then known as Osrhoene, was an important centre for the Syriac language and for religious studies. After the surrender of Nisibis in 363 CE, the school of Edessa had taken on the role as the principal centre for religious education for the whole region, but this was closed by the emperor Zeno in 489 and the main school returned to Nisibis. The development of Christianity in the Sasanian empire was sometimes the source of doubts at the Persian court in Ctesiphon concerning the loyalty of Christian subjects at times of conflict with the late Roman empire. However, especially after the first Council of Nicaea in 325 CE, the doctrinal splits within Christianity between monophysites and dyophysites (also known as Chalcedonians or Melkites) and the rise of Nestorianism especially in the east provided an identity for Persian Christians separate from that of the majority within the eastern Roman empire.[7] This permitted Christianity to flourish also in lands controlled by Persia.

It was the Council of Chalcedon in 451 which gave rise to serious divisions in Syria and Mesopotamia between monophysites and dyophysites. These are discussed by Hugh Kennedy. The monastery of Qartmin, once closely associated with the imperial court and situated just to the north of the area discussed here, was later especially active as a monophysite centre and ensured the failure of efforts to resolve the dispute which culminated in the council of Callinicum in 567 called by the emperor Justin II (Kennedy 2000: especially 599).

Mount Sinjar appears in an early saints' life of the sixth century and seems to have had a distinct identity - maintained through the occupation of the area by Yezidis from the fourth century CE until the recent past (Lescot 1938). The saint, known from an Arab chronicle as Abd-el Masih, was a young man from a Jewish family, who was martyred apparently in 391 CE and who had friends in the Zoroastrian and Christian communities of Sinjar.[8] Peeters, the editor of this 'Life', considers this reference to Zoroastrian ('*Perses mazdéens*'), Christian and Jewish communities living together in the later fourth century anachronistic,[9] but he does also mention some early Christian bishops in Sinjar and the visit of John, bishop of Tella (now Viranşehir), to the mountain in 536/7.[10] Northern Mesopotamia was a hotbed of religious innovation from the second century CE with the Elkasaites and Manichaeans also being active in this area.[11] From the mid-third century Sasanian monarchs sought to promote

[7] For a study of the impact of religious dissension on northern Mesopotamia see Hammond 1987: 294-314..

[8] La passion arabe de S. Abd al-Masih, Peeters 1926. See also Fiey and Conrad 2004 : number 10 (88 and 238 also had links with Mount Sinjar).

[9] Peeters: 281; anachronistic presumably because Ammianus tells us that Shapur had removed the population of Singara to Persia.

[10] In a remarkable instance of collaboration between the forces of the Sassanian marzban in Nisibis and those of the late Roman commander based in an expedition was mounted to capture John; when he was apparently seeking to spread Monophysite beliefs. *Vita Iohannnis episcopi Tellae, auctire Elia,* ed. EW Brooks, 1907, Corpus scriptorium christianorum orientaluium, Scr. Syri, Ser.3, Vol XXV, p66

[11] Socrates Scholasticus included an account of Mani which formed the basis of Western traditions concerning Mani for centuries, but his account appears to be largely false. No good modern account seems to be available. Mani's own writings were for the most part written in Syriac.

Zoroastrianism as the state religion, partly under the influence of a Zoroastrian priest called Kartir,[12] active during the reign of Shapur I.

Much later, in the twelfth century CE, the Jewish traveller Benjamin of Tudela does not appear to have visited Singara although he does describe journeys to Ras el-Ain, Cizre, Mosul and Carchemish, all of which still did have Jewish communities.[13] He must have gone past Singara on his way from Mosul to Raqqa. That is presumably an indication that at that time no substantial Jewish community remained in Singara, but also that the route east from Mosul on the Tigris to Carchemish on the western Khabur remained in use at least until the twelfth century.

In modern times the first European visitor to Sinjar was Forbes who describes the Yezidi villages in some detail but mentions no Christians then living on the mountain, although local people told him that it had formerly been inhabited by Christians and he did see the site of a monastery near Bukrah (1839: 417[14]). Already then the mountain was occupied by Yezidis, whose beliefs are monotheistic and stem originally from Mithraism and Zoroastrianism, at least in part.[15]

****

In regard specifically to the history of Roman occupation of north-east Mesopotamia up to the fateful year of 363, a Roman province of Mesopotamia was created firstly by Trajan in CE 115, but this was soon abandoned by Hadrian. The province was re-conquered, perhaps by the general Avidius Cassius (acting for the co-emperor of Marcus Aurelius, Lucius Verus), following his capture of Ctesiphon and Seleuceia in 165.[16] In the same year Cassius' colleague Martius Verus re-occupied Edessa and captured Nisibis, after which the Parthian king Vologases IV ceded parts of Mesopotamia to Rome. In 166 Cassius is known to have crossed the Tigris into 'Media' (Adiabene?), but this does not seem to have involved any permanent occupation.

There is then a thirty-year interlude for which no information is available concerning northern Mesopotamia. But in the year 197 CE Septimius Severus attacked Ctesiphon and, when he retired, he left two legions to defend the province. Singara was captured (at this time if not before) and was fortified by the Romans who made it the base of Legio I Parthica, as is attested by an inscription from a legionary veteran's funerary from Aphrodisias (Oates 1956; Speidel and Reynolds 1985): "...[I Parthica] *which legion is at Singara in Mesopotamia by the river Tigris*". Together with Nisibis, Resaina and Carrhae/Harran, Singara was given the status of a Roman colonia by Septimius Severus (Millar 1990: 38-9).

[12] Also called Kirder. For a discussion of his role see Panaino 2016.
[13] Benjamin of Tudela 1983
[14] Possibly the monastery of Bar Tura, mentioned by Fiey as existing near Singara town in the seventh century (2004: numbers 165 and 455)
[15] For the history of the Yezidis see Lescot 1938.
[16] For the possibility that Singara was already awarded colonial status see the following note and Gregory and Kennedy 1985: 385. Bivar believed that the frontier incorporated Singara from this time (1983: 94): '..as a consequence of the expeditions of AD 165 and 166, the Roman frontier was fixed on the line of the Jebel Sinjar, of the Chabora (Khabur) and of Dura-Europos'.

In around 226 CE the last Parthian ruler was defeated in Fars by Ardashir, the founder of the Sasanian dynasty, which was more aggressive in its attempts to regain control of northern Mesopotamia and may possibly have held ambitions to restore the boundaries of the Achaemenid empire (see sources included in Dodgeon and Lieu 1991: 16, especially Dio Cassius LXXX, 4, 1-2; however, the link between the external actions of the Sasanians and the Achaemenids is doubted *inter alios* by Shayegan (2011)).

Ardashir had attacked Armenia – apparently unsuccessfully - already in 226 and then turned his attention to the Roman empire. According to Herodian (VI, 2, 5-6) he overran Mesopotamia and besieged '*the Roman garrison camps on the banks of the rivers, the camps which defended the empire*'. Another Roman historian, Zonaras, says (XII, 15) that the Persians overran Cappadocia and put Nisibis under siege (Dodgeon and Lieu 1991: 17). In response, the emperor Alexander Severus (reigned 222-235) is said by Herodian to have organised a campaign; but the three armies sent to Persian territory did not fare well and the central thrust was defeated by Ardashir (Herodian VI, 5, 1-6). The final siege of Hatra, probably allied to the Romans, and its fall to the Sasanians under Ardashir's son, Shapur (known from this time as the shahanshah Shapur I, possibly in CE 240, is discussed by Hauser (2009). It appears to have set the seal on Sasanian control of southern Mesopotamia, while Rome remained dominant in the north. The end result seems to have been a stalemate (Palermo 2019: 43).

When Alexander Severus departed from Antioch to fight incursions across the Danube, Herodian states (VI, 7, 1-6) that he left behind a force which he considered strong enough to defend the Roman frontiers; he ensured that the camps and outposts were given more efficient defences and assigned to each camp its normal complement of troops. Alexander Severus even claimed in the Roman Senate that he had defeated Ardashir. Although this seems unlikely to have been true, the milestone found SE of Singara (see below) is an indication that the frontier road was held and used during his reign and that control of Singara, as well as Nisibis, was retained. The fall of Hatra to the Persians, despite possible Roman assistance, in 240 is briefly discussed below (for the sources see Dodgeon and Lieu 1991: 33).

Just two or three years later in 243, when Ardashir had been succeeded by his son Shapur I, the emperor Gordian III mounted a further expedition against Persia. Its success is disputed; following an initial Roman victory at Resaina (Ras el-Ain), the Persians claimed to have won a great battle at 'Meshike' (later renamed 'Peroz-Sabour'), apparently near the Persian capital at Ctesiphon, but this battle is not mentioned by Roman sources. Coins of Gordian were minted at Singara between CE 242 and 244; their reverses describe Singara as a Roman colony (Reverse: AVP CEΠ KOL C[I]NΓAPA – Aurelia Septimia Colonia Singara[17]). In any case, Gordian was then assassinated and replaced by Philip, who withdrew the army, but only after a large tomb had been constructed for Gordian near Circesium, at the confluence of the western Khabur and the Euphrates.[18] Philip apparently ceded much territory to the Persians, but at least Resaina and Nisibis remained in Roman hands until 252/3.

[17] According to Weissbach RE III A/1 col 232; Singara was made a Roman colony under Alexander Severus and Philip the Arab on the basis of the numismatic evidence; but according to Schachermeyer RE XV/1 col 1160 colonia status was awarded under Marcus Aurelius. If Schachermeyer is correct, then Singara may have become a colony as early as the campaigns of Lucius Verus.

[18] The position of Gordian's tomb is mentioned in the Historia Augusta (the three Gordians, 34.1) and placed by Eutropius, IX.2.3 at the 20th milestone from Circesium. It was also seen by Ammianus who puts it downstream from Circesium at 'Zaitha' (XXII.7) and it is mentioned by Zosimus (53.14.2) who places it at Dura.

The following years are murky. It seems likely that Singara fell under Persian control before or at the same time as Nisibis, since neither are mentioned in the list of Roman cities captured by Shapur I in his campaigns of 252 and 260 (*Res Gestae Divi Saporis*). Even Antioch had fallen to the Persians in 252 or 253. The emperor Valerian had mounted a further expedition but sought to buy off Shapur, according to Petrus Patricius (frag.9; Dodgeon and Lieu: 62). He was then defeated at the battle of Edessa in 260 and later killed by Shapur.

The position of northern Mesopotamia after the victories of Odaenathus of Palmyra in 262 is unclear, but he appears to have recovered all the Roman territory which had been captured by Shapur I between 252 and 260.[19] Presumably Singara was under Palmyrene control until Aurelian defeated Zenobia and later sacked Palmyra after a revolt in 273.

For many years thereafter Singara and northern Mesopotamia are not mentioned in the sources. The emperor Carus took Ctesiphon in 283 but the status of northern Mesopotamia is still unclear The account of the historian Zonaras (12, 30) is extremely skimpy: '*...he [Carus] immediately marched against the Persians and captured Ctesiphon and Seleuceia .... he returned towards Rome leading a multitude of captives and much booty*'. The 'Historia Augusta' states that '*without opposition he conquered Mesopotamia and advanced as far as Ctesiphon*' (The Lives of Carus, Carinus and Numerian).

At the time of Diocletian's accession (284 CE), all of northern Mesopotamia seems to have been in Roman hands. Ammianus Marcellinus (XXIII, 5,2) states that Diocletian fortified Circesium and organised '*the frontier defences in depth on the confines of the territory of the barbarians in order to prevent the Persians from overrunning Syria, as had happened a few years before to the great injury of the province*'. The Caesar Galerius suffered an initial defeat at the hands of the Persian king Narses but then won a mighty victory in 297 following which he captured Narses' family and many Persian aristocrats (see sources quoted in Dodgeon and Lieu 1991: 125-131). The outcome was the cession by the Persians of much territory to the north of the Tigris and the establishment of the frontier along that river. Nisibis was established as the 'place for transactions'. Once again it is unclear if Roman territory extended as far south as Mosul/ Nineveh, but Singara was certainly re-affirmed as an important military centre, which it remained until 360.

Towards the end of his life, the emperor Constantine, who had earlier fought in the East under Diocletian, is said by Eusebius to have planned a campaign against Persia. He had apparently also written at some point to Shapur II, apparently claiming the right to protect Persia's Christian subjects.[20] According to Garth Fowden, the 'Vita Constantini' of Eusebius and other accounts of the abortive campaign against Persia were expurgated because Christian writers of the fifth century wished to avoid 'engaging with the view that ultimate responsibility for the disastrous course of Roman-Iranian relations in the fourth century lay, not with Julian, but with Constantine' (1994: 153).

[19] The Historia Augusta (Life of the two Gallieni, 10) tells us that Odaenathis recaptured Carrhae and Nisinis and then moved on to Ctesiphon. cf Life of the two Valerians, 4: 'Odaenathus the Palmyrene gathered together an army and restored the Roman power almost to its pristine condition.'. Jerome's Chronicle (251st Olympiad) tells us that 'Odenathus, a decurion of Palmyra, having collected a band of peasants, so slaughtered the Persians that he set up camp at Ctesiphon.'

[20] Eusebius, Vita Constantini (VC) 4.8.14.

In response to border raids, Constantine had already sent his son Constantius to guard the eastern frontier in 335. The following year, Shapur II's general Narses invaded Armenia (which had been Christian since 301) and installed a Persian nominee on the throne. It was apparently this that decided Constantine to campaign against Persia himself. He treated the war as a Christian crusade, calling for bishops to accompany the army and commissioning a tent in the shape of a church to follow him. Persian diplomats came to Constantinople over the winter of 336–337, seeking peace, but Constantine turned them away. The campaign was called off, however, when Constantine became sick in the spring of 337.[21]

During the reign of Constantine's successor in the East, his son Constantius II, north-east Mesopotamia figures more largely than ever before, but the accounts of Constantius' campaigns are confused in the sources.[22] A major battle took place west of Singara, probably in 343/4 CE but the date is uncertain[23] and sources are divided in regard to the victor (Dmitriev 2015 concludes that it was a Persian victory). 'Alaina' is mentioned by Ammianus as the site of this battle. Constantius seems to have been defeated about this time in a battle which forced him to flee to Thebeta (Ammianus calls this 'Hibita'[24] – for Alaina and Thebeta, see below). After Shapur II's second failure to take Nisibis in 346/7, he marched the following year to Singara but failed here too after a night raid on his camp by the Romans. (But there seems to be overlap in the accounts of this battle with that of 343/4.[25])

Constantius II had to leave the east in 350 to counter the rebellion of Magnentius in Gaul, in which his brother Constans was killed. Shapur invaded and besieged Nisibis for a third time, on this occasion using elephants.[26] He was once again unsuccessful and had to withdraw. Both sides were then distracted by problems elsewhere and stalemate ensued for several years. But in 359 Shapur II besieged and eventually took Amida,[27] 230km north-west and a city strongly fortified by Constantius II, where several legions had been gathered. In the following year both the cities of Singara and Bezabde fell to Persian sieges. Although Singara was defended by two legions (I Flavia and I Parthica) the city was captured following a breach made in walls recently repaired where the mortar had not yet set.

This short review of the events leading up to the fall of Singara and Bezabde to the Persians is thus completed, but the aftermath was very important. Julian's rebellion against Constantius II did not come to any violent internal conflict because of the latter's death in 361. Julian inherited the empire and the conflict with Persia. His expedition into southern Mesopotamia in 363 resulted in catastrophe and his successor Jovian was compelled to surrender Nisibis and much of northern Mesopotamia, including the 'TransTigritane' territories acquired in 298, in order to extricate the army. The route of his retreat is discussed below.

[21] Eusebius, VC,, Book 4.9 and 56; Barnes 1985, Fowden 1994

[22] See especially Barnes 1980 and Harrel 2016

[23] See especially Mosig-Walburg 1999

[24] AM XXV, 9.3

[25] Barnes, followed by Farrell, speaks of two battles near Singara in respectively 343 and 348. In both cases night raids are mentioned and it seems possible that the battles have been confused in the sources, principally Pestus (Breviarium 27). The latter mentions 9 battles in the reign of Constantius II for which the emperor was present in person at two, both near Singara. Julian (Orat. 1,26 B) mentions only one but he may have compressed the two. See Mosig-Walburg 1999 and Dodgeon and Lieu 1991: 386 n.25

[26] See especially Lightfoot 1988

[27] Ammianus gives a detailed description of both this siege and those of Singara and Bezabde (:XIX and XX.6.1-7). Dodgeon and Lieu 1991

Singara, together with Castra Maurorum and Nisibis itself, was formally surrendered to the Persians by the treaty of 363, thus bringing the involvement of Rome in north-eastern Mesopotamia to a close. The frontier in Osrhoene and Mesopotamia thereafter was much less central to the rivalry between Rome and Persia.

Following the surrender of territory by Jovian, this frontier between the two empires south of the Tur Abdin followed the Jaghjagh river southwards from a point somewhere west of Nisibis. Dara was not built by the emperor Anastasius until 505 and the Roman (or Byzantine) military commander was based at Tella (now Viranşehir). How the frontier south of Nisibis was defended during the period 363 to 505 is uncertain but some forts apparently continued in use, in particular Thannouris. After a comparatively calm fifth century Amida was again captured by the Persians in 502 and it was this that spurred Anastasius to fortify Dara.

The sources for the historical geography of the region in the reign of Justinian include Procopius (especially '*On Buildings*') but also the *Synekdemos* of Hierokles and the *Descriptio Orbis Romani* of George of Cyprus. The latter work especially provides the names of fortresses of this frontier region but many of these have not been identified. Those along the post-363 frontier line of the Jaghjagh and Khabur rivers are discussed below.

Chapter 3

Forts and fortresses[1]

The terms 'forts' and 'fortresses' and their equivalents in Latin are discussed in Kennedy and Riley 1990: 19-20. In this book the term fort is used for a fortification up to 2.5 hectares in size (25 000 m^2).[2] It is generally accepted that beyond the Euphrates large Roman military units were frequently based inside fortified cities and legionary camps of a playing card shape were rare.[3] There are no long walls separating the two empires similar to the Gorgan Wall defending Sasanian Persia's north-eastern frontier (Nokandeh, Rekavandi Omrani et al. 2012), and the concept of a frontier consisting of a Roman road studded by fortifications applies only to the fortified line heading north-east to the Euphrates from Palmyra and Damascus, constructed for the emperor Diocletian (the '*Strata Diocletiana*').[4] The reasons are discussed in chapter five below. In the area examined here (north-eastern Mesopotamia between the Tigris and western Khabur) there is one short stretch of wall only, situated on the Jebel Cembe west of Mount Sinjar, and its defensive purpose is unclear (see discussion below).

The construction materials of fortifications in this region were usually mudbrick, but in a few cases (especially Singara, Serjihan and the 'fort' at Tell Brak) the walls are constructed, at least In part, of ashlar limestone blocks. The 'Castellum' at Ain Sinu may have also had some parts built of ashlar masonry but Oates records rough limestone blocks and mudbrick as the principal materials (1968: 81-88). Although the Jebel Sinjar behind the Roman town of Singara has sedimentary formations which may have provided some good building stone, it is likely that for the fort at Tell Brak the limestone blocks would have had to be brought by river from the Tur Abdin. At the fortress of Thannouris and at Tell Bizari Poidebard reported walls made of '*blocks of calcareous stone or basalt pebbles set in a very hard lime mortar*' (see below).

A major difficulty for archaeologists studying the region of the frontier between Rome and Persia is identifying dates of construction. Even for those generally thought to date from the period 100 to 600 CE there is also frequently doubt about the identity of the state responsible – Rome or Persia (whether Parthian or Sasanian). Some of the fortifications mentioned below are likely to have been already occupied by the Seleucids, but no information is available concerning the detailed history of the area under Hellenistic occupation when the main city

[1] This section does not include a study of Nisibis, the most important fortified city of the region situated in the north-western corner of the area under review, nor of Dara, the large fortress created by Anastasius in 506 CE. The available details for Nisibis are referred to in Comfort 2017b: 208-211, but the ancient city is actually on the border between Turkey and Syria. Much of it is mined and even the line of the fortifications is unclear. Recent studies of its role as a fortress and of the three unsuccessful sieges by Shapur II in 337, 346 and 350 CE are included in Harrel 2016 and Demir and Keçis 2017 . The third siege is discussed in Lightfoot 1988. Palermo has provided a clear summary of its role in Late Antiquity (2014). The disappointing archaeological remains that are still visible are also discussed in an unpublished master's thesis (DEA) by Jean-Baptiste Yon (Yon 1992: 70-75). For Dara a copious literature is available: see especially Sinclair 1989: vol3, 219 and other authors listed in Comfort 2009: 383, n826). Keser-Kayaalp has also reviewed recent discoveries outside the fortifications of Dara (Keser-Kayaalp and Erdoğan 2017).

[2] Sauer (pers; comm.) believes that the term 'castellum', often employed by Ammianus Marcellonus, refers to a small fortification up to a hectare in size.

[3] Gregory 1989. However, two large rectangles have now been identified on the east side of the Tigris at Shakh. These could possibly be a Roman. For soldiers in cities see Pollard 2000.

[4] See especially Konrad, 2001.

of Nisibis[5] was known as '*Antiochia in Mygdonia*'. For the eastern side of the frontier there has been a major increase in the information available concerning Sasanian fortifications, especially following the excavations on the Gorgan Wall on Persia's north-eastern frontier.[6] Farrokh's book on the armies of ancient Persia reviews what is now known concerning Sasanian fortifications but he notes in his chapter on 'Military architecture' that no long walls were constructed by them on the frontier with Rome (2017: 230).[7] The reasons for this are discussed in Chapter 5 of this book.

The most detailed analysis of the Roman sites known to exist in the 'Middle East' is Shelagh Gregory's long article in '*The Roman army in the east*' (Gregory 1996).[8] She discusses the problems of dating (p176) and the issue of the comparative absence of forts in a playing card shape. Although very welcome as a source of comparison for some of the fortifications described below, this article does not discuss the area of northern Mesopotamia in depth because of the doubts concerning the dating of those sites identified by Poidebard and Stein as 'Roman' and the absence of corroboration.

This book therefore addresses a difficult subject: it is likely that at least some of the fortifications on this frontier were Sasanian or Roman, since it was the scene of heavy fighting between the two empires on many occasions, but what were the forts and fortresses concerned and how may they be distinguished from fortifications of earlier and later periods?

Dating the fortifications

In fact, for the period following that examined here, little has been published which concerns fortifications in Mesopotamia. Kate Raphael's '*Muslim fortresses in the Levant*' (2011) does provide some basis for comparison with later periods and includes discussion of two fortresses on the upper Euphrates:[9] al-Bira (now Birecik) and Rumkale, 30km to the north. The former was originally constructed in the 11th century CE and included an octagonal tower in the south-east corner which has now disappeared (Figure 4:34, p177 of electronic edition).[10] The photographs of al-Bira reproduced by Raphael[11] also showed 8 square towers; most of these seem to have been constructed in the thirteenth century by Baybars, the fourth Mamluk sultan of Egypt, but at least one was re-constructed in the early fourteenth century.

Rumkale, in its existing state, is a construction largely of the 13th century CE. Its position high above the Euphrates did not require towers for defence, even though Raphael states that

[5] See n38.

[6] See especially Nokandeh, Rekavandi Omrani, Sauer and Wilkinson 2012

[7] Without citing examples other than Nisibis and Ctesiphon itself, Farrokh states that 'Instead of defensive walls, the Sassanians relied on a system of powerful fortresses along the Romano-Byzantine frontiers for defence '.

[8] Gregory's conclusions are discussed in the chapter on the frontier below. Her article is based largely on her doctoral thesis published as 'Roman military architecture on the Eastern Frontier' (Gregory 1995).

[9] Regrettably the Muslim fortifications of Besni (Bahasna), the impressive castles at Ravendel and the less impressive Turbessel (Tilbaşhar), south of Gaziantep and built at least in part by the Crusaders, are hardly mentioned, neither in Raphael 2011 nor in Kennedy 1994..

[10] The tower is reminiscent of another one that used to be visible at Zakho in Iraqi Kurdistan close to the modern frontier between Turkey and Iraq (see drawing by Maunsell (1890),reproduced in Comfort and Marciak 2018: 80).

[11] These were originally taken by Creswell who visited the fortress in the early 20th century when it was much better preserved.

towers were one of the most common features of fortifications of this period and a 'Mamluk trademark'.

Much closer to the area of north-east Mesopotamia is Soukara, a castle on the northern edge of the range of hills known as the Jebel abd-al Aziz, some 100km west of the Jebel Sinjar. Most regrettably no detailed information is available about this castle on the internet, but it seems possible that it was fortified by the eponymous abd-al Aziz, a descendant of a general of Saladin.

Earlier Muslim fortresses are known (especially of the Artukids in north-east Mesopotamia and those in the Levant constructed by the Ayyubids during the twelfth and thirteenth centuries) but during the period following the Arab invasions most fortification appears to have involved cities.[12] Constructions by the Artukids are especially well-known at their capital of Hasankeyf on the Tigris, granted to them by the Seljuk sultan in 1102 CE, but fortifications here and at Diyarbakır may have frequently involved renewal of walls inherited from antiquity.

Specifically in north-eastern Mesopotamia south of the Tur Abdin, the area of this study, there are no published fortifications known to be originally from the early Islamic period, although fortifications at Singara itself and at Rhabdion (Hatem Tai Kalesi),[13] just to the north in the Tur Abdin, were renewed after the Arabs took control. Many of those described below and thought by Stein or Poidebard to have been Roman may nevertheless be Islamic, although the information so far available indicates that those over a certain minimal size are more likely to be either Sasanian or Roman. In fact, most of the fortifications discussed below other than Singara, Thannouris and the Sasanian camp at Gohbal (see below) are fairly small.

In a conference paper delivered at Durham in 2001, Howard-Johnston spoke of '...the ancient form of an arms race [between Rome and Persia], construction of forts...' (2001/2008). In a later paper on 'The Late Sasanian Army',[14] he included a map (p97) concerning the linear defences of the Sasanians. He cites Wilkinson and Tucker 1995 and Simpson 1996 to support a dashed line showing a 'screen of defences' marked on his map to the east of Singara.[15] A second such screen is shown to the north in Arzanene (a region north of the Tur Abdin and the Tigris river, which follows a west-east course from Diyarbakır/Amida to Çattepe, where it turns south).

But according to the current state of our knowledge, that in Arzanene consisted of just two known forts (Akbas and Aphoumon), compared to a much larger number on the Roman side of the frontier (Comfort 2009, 2017). The 'screen' to the east of Singara was also rather thinly held if one follows the evidence available until now. Apart from Ain Sinu east of Singara and Saibakh across from Tell Brak, both discussed below, little was known of Sasanian fortifications in north-east Mesopotamia. The survey conducted by Wilkinson and Tucker cited by Howard-Johnston did provide evidence for at least one other fort or, rather, camp near the road from Nisibis to Niniveh (see their 'site 54' discussed below), but it is only Aurel Stein's large camp at

[12] The crusaders also constructed well-known fortifications such as Krak des Chevaliers and some are known further east but non east of Edessa (see Kennedy 1994).
[13] For Rhabdipn see Comfort 2017: 215-217.
[14] Howard-Johnston 2012
[15] Simpson's evidence for Sasanian occupation in northern Mesopotamia does not refer to fortified sites.

Ghobal, here re-assigned to the Sasanians (below), which confirms the substantial presence of at least one possible component of Howard-Johnston's 'screen of forts' in this area.

Various fortifications were found in eastern Syria and northern Iraq by Poidebard and Stein. Especially if they were square in shape, they usually ascribed these to the Roman period. Since the 1930s such identifications have frequently been called into question,[16] but few excavations have been conducted which would allow the dating to be decided with precision. In any case ceramic sequences for the period from the Achaemenids through to the Muslim invasions have still not been settled satisfactorily.[17]

The discussion of the sites below therefore relies for the most part on stylistic criteria, even though these are far from certain. A photograph of a square camp or fort without towers, seen from the air, provides insufficient information to hazard even a guess, unless there are nearby sites associated with it. Kennedy and Riley's 'Rome's desert frontier from the air' (1990) and Shelagh Gregory's book 'Roman military architecture on the eastern frontier' (1995) provide some pointers but few fortifications have until now been available for study in this region.[18]

In many cases the dating of fortifications in this region therefore has to be left open. Bronze Age 'Kranzhügeln' - or round sites with embankments - can clearly be identified and are not included in the discussion below. It would also appear that some fortifications were also constructed by the Seleucids during their long retreat from the eastern limits of Alexander's conquests. Thus, some square camps without towers, such as that south-west of Tell Brak at Tell Zenbil (see below), seem to have been Hellenistic rather than Roman. But others were probably small wayside forts built in the Middle Ages.

The problem of distinguishing Roman from Sasanian fortifications is particularly difficult at Ain Sinu, which may be entirely Sasanian. It is only recently that the importance of Sasanian fortifications has been recognised and it seems clear now that at least one of the fortifications found by Poidebard at Tell Brak and the large rectangular fortification of Ghobal, initially identified by Aurel Stein, are Sasanian in origin.

The city of Singara

Following his description of the siege of Singara in CE 360, Ammianus Marcellinus states (XX.6.8): 'This place [Singara] had been fortified in days of old as a convenient outpost to

[16] For example, firstly by Diillemann (1962: 189-203). In Figure XXVII he shows more than 20 castella in the region between Mosul and the Khabur river identified by Stein as Roman. Many of these are likely to be early Islamic but regrettably it is not yet possible to be precise. For a discussion see Gregory 1996.

[17] Dark's study of Byzantine pottery (2001) begins only in c.400 CE. His chapter 2 ('Byzantine coarse-wares 1000 years of contenuity in pottery production?') shows that these cannot be used for dating purposes. Fine-wares are treated in his chapter 3; fourth and fifth century fine-wares were apparently not traded widely and there is no discussion of such fine-wares in, for example, Oates. Glazed Byzantine pottery only appears from the seventh century. See also Oates 1956: 191-2., Palermo 2018, Palermo 2019: 175.

[18] Those listed in Gregory's book and potentially relevant here are Diyarbakır (Amida), Silvan (Martyropolis), Tilli, Kale I'Zerzevan,Dara, Tell Fakhariya (Pesaina), Tell Brak, Jebel Cembe, Beled Sinjar, Ain Sinu, Eski Hisar, Samsat (Samosata)and Belkis (Zeugma) – but not Circesium. Konrad (2001) adds Sura, Tetrpyrgiium, Cholle and Resafa. Other well-known sites with Roman fortifications included Dura Europos and Nikephorion (the latter is now covered by the modern city of Raqqa). For a complete survey of the historical geography of the Middle Euphrates, see Gaborit 2007. For plans of various forts from late antiquity on the Lomes Arabicus in Syria and Jordan see Arce 2015.

obtain advance information of any sudden enemy movement, but in fact it had proved a liability to Rome, because it was taken on several occasions with the loss of its garrison'.

However, the city was more strongly fortified than almost any other in north-east Mesopotamia.[19] At the final siege in 360 CE (Ammianus Marcellinus XX,6.1-8) it was defended by two legions (First Flavian and First Parthian).

Sir Aurel Stein's 'Limes Report' was published by Shelagh Gregory and David Kennedy only in 1985, although his work in northern Iraq was carried out before the Second World War (Stein: Gregory and Kennedy 1985). Stein admitted his debt to Poidebard who between 1925 and 1932 surveyed the 'limes' on the Syrian side of the frontier with Iraq, Syria being then part of the French mandate. Stein saw the interest in extending this work to the Iraqi side, then under the control of the British. He began his survey in 1937 at Singara, having already made a preliminary visit in 1929, Chapter 1 of his report is dedicated to the town and its surroundings (pp1-29). Unlike Poidebard, who was able to conduct occasional soundings, Stein did not excavate because of a shortage of time. However, he did examine the remains of Singara carefully, also on the ground, and his report contains many interesting photographs.[20] A plan was drawn up by his Indian surveyor and recently re-discovered in the archives of the British Museum. His text also contains reflections on the siege of Singara by the Persians in CE 360, recounted by Ammianus Marcellinus (XX.6.1).

Many interesting aerial photos by Stein of Singara and the surrounding area have been scanned by APAAME[21] for the British Academy, which houses an archive of Stein material.[22]

The first excavations were carried out by David Oates, who had read Stein's report although this was not published until much later.[23] The Roman town, investigated by Oates in the 1960s, was largely covered by debris of an Atabeg city from the twelfth and thirteenth centuries CE, as well as by a smaller modern town. He found that only the line of the main north-south street was detectable to indicate its internal plan (Oates 1968: 97-106 and plates VII to XII). Much of the Roman masonry was thought by him to have been burnt in limekilns but he was able to trace the line of the walls and study a few U-shaped bastions which were more or less well-preserved and allowed him to draw parallels with the walls of Diyarbakır (Amida) in particular, confirming a date of construction in the fourth century. There was an outer ditch cut into the solid rock which was 15m wide and about 3m deep. In the 1960s the Roman

[19] The fortifications of Nisibis, which successfully withstood three sieges by Shapur II, must have been strong but nothing is visible (Lyonnet 1996: 353; she states 'As far as the Roman limes is concerned , we do not have any evidence of 'fortresses' lying under the shapeless mounds where Roman material is attested'.

[20] Other unpublished photos are available in the British Library.

[21] Aerial Photographic Archive for archaeology in the Middle East. APAAME is a research project founded by David Kennedy and now based at the University of Oxford (School of Archaeology). The project is designed both to develop a methodology suited to the region, discover, record, monitor and illuminate settlement history in the Near East. The archive currently consists of over 115,000 (mainly aerial) images and maps, the majority of which are displayed on the archive's Flickr site.

[22] https://www.flickr.com/photos/apaame/albums/72157652009016911/. It is from this archive that the photograph of the fortifications of Singara used to cover this book has been drawn.

[23] At the request of the British Academy Oates visited northern Iraq, a visit recorded in an unpublished summary report submitted in November 1954 (British Academy 'Aurel Stein Archive' - ASA/2/13). Unfortunately, this is poorly typed and several lines are missing. Oates was highly critical of Stein's report: '...His description is incomplete and in some places seriously inaccurate ...' In particular, Oates says that '...several of the castella along the principal caravan tracks are undoubtedly ruined medieval khans'.

'enceinte' enclosed an area substantially larger than the area of the modern town, but the Roman ruins were covered by medieval debris or by modern houses, which prevented him from carrying out further investigations.[24]

'Balad Sinjar' is also discussed in Kennedy and Riley 1990: 125-131, where several further photos and plans are provided, and in Gregory's 'Roman military architecture on the eastern frontier' (1995: Vol 2, 104-108). The satellite photos from 1967 and a recent one from Google Earth are included below. A detailed review of its history in the Roman period is included as chapter 5 in Rocco Palermo's doctoral thesis (2011-2012).

The Sasanian Persians retained control of Sinjar from 363 CE until it was captured by the Arabs in 630s.[25]

The forts at Ain Sinu

30kms due east of Singara lie two adjacent ancient fortifications at Ain Sinu, first visited by Sarre and Herzfeld who called the site 'Ain al-Shahid' and published a plan (Herzfeld, Sarre et

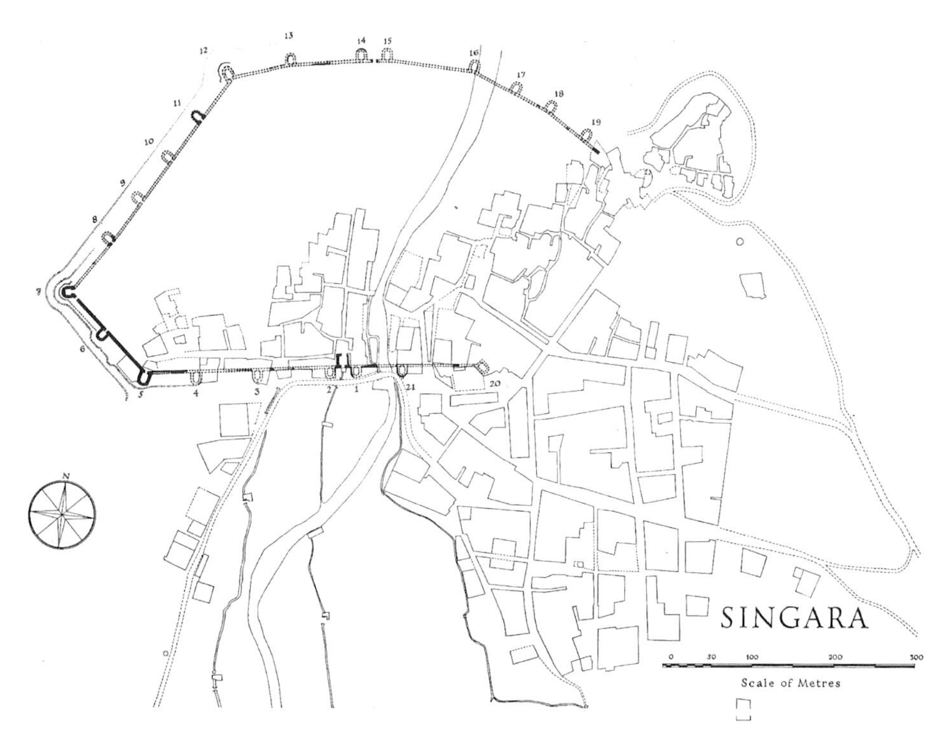

Figure 1. Copied from Oates, 1968 Fig 8. Also in this publication are plans of the Roman south gate and Bastions 5, 6 and 7

[24] A detailed description is also included in Gregory 1995. She drew attention to parallels at Pagnok Oreni and possibly Ain Sinu – p108).

[25] For the Islamic history of the town see the article by C.P. Haase in the Encyclopaedia of Islam, new edition, vol. XI: San-Sze.. Much of this is article is repeated in Wikipedia (Sinjar). In 1186 Ibn Shaddad noted that the town was protected by a double wall under the Ayyubids but that this was destroyed by the Ilkhanid Mongols in 1262.

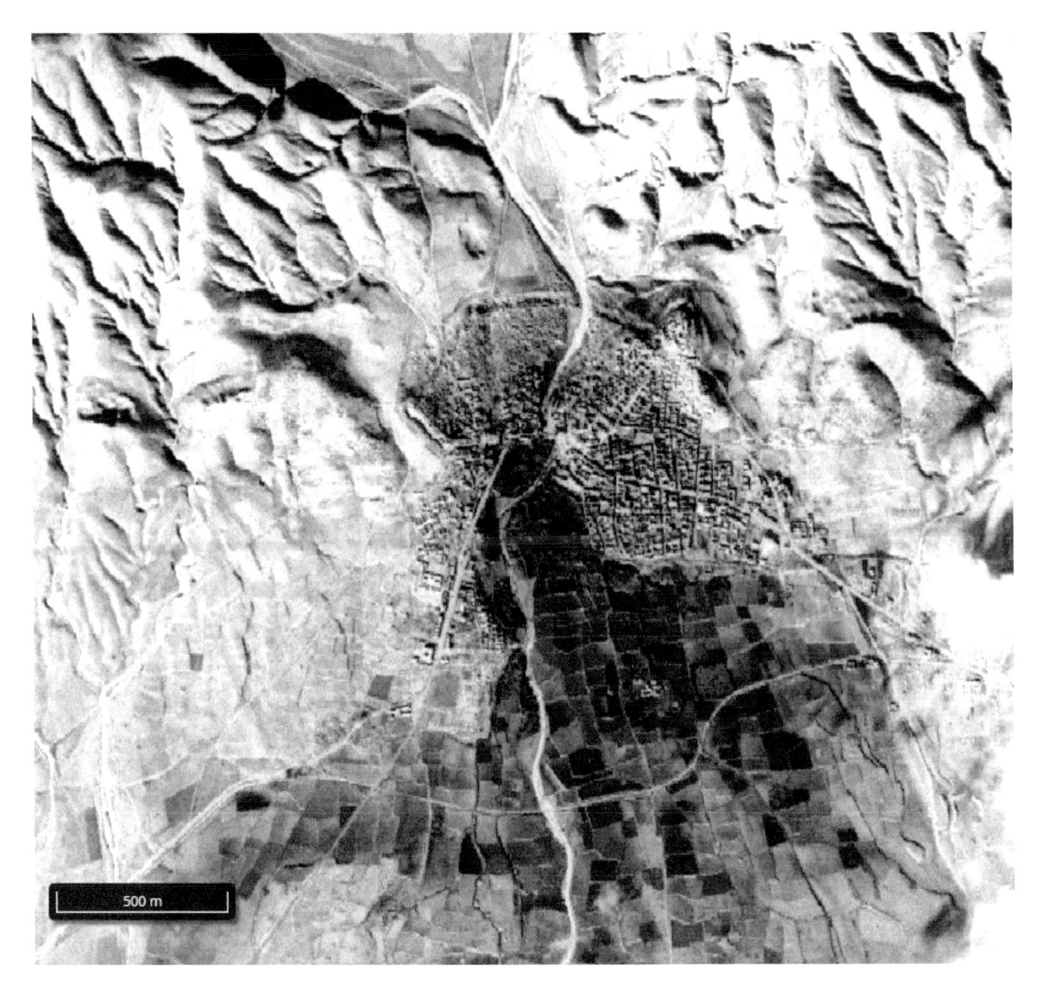

Figure 2. Singara Corona 11 Dec 1967

al. 1911-1920: vol2: 305). They proposed the identification with *Zagurae* of the Peutinger Table. Ain Sinu was also investigated by Stein in 1937 and by Oates in 1957; the latter confirmed this identification. The PT shows *Zagurae* as lying 21 Roman miles beyond Singara (or 31 kms) and 18 miles (26.6km) before *Ad pontem*. The modern town of Tell Afar is usually identified with this last station of the PT; it is situated on a deep river valley which would have required bridging and lies 25 kms beyond Ain Sinu. These exceptionally good correspondences, together with the presence of the old modern road which here followed the course of the ancient road, just below the site of Ain Sinu, and the Gaulat pass to the north, seem to leave no room for doubt concerning the identification of Ain Sinu with Zagurae.

The soundings made by Oates revealed two major buildings described by him as a 'barracks' (AS1) and 'the castellum' (AS2). AS1 was substantially larger than AS2 being approximately 340 by 310m (about 105 000 m^2), while AS2 was 175 by 210m (about 37 000 m^2) with a slight projection for the west-facing wall (Oates, 1968: 83). The current state of these structures as

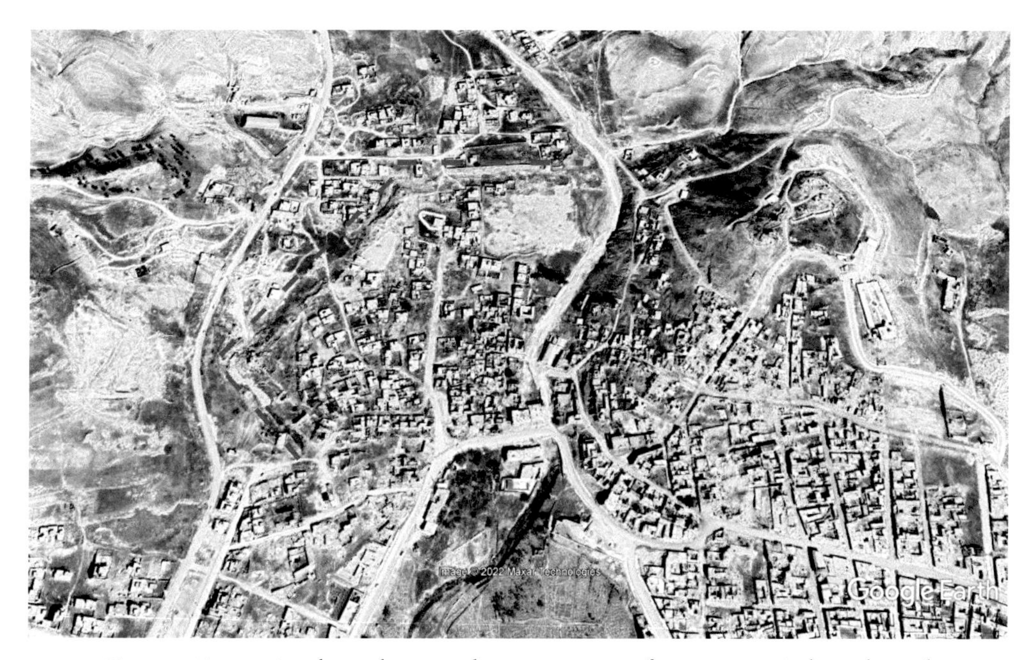

Figure 3. Singara Google Earth 13 March 2021. Rampart of Roman town indicated in red

seen in the satellite imagery appears to be fairly good for AS1, but little can be seen of AS2 (see figure 32 below). The images confirm for AS1 the presence of the barracks blocks seen by Oates and the absence of the 'praetorium' or administration building often associated with Roman forts.

It now seems probable that, despite the Roman coins found by Oates from the early years of the third century, at least AS1 must be ascribed to the Sasanians on the grounds of the similarity with other forts found on the Gorgan Wall to the south-east of the Caspian Sea (Sauer, Rekavandi, Wilkinson and Nokandeh 2013; St John Simpson, 1996: 92). Oates suggested that the forts at Ain Sinu were probably captured by Ardashir in around CE 237 but it now seems probable that both were constructed after this date; the area between Singara and the Tigris could have been part of the territory known to have been surrendered by Philip the Arab in 242.

Although Oates was convinced that AS 2 was of Roman origin it should be noted that Wilkinson and Tucker's survey in the 1970s of the area to the north-east found a similar pentagonal structure (site 54) between Tell Hawa and the Tigris, 3km ESE of Gar Sur with mounds of the Sasanian/Early Islamic period. The surrounding enclosure '*... was not dated directly, but probably dates from first major period of occupation i.e. Sasanian/E.Islamic*' (Wilkinson 1995: 128 and figs 6 and 7). This fortification is discussed below and a Corona image from 1967 is reproduced at figure 64. It now seems possible that Zagurae was at the southern end of a protective screen of Sasanian fortifications built by the Persians to defend Nineveh and important Tigris bridgeheads here and at Eski Mosul against the Romans.

Thus, Ardashir and Shapur I may have created a defensive line running north-east towards the Tigris, which could have included the fortified enclosures seen by Wilkinson and Tucker (1995: 70). Such a line ('a screen of forts') has already been proposed by Howard-Johnston (2012) as discussed above, although the evidence found so far is not conclusive. In Chapter 5 below the idea of such a line defended by fortifications, comparable to the 'Strata Diocletiana' north-east of Damascus, is rejected.

The fortifications at Ain Sinu are discussed by Gregory 1995: 109-115. She stated that both structures examined by Oates '...seem to be unique in the field of Roman fortifications'. She noted in particular the absence of 'principia' buildings. Although she says that the Roman coins found from the Severan period could confirm the presence during that time of a Roman military unit, she does not accept Oates' identification of AS 2 ('the castellum') as a type regularly occupied by auxiliary forces (page 113). Although she considered AS 1 ('the barracks') to be 'much more convincing as a purely Roman structure', the parallels which she herself draws with Tell Bati and near Tell Brak (p111) now argue for a Sasanian structure and not a Roman one.

After the fall of Singara in 360 CE the frontier appears to have moved westwards to the north-south line of the Jaghjagh and Khabur, but evidence is scarce. As Gregory says, a similar fort to the AS1 at Ain Sinu, is now under a village called 'Saibakh' on the east side of the Jaghjagh, opposite Tel Brak (see below). This is 200m square with four barracks blocks and was photographed by Poidebard in the 1920s (1934: 144 and pl CXXII). A third such site lies 28kms further to the west at Tell Bati (1934: 150 and PlCXXXIX). Now destroyed, this site is more difficult to explain - if it is indeed a Sasanian fortification - since it lies beyond the line which probably constituted the border between Rome and Sasanian Persia for most of the period CE 363-640. These two sites, together with that at Ain Sinu 1, and their identification as Sasanian barracks are discussed in Sauer, Rekavandi, Wilkinson and Nokandeh 2013: 234-9 and are further examined below in relation to Tell Brak.

The 'castellum' and 'barracks' at Ain Sinu, as well as the 'barracks' at Tell Brak 2, are also discussed by Kennedy and Riley 1990: 168-170 and 213-215 with aerial photos and plans. At that time the possibility of Sasanian parallels had not been raised.

Alaina

This is the name of a site mentioned on the Peutinger Table as a station on the road from Singara to the Khabur via Batitas. There was a second road shown on the PT from Nisibis to Singara via Thebeta and Baba. Depending on the location of Thebeta and Baba (see discussion below) this may or may not have passed via Lacus Beberaci - now Lake Khatuniye,[26] situated just over the modern border between Iraq and Syria.

[26] Honigmann 1934: 479

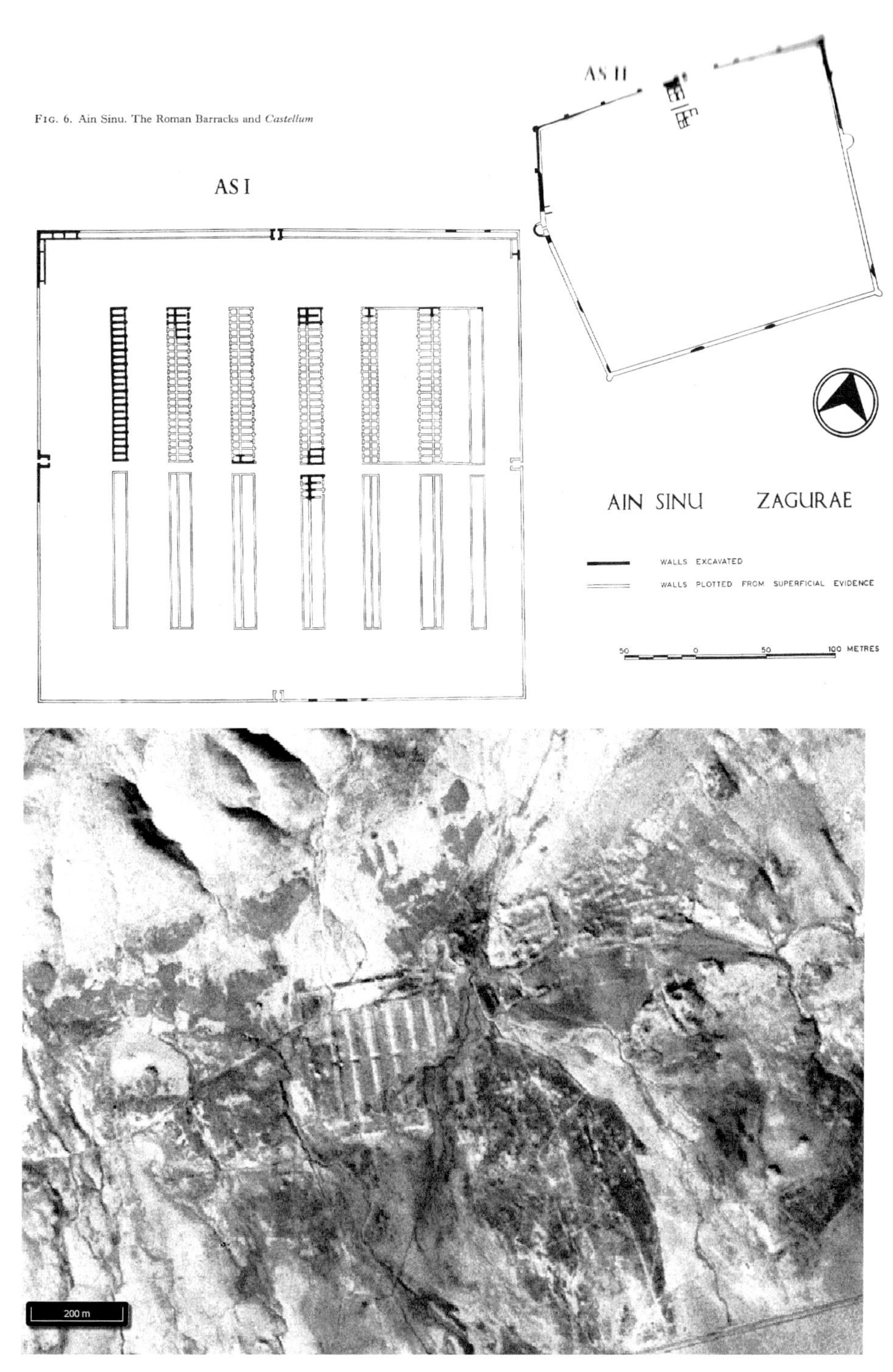

Figures 3a and b. Ain Sinu/Zagurae. a) Plan copied from Oates 1968 p83. b) Corona 11 December 1967.36°27'07"N, 42°10'43"E

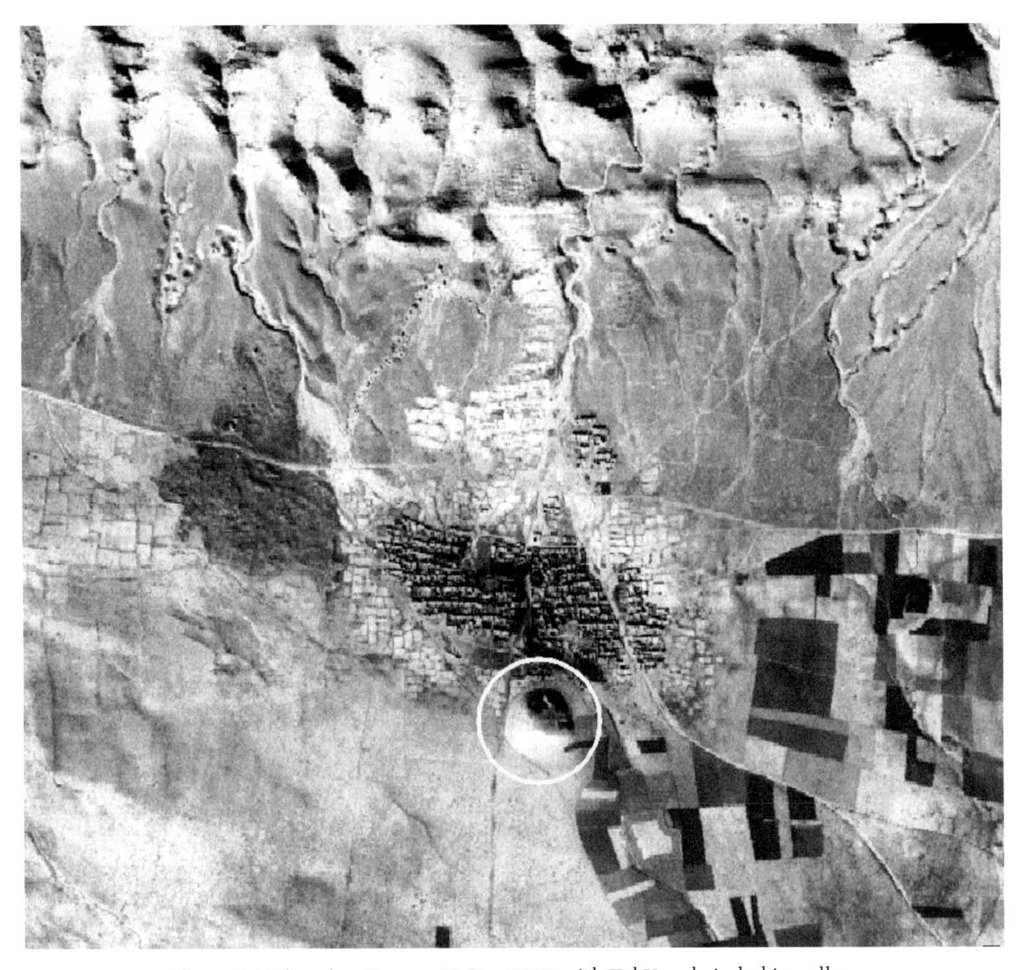

Figure 4. Majnuniye. Corona 11 Dec 1967. with Tel Hayal circled in yellow

Alaina has usually been identified with the 'Eleia' of Ptolemy,[27] thought to be the same as the Hileia of Ammianus Marcellinus,[28] the site of two battles between Romans and Persians in 344 and 348 (see above).[29] It is probably located near the point at which the modern and ancient road crossing the western end of the Sinjar mountain chain via the Bara pass emerges onto the plain to the south and joins the road coming from the Khabur river. There is currently a substantial village known as Masnuniyah (now 'Sariyatak' according to Google Maps) a little to the east. Near this village is Tell Hayal which Sarre and Herzfeld identified with Alaina.[30]

[27] For example, by Dillemann 1962: 181. Stückelberger and Grasshoff 2006 identify Eleia with 'Tell Hajjal' (p585) and place it west of Singara with an intervening place mentioned by Ptolemy called 'Baxala' - otherwise unknown (map on p861).

[28] XXV.9.3

[29] Dillemann assumes (1962: 212) that Constantius was defeated here and fell back on Thebeta.

[30] Herzfeld, Sarre et al. 1911-1920: 201

In agreement with Dillemann (1962: 178), Oates (1968: 79) states that Alaina may now be firmly identified with Tell Hayal, 'a high mound situated on the south side of the village of Majnuniye'. He says:

> The Roman site lies about 500m east of the tell where a partly effaced ditch and the debris of a massive stone wall can be traced from east to west for a distance of over 200m.This was probably the exterior wall of a *castellum*, for among the piles of stones collected by ploughmen near the site was found, in 1956, a brick bearing the stamped inscription COH[ORS] VI I[TURAEORUM].[31]

Regrettably, nothing of this is visible on the satellite imagery (see figure 4) and Oates published neither plan nor photo apart from a general view of Majnuniye.

However, some 3.5 kilometres to the north-west of Sariyatak/Majnuniye there is a gorge emerging from the mountain with some houses at its foot. Behind the gorge, on the mountainside, there are the remains of a substantial town, now entirely abandoned but of which the ruins of several hundred houses are still clearly visible both on Google Earth and especially on a 1967 Corona image (figure below). This town is given the Kurdish name of 'Sikeniye' on map II (opposite page 194) of Lescot's '*Enquête sur les Yezidis de Syrie et du Jebel Sindjar*' (1938). The text of his book provides little information about the town, which was perhaps already then in decline, but it was at that time the major place of the Xiran tribe with 230 houses divided between three settlements (Hekresiya, Savi u Bavi and Eli Sekoli – page 256). (At this time Mehmé or Majnuniye had 60 houses, while Balad Sinjar itself had apparently only 200 houses belonging to the Hebbabat tribe - p260).

Aurel Stein (page 27 of the Limes report) stated that he visited Sikeniye (which he spells 'Sukainiye') in 1938, when it was still a 'large village'. He also saw Tell Hayal, 'a conspicuous mound' rising to 15m, and visited 'a large area 2km SW of Majnuniye' with debris of walls but no firm evidence of a Roman station. He apparently did not see the wall described briefly by Oates but: '*...It was probably about [3km] further to the south-west and on ground cultivated with water of the stream descending from Sukainiye that a fairly large square site marked by lines of much decayed walls enclosing it was observed from the air'.* However, although Stein's Limes report shows a rather nondescript aerial photograph of this site (Plate 6b), he was uncertain of its exact position and did not visit it on the ground. 'Alaina' may – according to Stein - have been either this square site or another smaller enclosure called Tall Rafsi (1.5km west of a police post at a road junction for Sikaniye and, further on, for the Bara pass.[32] The modern road follows a course to the north, but that used in Stein's day – and probably also in the Roman period – is clearly visible, especially on the Corona imagery from 1967/8. But no such enclosures can be seen on these images.

[31] For this information Oates cites as source 'Information from Sayyid Fuad Safar and Sayyid Kadhim al-Jenabi'. Cohors I Ituraeorum was present in Syria ('Ituraea' included Palestine) and is listed on military diplomas in the years 88 and 93 CE but not later. Another possibility could be 'Illyricianorum' since units including this name figure in the 'Notitia Dignitatum' under the *Dux Mesopotamiae*. At plate Via Oates published a photograph of Majnuniye taken from the top of the tell, but nothing else concerning the *castellum*.

[32] Stein's description of Tell Rafsi is as follows (1985: 27): '*The walls of which the lower courses built with rough stones and hard mortar emerge clearly on the west, north and south but are partially effaced along the canal skirting the east side , form a correctly orientated rectangle of about [51 x 41m]. The interior covered with stones from completely decayed structures rises about [2m] above the fields around. In the southern portion of the interior a small approximately rectangular mound formed by stone debris rises some [2m] higher and bears near its south-eastern corner a roughly bult modern tower.*'

Figure 5. Sikeniye. Corona 11 Dec 1967. Abandoned town circled in yellow

Nevertheless, it seems very possible that the now abandoned town of Sikaniye,[33]with the associated squares seen by Stein, corresponds to Ptolemy's placename and to the PT site of Eleia/Alaina and therefore that the settlement mentioned by Oates at Majnuniye was less important.

The identification of Sikeniye with Alaina is strengthened by an additional discovery made by the writer using recent satellite images of the area. 5.3km due west of Sikeniye it has been possible to identify the remains of a substantial fort at the foot of the pass leading north to Bara[34] and Lake Khatuniye (figure 6; here called the Bara pass but 'Col de Chillouh' on Dillemann's Fig. XXIV, 1962: 186 and the 'Shilo pass' for Stein (1985: 40)). This fort was apparently seen by neither Poidebard nor Stein and is not mentioned in other accounts of early travellers. It is located near the modern tarmac road descending from the Bara pass but is not near a village. Its size is about 40x60m. Although the Corona imagery is here too poor

[33] Sikeniye is situated at 36°18'30"N, 41°33'36"E.

[34] Bara was first identified with the Baba of the PT by Dussaud (1927: 493). The spelling Baba is apparently a scribal error. See also the 'Bara' of the Ravenna Cosmography (Mesopotamia) and Honigmann 1934: 179. There are substantial remains of abandoned villages nearby visible in the satellite imagery both here and at Lake Khatuniye ('Lacus Beberaci'), for which Poidebard published some photos (1934: Pls CLII and CLIII).

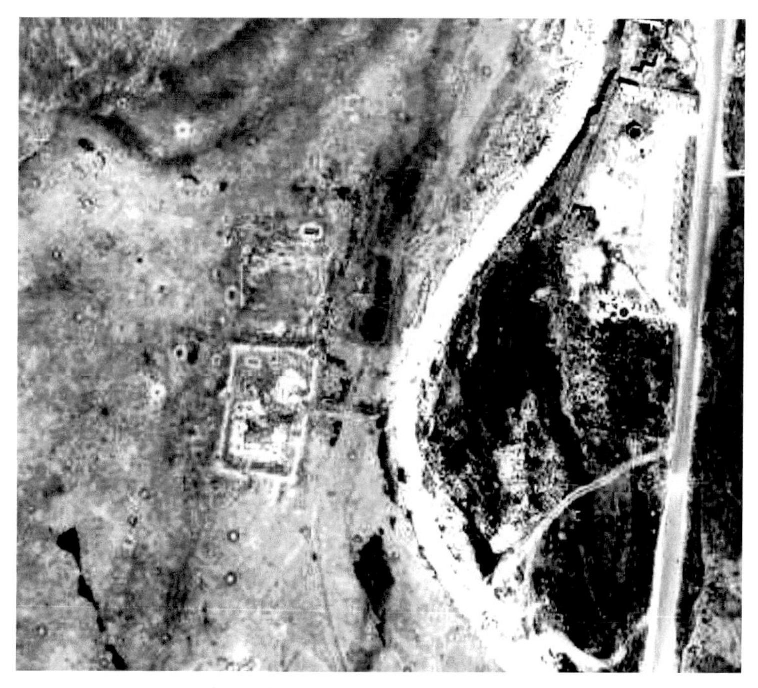

Figure 6. Fort at foot of Bara pass. CAST and Google Earth 5 Sept 2020

to be of use, it is shown on a Google Earth image of September 2020. Towers are visible on the north-east and possibly the other three corners; a gate is in the middle of the east-facing wall with what may be a road leading to the wadi 35m east. Another substantial structure can be seen immediately to the north together with the foundations of various houses.

The closest parallel to this fort in Kennedy and Riley, seems to be 'Khirbet el-Beida' (1990: 128). Although the latter was considered by Poidebard to be Roman, it was thought by Gaube to be a Ghassanid palace-fortress of the Late Empire (1974). In this case the strategic position at the base of a pass seems to indicate a military role, but its dating must remain uncertain until the remains can be investigated on the ground. Evidently the fort near Alaina would have to have been built before 363 CE if it was Roman.

The fort is 32.5km west of Balad Sinjar. The PT indicates a distance of XXI Roman miles from Alaina to Singara and thus offers an almost exact equivalent, although the main ancient west-east road lies 3km to the south of this fort.

Thebeta

The position of Thebeta ('Tabite' in Assyrian sources)[35] is of great importance for the discussion of roads between Nisibis and Singara. The location is also examined below in the section on roads. Unfortunately, there has been considerable disagreement amongst scholars and modern surveys have yet to identify its position convincingly. It seems that the most probable

[35] Dillemann 1962: 167

site lay to the south of the survey area examined by Meijer (1986), but 25 kilometres to the north-west of the border of Syria with Iraq. The survey of Wilkinson and Tucker (Wilkinson 1995) was confined to the Iraqi side of the border and centred on Tell al-Samir and Tell al-Hawa to the north-east of the area surrounding Mount Sinjar.

According to the PT, Thebeta was a station on the route from Nisibis to Singara, possibly via the western end of Jebel Sinjar and the Bara pass. Ammianus Marcellinus says that the emperor Constantius II took refuge here once from the Persians.[36] Dillemann reviews (1962: 196n3) the mentions of Thebeta in ancient authors: Arrian's Parthica refers to it as a φρούριον of Parthia, Ammianus Marcellinus as the Roman 'unprotected[37] post' (*stationem intutam*) to which Constantius fled (in 348 CE?). There are also mentions of the town as a Sasanian fortress attacked by the Romans on several occasions after 363 CE.[38] He also raises the possibility that this was one of the fifteen unnamed fortresses surrendered to the Persians by Jovian (1962: 220).

The proposal of Oates that Thebeta lay on the Jaghjagh near Tell Brak has much to recommend it,[39] despite the dogleg involved in a route heading south from Nisibis to Tell Brak and then south-east to the Jebel Sinjar, but this is far from the positions assigned to it by Poidebard in his map (figure 3 above) and by Dillemann (Fig. XVIII, p149).

Poidebard indicates as a first possibility the village of 'Tell Hader', south of Tell Garasa, where there used to be visible remains of an old bridge, now disappeared (1934: 162). This route would have continued to Bara and the western end of the Jebel Sinjar but is not shown on his map. Tell Hader has not been identified on the satellite imagery, but Poidebard says that it was not fortified.[40] We know that at least for some parts of its history Thebeta was a φρούριον or citadel and therefore fortified. This site's distance from Dara (65kms as the crow flies) would however correspond fairly closely to that of 15 parasangs (or 75-90km, depending on the source) provided by Pseudo-Zachariah Rhetor (Greatrex 2011: 117 and n24), taking into account a detour around Nisibis.

Poidebard mentions a second possible route from Nisibis to Singara further to the east via a site at Lelan, 28km SE of Nisibis, where he found a fortified town (also spelt Leilan and discussed below on page [92] and figs.58/59; for the pre-history of this important site see Weiss 1983); he apparently heard of another such site along this route to the north-west of the 'Zerwan pass', also with fortifications (see 'Qohbal' below). Poidebard correctly indicates in his text that Bara/Baba is at the western end of the Jebel Sinjar at the foot of a pass (which he calls 'Samouka', but which is generally referred to in this book as the Bara pass). However, his

[36] As mentioned above, Dillemann considered that this incident took place after a Roman defeat at Hileia/Alaina in 348 CE.
[37] Or perhaps 'unguarded'.
[38] In particular, by the author now known as Pseudo-Zacharias Rhetor(Zachariah 1899: 9.1) and Greatrex 2011.. In the beginning of the reign of Justinian in 526 CE an attempt to recover Nisibis failed: *'when the magister militum Timostratus was dux on the frontier those assembled [under] him an army with its officers [in order] to fight Nisibis. Though they attacked they did not capture it, and they moved on from there to the fortress of Tebetha. The army approached the wall and breached it, and this was during the period of the summer, but for some reason they were dislodged and did not take the fortress, which was a journey of some fifteen parasangs from Dara...* '(Greatrex edition). The parasang is a flexible term of measurement equivalent to the 'league' and roughly 5 kilometres. So according to Zachariah Thebeta was about 75km from Dara.
[39] See discussion below under 'Jaghjagh'.
[40] 'Ville agricole sans défense'.

map - reproduced at Figure 3 - places Baba at the eastern end at Qohbol, where a pass crosses to Ain Sinu. This must be the Gaulat pass mentioned by Oates (1968: 80; 'Qaulat' in Stein), but Poidebard calls it the 'Zerwan - or Zirwan - pass'.

His positioning of Baba on the map is apparently offered as an alternative possibility to the Bara at the western end of the chain although it is generally considered that the Baba of the PT is a scribal error for 'Bara'.[41] Despite the probably mistaken identification with Bara/ Qohbol – followed also by Aurel Stein - this second possible identification of Thebeta with a site about 41km to the north-west of Qohbol, on the road towards Tell Lelan and Nisibis seems to this writer to be the most probable. The photograph published on Plate CLX of *'La trace de Rome dans le désert'* is reproduced below; it is not very clear but corresponds to a site located on the satellite imagery 60kms to the north of the Gaulat pass. The position of his 'Tell Lelan' is certain since it has kept this name since the 1920s when Podebard did his research and a Corona image is also reproduced below (figure 59).

On page 164 of *'La Trace de Rome'* Poidebard, who does not appear to have made a ground visit, described the site – together with another one a few kilometres to the west - briefly as follows:

> A Thebeta, ville romaine avec bastions extérieurs en étoile. Même type de ville, dans le site situé entre Thebeta et Garasa.

No Roman towns in the shape of a star are known elsewhere, but in any case this is not in fact the shape of the town visible in Poidebard's photograph reproduced below and the walls might well be a Sasanian. The accompanying Corona image shows the same shape but not as a star. The other site towards Garasa has not been identified.

Dillemann is sceptical of Poidebard's second identification of Thebeta with this site (1962: 106). In his maps of the 'vallée du Radd' (Fig VIII, p61) and of 'Routes antiques de Mésopotamie (Est)' (Fig. XVIII, p149), Dillemann shows Thebeta with a question mark south of an ancient

Figure 7. Poidebard's photograph of 'Thebeta'. La Trace de Rome dans le désert', Pl.CLX.3

[41] Dillemann 1962: 137

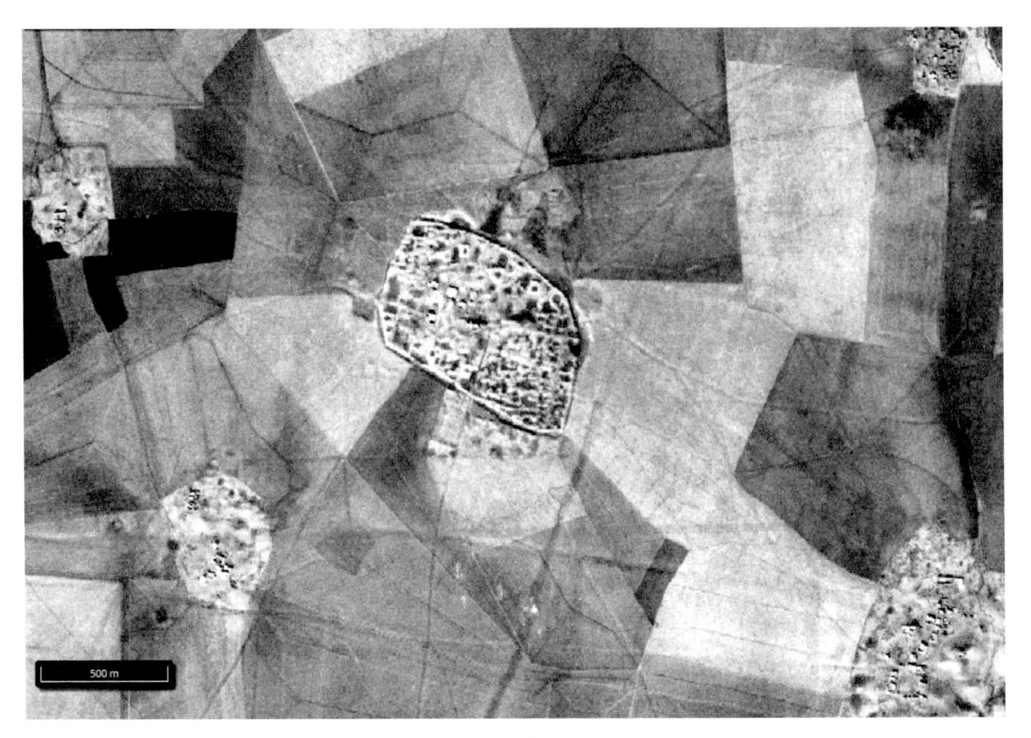

Figure 8. Thebeta, according to Poidebard. 36°49'25"N, 41°41'43"E. Corona 1967

bridge[42] near Tell Garasa at 'El Aouinet',[43] presumably close to Poidebard's first possible location at Tell Hader, but nothing suitable has been found on the satellite imagery in this area. Dillemann shows his route 3 descending south from Nisibis to this bridge, which has now sadly disappeared, and then continuing south to Bara. El-Aouinet's position does indeed correspond to a likely location for Thebeta, but the name appears no longer to be in use and there is nothing yet found to corroborate this identification, although there are other possible ancient sites in the area.

Qohbol/Ghobal

The other fortified site north of the Jebel Sinjar of which Poidebard was informed[44] lay north-west of the pass of Zerwan – or Gaulat. It was not apparently seen by him, presumably because it lay on the Iraqi side of the border. A very large rectangle is visible on the Corona imagery around the small town of Ghobal which must correspond to this site (see figure 9 below). Its great size (about 1700 by 1400m or 238 hectares) could indicate a Sasanian camp,[45] but

[42] 'Le 'pont du Djerrahi', Dillemann 1962: 166.

[43] This may correspond to the first of Poidebard's identifications at 'Tell Hader'. Tell Gharassa is the 'Tell Qarassa' shown at 36°49'49"N, 41°27'44"E on the University of Arkansas CAST site for Corona imagery, also site 98 of Meijer's survey (1986). Locations and naming conventions used by CAST are obtained from Oxford Encyclopaedia of the Near East, Atlas of PreClassical Upper Mesopotamia (APUM) and ANE Placemarks for Google Earth of Uppsala University.

[44] *'...une grande ville fortifiée signalée au N-O de la passe de Zerwan'* (Poidebard 1934: 162).

[45] Sauer has kindly remarked to the writer on the similarity with Qal'eh-Ye Pol Gonbad (Sauer, Omrani Rekavandi et al. 2013: 358-9 – see also the campaign bases discussed on his p370). The empty interior is typical of such Sasanian

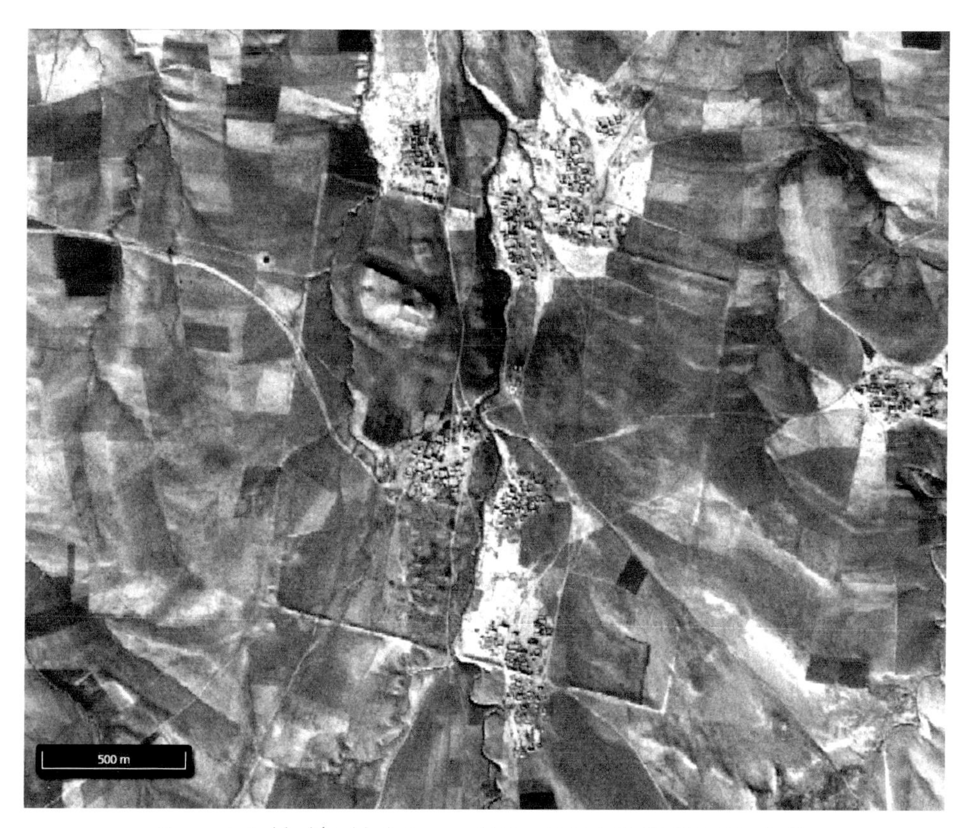

Figure 9. Qohbol/Gohbal. Corona 11 Dec 1967. 36°30'52"N, 41°57'24"E

no barracks blocks are visible in the Corona image of December 1967 so it was presumably designed to harbour tents. The substantial modern development of the town seems to have destroyed many of the ancient features since the 1960s.

Qohbol is situated 25km north-west of Ain Sinu/*Zagurae* and must be the 'Kohbol', mentioned by Stein on pp29-37 of his report, in which he specifically mentions a 'large rectangular enclosure', seen initially from the air.[46] None of his photographs of this site, neither from the air nor on the ground, have yet been found, but it has been possible to identify it on the satellite imagery and provide co-ordinates.

Stein was not able to identify the period of construction, but he mentions a mound of 9m in the north-west corner. The walls had already then (1937), according to Stein, been robbed of much of their stone for construction of the modern village.[47] Despite the absence of datable remains on the surface, he concluded that the circumvallation was of 'considerable antiquity'

campaign bases.

[46] In Stein 1938:63 he calls this 'the ruined town site' of Qohbal and identifies it with Baba, presumably on the strength of Poidebard's map of which an extract is reproduced at Figure 69 below. Dillemann rejects this identification (1962: 167).

[47] However, Sasanian forts further east are often built exclusively of mud brick – see, for example, Nemati, Mousavinia et al. 2019.

because of the 'far-advanced decay of the ramparts' (p30). The latter were 9-11m wide on the top and 1.8 to 2.4m high. Stein also saw the remains of a gate in the west wall suggested by 'plentiful debris of large rough stones'. The structure is rectangular and not pentagonal like site 54 ('a low earthen bank') of the Wilkinson/Tucker survey, although it is of a comparable size.[48] This site is visible on the Corona imagery of 1967 but not on more recent satellite images (see figure 7 below).

Qohbol must also have been visited by Oates because he states (1968: 35-6 n3):

> ...North-west of the Gaulat pass in the direction of Šubat-Enlil[49] lies another prominent mound, Gohbol, surrounded by a walled enclosure nearly 1500m square. The pottery indicates occupation of the mound and its immediate vicinity from the second millennium and perhaps earlier down to the Hellenistic period, and again in Islamic times, but the walls cannot be dated....

The site is not mentioned by Ptolemy, unless it be the otherwise unidentified site of Baxala (Stückelberger and Grasshoff 2006: 585). It seems possible that the camp at Qohbol is also the Persian fortress mentioned by Ammianus Marcellinus at 'Ur' (XXV, 8.2). He describes this part of the retreat of the Roman army from Hatra to Nisibis as follows (translation by Walter Hamilton in the Penguin edition):

> ...we arrived by forced marches in the neighbourhood of Hatra, an old town lying in the wilderness and long since abandoned. On various occasions the warrior emperors Trajan and Severus had attacked it and themselves almost perished with their armies.... We learned that for a distance of seventy miles [in the direction of Nisibis] over the arid plain we should find no water that was not salt and stinking, and nothing to eat but ... bitter herbs. All the receptacles we had were filled with fresh water, and food of a sort, however unwholesome, was provided by slaughtering camels and baggage-animals. After we had marched for six days and could no longer find even grass, the last resource of the destitute, Cassian, the commander in Mesopotamia, who had been sent on some time before for this purpose with tribune Mauricius, met us at the Persian fortress of Ur and brought us food from the stores which the army left with Procopius and Sabinus had saved by strict rationing.

Dillemann, however, identifies Ur with Ain Sinu[50] despite the fact of it lying only 100km from Hatra, which seems little for the army to have covered in six days.

The route followed by Jovian's army seems very probably to have included that proposed by Poidebard and the distance of six days' march would seem to correspond better to the 130km distance to Qohbol from Hatra. The road concerned which links the three sites discussed above (Tell Lelan, Thebeta (?) and Qohbol) may thus have been another important connection

[48] Wilkinson and Tucker's pentagonal enclosure (site 54) is approximately 1300x1100m, I.e. 143 hectares. No Parthian or Roman pottery was found. It was probably 'a large defended settlement' and may have been a part of a Sasanian 'limes' (pp70-71) defending the frontier against the Roman empire.

[49] Now identified by Weiss with Tell Lelan (see discussion of Castra Maurorum below).

[50] Dillemann 1962: 171. He also links Ur on linguistic grounds to the 'Oruros' of Pliny (VI.120), as well as to 'Zagurae' (Ain Sinu). Pliny says Oruros was on the Roman border in Pompey's time and was 250 Roman miles from Zeugma, which is about the right distance for either Qohbol or Ain Sinu.

between Nisibis and Singara, but passing to the east of the Jebel Sinjar via Ain Sinu/*Zagurae* and one not mentioned in the PT.

Towards the Khabur

Heading west from Singara and Alaina, Poidebard found various fortified sites along the old roads to the Khabur (see Chapter 4 below) and around the low mountain massif of the Jebel Cembe, which lies to the west of Jebel Sinjar. Some of these it has been possible to identify on the satellite imagery. In particular, those so identified are: a substantial structure with three forts north of Al Hol, small forts at al Han and Touloul Mougayir and a square camp at Hirbet Hassan Aga.

A detailed study of this area follows with the aim of revealing the problems as well as the achievements of Poidebard's work. As far as the writer is aware, no archaeological work in this area has been undertaken apart from the excavation of a few sites affected by the Hasaké South dam on the Khabur river (see below). The CAST website of the university of Arkansas is particularly helpful for this exercise because it permits an easy comparison of the Corona imagery from 1967/1968 with Google Earth and other recent images and also because it allows the viewer to see on the Corona images the superimposed names and locations of some archaeological sites.

These names are taken for the most part from Olof Pedersen's 'Ancient Near East Placemarks', a project he has carried out for the University of Uppsala.[51] Although this latter project is principally concerned with Assyriology, several of the placenames correspond to those used by Poidebard for 'La trace de Rome dans le Désert de Syrie'. Unfortunately, Pedersen's collection of names of ancient sites is incomplete for the Roman period.

The river valley of the Khabur has recently been irretrievably damaged from an archaeological viewpoint.[52] The south Hasaké dam has inundated the part of the valley from above Tuneynir (Thannouris) in the north to below Tell Matariya (Amostae). Once again, the damage caused by such dams in the Near East to the historical record has been incalculable, although it has contributed to making the Khabur valley into the principal grain-producing area of Syria.

Sadly, the Corona images available from the CAST site of the university of Arkansas are here of relatively poor quality. At the time of writing a few images available from the Zoom Earth website, taken before complete inundation of the valley, permit study of the northern sector of what is now a reservoir, in particular Thannouris/Tuneynir). But some of the sites seen by Poidebard in the 1930s have been destroyed and are no longer visible. Google Earth is of little help because the reservoir had already been filled at the date from which their imagery becomes available and even Thannouris is now largely below water.

In this area centred on the Jebel Cembe, Poidebard's map of the Khabur bend (see figure 13 below) shows various major and minor forts. Starting from the point nearest Alaina and following a clockwise path, the major ones ('fortified towns') are Batitas (Qseybe), al-Han, Mesnaya (Tell Mashnaka), Amostae (Tell Oumtariye), Thannouris (Touneinir) and an

[51] See http://www.diva-portal.org/smash/record.jsf?pid=diva2%3A891535&dswid=951. Accessed 26/01/2022.
[52] See Bounni 1990.

Figure 10. Al- Han – situation to the east. Corona 5 Nov 1968

Figure 11. Fort at al-Han. Google Earth 23 November 2020. A modern structure has been superimposed.

Figure 12. Fort at al-Han. Corona 5 Nov 1968. 36°17'36"N, 41°04'14"E

unnamed fortification NE of Thannouris. Four smaller forts ('posts' or castella) are shown between Mesnaya and Thannouris on the Khabur and five others within the Jebel Cembe area, including Lake Khatuniye and what must be the fort north of al-Hol, shown below in images from Google Earth and Corona.

al-Han

Poidebard's distinction between small 'castella' and large 'fortified towns 'is doubtful, since the 'fort' at al-Han is hardly any larger than that the supposedly smaller 'Roman post' or castellum at al-Hol, also discussed below.[53] Al-Han is on the course of the old road from Batitas to Amostae, but those north of al-Hol have no such road apparent nearby and one fort seems to have been constructed inside a much larger - and presumably more ancient structure. No archaeological investigation of any of these has yet been possible.

Poidebard mentions at al-Han (p155) '*...camp important et, un peu à l'E[st], ville forte gardant une source*'. What is now to be seen on the satellite imagery is a fort 130x130m in size or 17 000m^2,

[53] Al-Han is about 17 000m^2.The three fortifications north of Al Hol are respectively; A - 8000, B - 64 000 and C-25 000m^2. However, Poidebard may have seen a 'fortified town' near al-Han which is simply not visible to us.

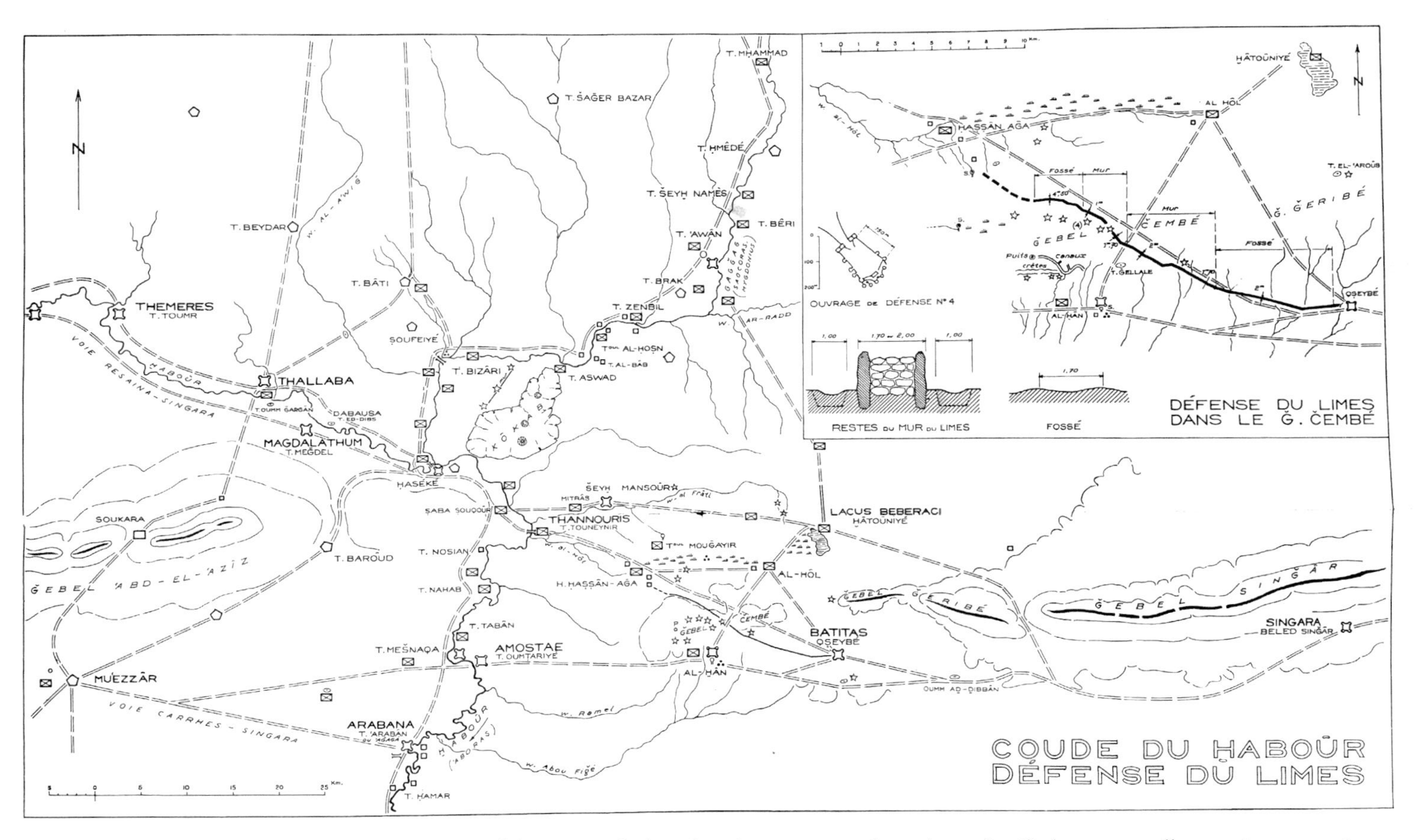

Figure 13. Poidebard's map of the Khabur bend (Pl CXL, 'Coude du Habour' Large rectangles indicate fortified towns; small ones = Roman posts (castellum/castrum).

probably of mudbrick, with a modern addition on the highest point. It is thus one of the larger forts of the area discussed here.

The old fort is not strictly aligned with the adjacent old road but is very close to it. No '*ville forte*' protecting a spring is visible to the east neither in the Corona imagery from 1967/8 nor in the recent images on Google Earth and Zoom Earth. The extract from Corona shown below gives the situation of the 'Roman' fort in relation to the neighbouring village to the east. There were some interesting small structures south of the village (circled in yellow), but nothing to justify the description as a fortified town. Regrettably these small structures are not now visible on Google Earth.

Apart from his description of this site as a fort, Poidebard also describes a system for collecting water from the Jebel Cembe to the north (p181).[54]

al-Hol

This is a village west of Lake Khatuniye which has undergone a remarkable expansion in recent years because of the construction of a large refugee camp. On the Corona imagery of 1967/68 it was a village with no sign of the Roman post indicated here by Poidebard.[55] But 4.5km to the north-north-west there is an interesting group of three fortifications which are

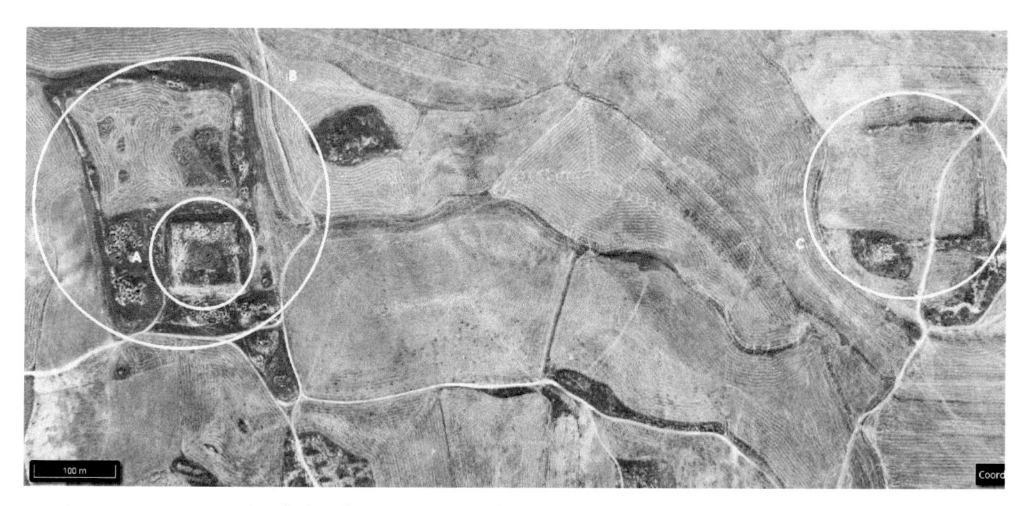

Figure 14. Forts North of Al-Hol. CAST accessed 22.01.2022. A is 94x84m, B is about 294x219m, C is 160x160m. A tower is visible in the SW corner of C in the Corona image below.

[54] *'Derrière le camp d'Al Han, situé sur la voie du limes Habour-Singata, on remarque, dans le Gebel Cembe une canalisation en forme de V qui captait l'eau pour alimenter la source du camp. La canalisation (canal à talus de terre de 8m. de largeur dans le fond) longe une région de dépression du Cembe séparée d'Al-Han par une crête rocheuse. A l'O, elle part d'un centre de puits; à l'E, le canal est précédé d'un système de fogaras collectant toutes les eaux du bassin. Eaux des puits et des fogaras, renforcés au moment des pluies par celles du plateau et des fogaras, convergeaient vers le wadi d'Al-Han qui s'est creusé dans la crêtes rocheuse du S. La photographie aérienne semble indiquer que l'eau était amenée au camp par un canal, dont il apparaît des traces , ou par un petit wadi passant contre le poste....'*

[55] Poidebard says (p157) that Aurel Stein had drawn his attention to Roman fortifications here, which he (Poidebard) then saw from an aeroplane. Since Stein only began his survey in 1938 and Poidebard's '*La Trace de Rome*' was published in 1934, Stein must have passed this information on after his visit to the area in 1929. But we have no record of this visit.

Figure 15 a and b. The fort north of al-Hol. a) Zoom Earth (accessed 26/01/2022) 36°25'52"N, 41°07'56"E. b) Extract from Poidebard Pl. CLI - Fort to east not visible

Figure 16. The forts at al-Hol. Corona 5 Nov 1968

shown below. Of these, C (25 000m^2) seems the most likely to be of the Roman period, but all need to be verified on the ground.

Although there is no road apparent on the satellite imagery in the vicinity of these three fortifications, it is interesting that they lie at the headwaters of the Wadi el-Frati, which Herzfeld investigated when looking for Chaikh Mansour.

Batitas[56]

Amongst the major fortifications shown by Poidebard on his map reproduced at Fig,13, Batitas appears in fact to be without walls - if it does in fact correspond to the abandoned village of Qseybe, as Poidebard believed. It is unclear why he should use the symbol for a major fortified town on his maps. The road to the Khabur from Singara passes through the former town.

Amostae

This placename occurs in the Peutinger Table as a station between Magrus and Batitas. Poidebard identified it as Tell Oumtariye (now called Tell Matariya and beneath the waters of the Hasaké South dam on the Khabur river). No recent photos are available and no excavations there are mentioned on the internet. Poidebard's Tell Mashnaqa lies less than 2km to the south-east. The latter was a fifth millennium site of the Ubaid period, excavated

[56] Written 'Ibatitas' in the Ravenna Cosmography (Mesopotamia 13).

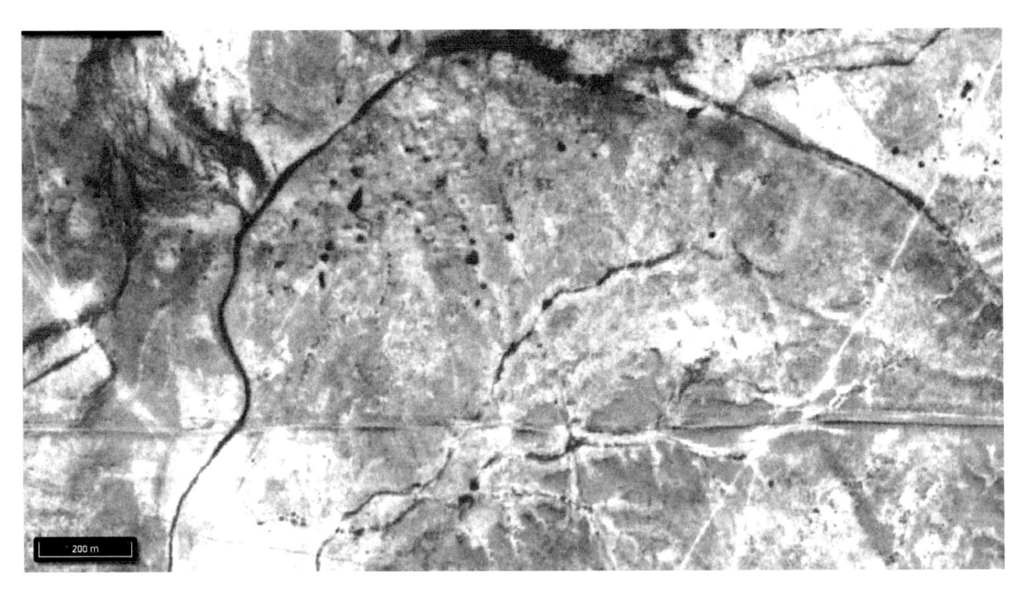

Figure 17. Batitas Corona 11 Dec 1968

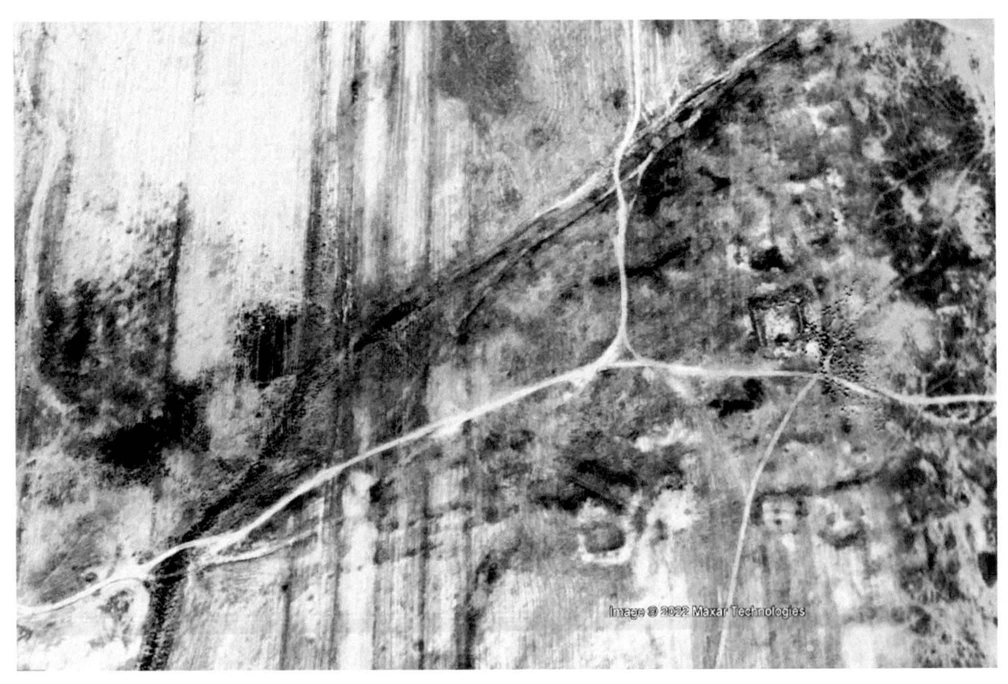

Figure 18. Batitas Google Earth 23 Nov 2020 Extract of mosaic (2 images) for part of the town 36°17'20"N, 41°14'00"E

Figure 19. Batitas CAST accessed 26 Jan 2022

by a Danish team in the from 1990 to 1995 and now also wholly drowned by the Hasaké South dam. Hellenistic and Roman levels are mentioned in the French version of Wikipedia but the excavators were interested in prehistoric periods. There is nothing visible which might justify Poidebard's fortress symbol.

An extract of Poidebard's photo of Oumtariye is reproduced below together with a rather blurred Corona image (Tell Matariya). This would have been close to an important crossing point of the Khabur on the route shown on the Peutinger Table from Carrhae via Tigubis to Singara and Hatra. This road must have passed south of the Jebel abd al-Aziz and is discussed below. Tell Mashnaqa is sadly even less is visible on Corona.

In fact, the satellite imagery shows another old road approaching the Khabur 4.5km to the north of Matariya, apparently arriving at a site which seems to correspond to Tell Taban, Assyrian Tabetu, shown on Mapcarta. This was on dry land a few years ago but is now surrounded by water. Archaeological excavations were also conducted here but Hellenistic and Roman remains are not mentioned. The four small forts between Oumtariye/Matariyah and Thannouris seen by Poidebard correspond to this and other tells in the valley,[57] but no fortification walls are apparent. Yet Thannouris, a really major fortification (see below) is shown with the same symbol on this map.

[57] Tell Mesnaya, Tell Taban, Tell Nahab, Tell Noseim are the names shown in Poidebard's maps of the valley (Figure 13). Only Tell Taban is listed on the map of Kühne (1977: 250).

Figure 20. Oumtriye/Tell Mashnaqa/Amostae? An extract from Poidebard's plate CXIV.

Figure 21. Oumtariye/Tell Mashnaqa/Amostae. Corona 11 Dec 1967 36°17'49"N, 40°46'39"E (approx.)

Of the other small 'castella' shown by Poidebard there is now nothing to be seen on the satellite imagery, but it seems likely once again that what he saw were tells in the river valley, several of which are shown on the CAST website as ancient sites. These may or may not have been used during the Roman period but calling them 'castella' seems to be going too far. It seems unlikely that even mudbrick walls would have so deteriorated in the century since Poidebard's research along the Khabur valley as to render them invisible.

Thannouris (Tell Tuneynir)

This was the principal Roman fortification along the Khabur after 363 CE, although the first available reference to it is in the Notitia Dignitatum (thought to date from c. 390 CE for the eastern Roman empire) at which time it was the base for a unit under the *Dux Osrhoenae* called '*ala prima nova Diocletiana*'.[58] It was refortified by Justinian following a failed attempt to do this under his uncle, the emperor Justin.[59] Pseudo-Zachariah recounts that a Roman army

Figure 22. Tell Taban. CAST - accessed 26 Jan 2020

[58] In fact, this unit is stated to be between Thannuris and 'Horobam'. A second (?) unit is mentioned under the *dux Mesopotamiae* at Thannuris itself called the '*Equites sagittarii indigenae*'. Possibly this is an indication that the line of responsibility between the two duces for Osrhoene and Mesopotamia changed during the fourth century.

[59] Pseudo-Zachariah Rhetor 9.2 (Greatrex 2011): "*... the works that had begun* [probably in 527 CE] *were destroyed by the*

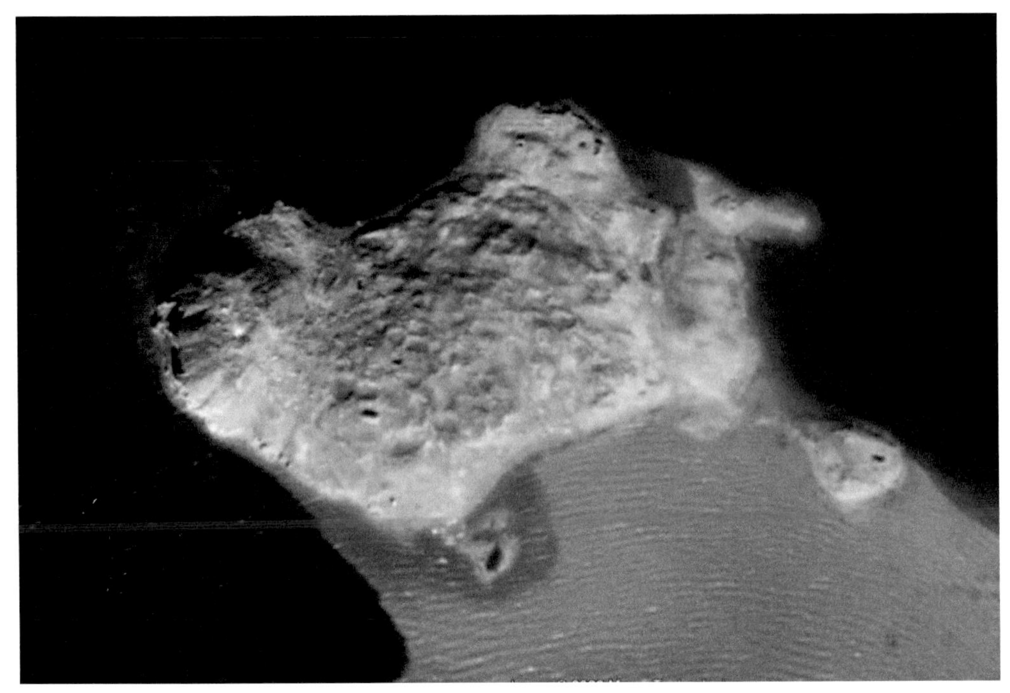

Figure 23. Tell Taban. Google Earth 5 Jan 2019. 36°20'08"N, 40°47'16'E

under Belisarius was sent[60] to Thannuris and '..*when the Persians heard of [the army's plans] they dug several pits among their defensive trenches by way of a stratagem and on the outside they drove in wooden tripod-like stakes* [or, possibly, caltrops],[61] *and they left an interval [between them].* The Roman army, which included amongst others Al-Tafar, a commander of the Tayyaye (Arabic-speaking nomads), was caught in the trap. Many were taken prisoner in the ditches and some of the cavalry which escaped fled to Dara.

The first attempt to re-fortify Thannuris must have been repeated because Procopius says (*On Buildings* 2.6.15, Loeb trans. Dewing) that Justinian made this fortress, with others in Mesopotamia ' ... *truly formidable and altogether unapproachable for their assailants'.*[62] The extract quoted below in note 62 indicates that the purpose of the fortification was to deter Arab raiders; attacks by a full Persian army are not mentioned. It is also interesting that in

Tayyaye and the Qadishites who were in Singara and Tebetha. Since the Romans ... had planned to attack Nisibis and Tebetha, henceforth the Persians were also prepared and made a defensive trench in the wilderness of Tannuris'. Greatrex states (n31) that the Qadishites were a highland people who lived in the vicinity of the Jebel Sinjar. 'Tayyaye' was simply another word for nomadic, Arabic-speaking tribes, some of whom supported the Persians, others the Romans.

[60] According to Greatrex 2011: 317 (n37) the next year 528 CE.

[61] Greatrex 2011: 317 (n40)

[62] Procopius, *On Buildings*, 2.6.15-16: "*... and two named Thannourios, one large and one small...and there was a certain spot near the larger Thannourios at which the hostile Saracens, after crossing the Aborrhas river* [Khabur] *had complete freedom to resort, and making that their headquarters they would scatter through the thick leafy forests and over the mountain which rises there and then they would descend with impunity upon the Romans who lived in the places round about; but now the emperor Justinian has built a very large tower of hard stone at this point, in which he has established a very considerable garrison, and thus has succeeded completely in checking the inroads of the enemy by devising this bulwark against them.'*

Figure 24. Tell Tuneynir (Thannouris) Zoom Earth, accessed 28/01/2022. 36°24'N, 40°53'S

this period the nearby mountain to the west (the range of the Jebel abd el-Aziz) was heavily wooded. Poidebard published an aerial photograph (Pl. CXXXVI – Soukara) showing there to be a sprinkling of trees and bushes in the 1920s; today there seems to be no vegetation at all.

The site of Thannuris was photographed from the air by Poidebard (1934: Pls CXV and CXVI), who also drew up a plan (Pl. CXVII). His description of the site is on pp.140-141 and is too long to reproduce here in its entirety, but he found plentiful evidence for the Roman fortress. One plate was reproduced and the plan redrawn by Kennedy (Kennedy and Riley 1990: Figures 68/9, pp118-121).

An image from Zoom Earth is reproduced below. Those on the CAST website from Corona and on Google Earth are unsatisfactory because blurred in the case of the Corona image and partly under water in the case of Google Earth (10/10/2019). The site was excavated in part by Michael and Neathery Fuller in the 1990s (see trenches on Zoom Earth image below).[63]

The plan shown above has north to the bottom. The ruins of the bridge noted by Poidebard (e.g. Pl. CXVI, where a pier can be seen in the river) and shown in the plan above is regrettably not visible in the Zoom Earth image and seems to have disappeared during the last century (Dillemann 1962: 130 notes that Poidebard published neither photo nor description). Presumably, the tower on the west bank (to the right above) is that built by Justinian and the Arab raiders would have crossed by this bridge.

[63] Fuller and Fuller 1998. Their interest appears to have been primarily in the prehistoric periods of occupation and their principal publication is difficult to obtain, the issues of the periodical concerned prior to 1999 being unavailable in the Bodleian Library

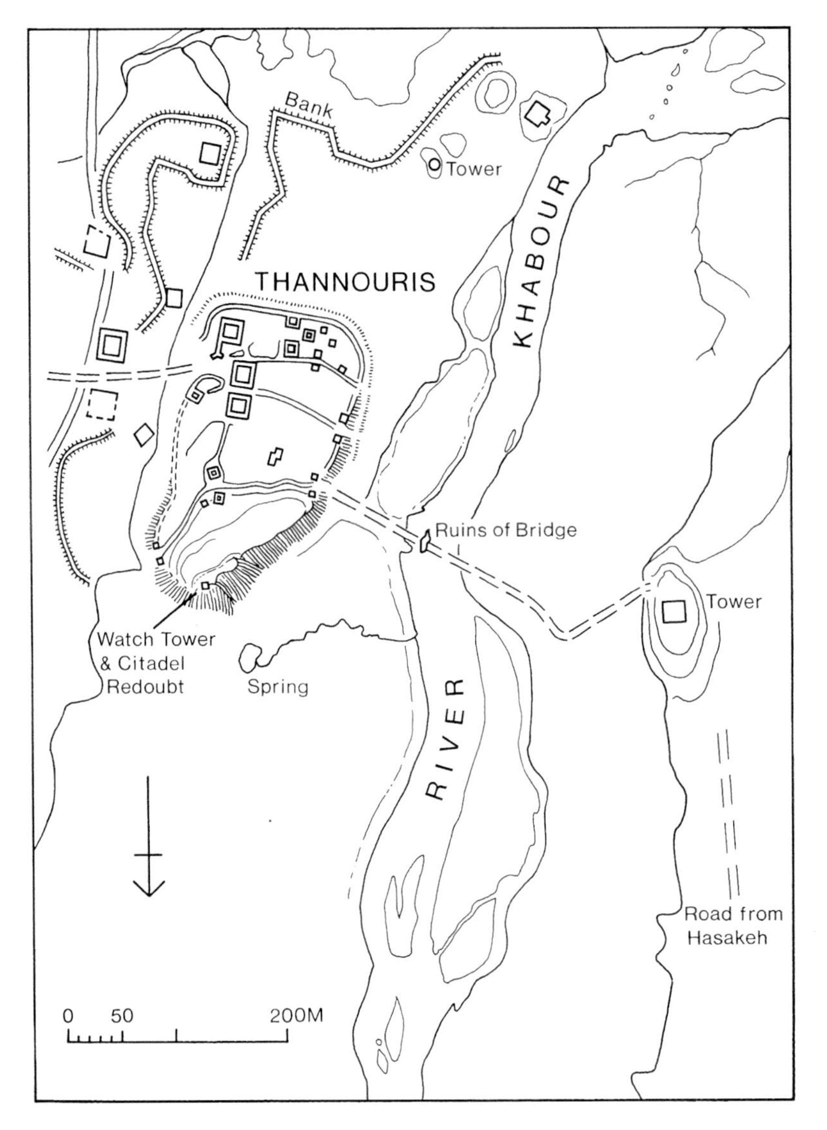

Figure 25. Thannouris. Plan by Kennedy traced from relevant portions of Poidebard, 1934: Pl CXVII. Note north to bottom.

Touloul Mougayir and Hirbet Hassan Aga

Poidebard describes the fortified road from Thannouris to Singara via the Jebel Cembe as '*la ligne principale du limes*' (La Trace, p162). Various sites to the north-east of Tell Tuneynir were mentioned by early travellers. In particular, Sarre and Herzfeld, who passed through in 1908-10, visited Mitras and Shaikh Mansour;[64] one of these might correspond to the 'Thubida'

[64] Herzfeld, Sarre and Berchem 1911-1920: Vol 1, 196

mentioned in the Ravenna Cosmography and shown on the Peutinger Table as the station preceding 'Lacus Beberaci'. Since the site of the latter is firmly identified as the existing Lake Khatuniye, and the distance shown is XVIII miles, it should be an easy matter to identify. But regrettably it has proved difficult to locate these sites on the satellite imagery.[65] Since Herzfeld found a four-cornered structure at Mitras, which he thought might be a Roman camp, and Shaikh Mansour was only 4 km further east, it seems unlikely that both could be important sites of the Roman period. Both sites were situated close to the 'Wadi el-Frati', whose course leaves the Khabur just to the north of Tell Tuneynir/Thannuris and arrives at al-Hol, 24km due east. Dillemann (1962: 176 and Figure XXIV) identifies Thubida with Herzfeld's Shaikh Mansour (he spells Shaikh 'as 'Cheikh').

14 km from Thannouris on a road slightly to the south Poidebard found Touloul Mougayir (1934: 157). He published an aerial photograph at PL. CXLIX and a plan at Pl.CL. He describes it as a

> Castellum de 50x50m, bâtiments alignés à la face intérieure. Tours d'angles circulaires de 3m.30 de diamètre. Deux tours rondes intermédiaires à chaque face. Orientation

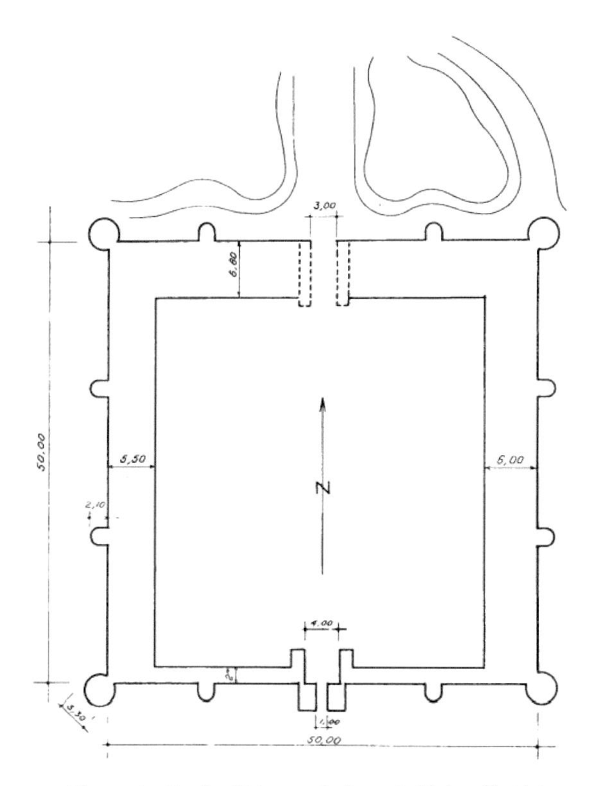

Figure 26. Touloul Mougayir from Poidebard's Pl CL

[65] A hint of such a structure is located at 36°26'26"N, 40°54'43"E but this is doubtful. It may correspond to the sketchmap of Shaikh Mansour made by Herzfeld at his Fig; 96. This site is 30km or 20 Roman miles west of Lacus Beberaci/Lake Khatuniye.

Figure 27. Touloul Mougayir a) Google Earth 20/08/2020 and b) Corona 5 Nov 1968
36°24'30"N, 41°01'27"E.

> N-S. Porte au N. et au sud. Le poste disposé pour avoir des vues étendues sur tout le Wadi el-Hol et le Cembé, gardait les sources.

This structure (2500m^2) has now been identified near the modern tarmac road between Hasaké and al-Hol. The satellite images are unfortunately not of good quality. No further information is available concerning the date of construction.

12.6 kilometres to the east-south-east of Tell Touneynir and just 3.8km south-west of Touloul Mougayir is the fortified camp of Hirbet Hassan Aga. This is mentioned by Poidebard on p154 of 'La trace de Rome':

> Le camp de Hirbet Hassan Aga, muni d'un point d'eau fortifié, gardait l'extrémité du long marécage d'Al-Hol qui longe les pentes N. du Gebel Cembe et forme un rempart naturel.

He published a plan at plate CXLII. The camp is about 200x120m or 24 000m^2. His plan also shows a fort protecting a spring situated 2.5km SSE. The camp and the likely site of the small fort are circled in yellow on the Corona image shown below. For the fort only 2 walls are now visible and only on an extract from the CAST image accompanying the Corona one.

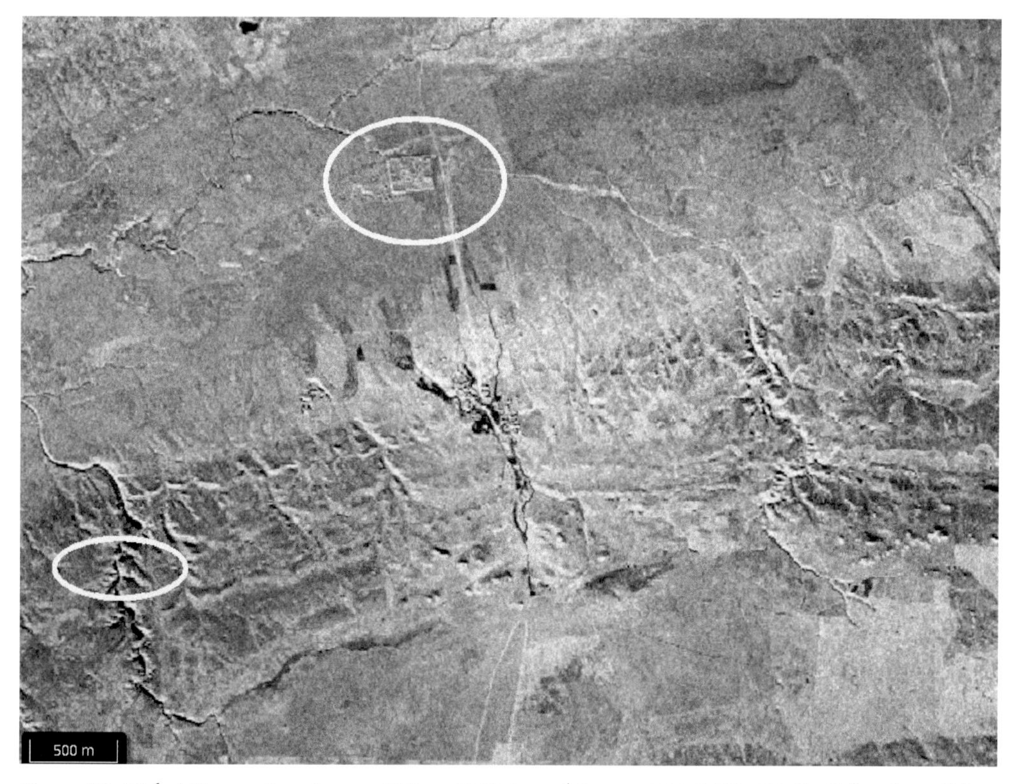

Figure 28. Hirbet Hassan Aga. Corona 5 No=v 1968 Camp (above – 36°22'48N, 40°59'51"E) and small fort (bottom left circled on yellow).

Figure 29. a) Enlargement from Figure 28 above showing the camp (Corona 1968) and b) Situation of fort guarding spring - CAST accessed 27/012022

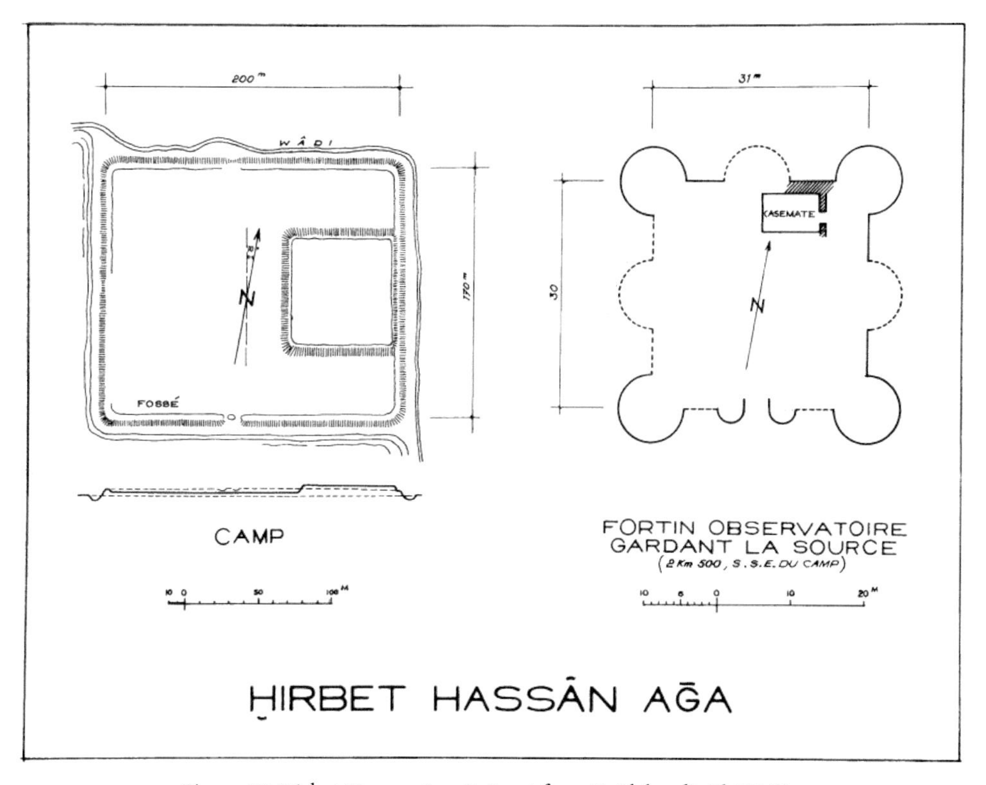

Figure 30. Hirbet Hassan Aga. Extract from Poidebard's Pl CXLIII.

The camp is situated on an old route from Tuneynir (Thannouris) to Batitas and Alaina. So far there is no evidence concerning the date of construction for this fortification either. There are no towers to be seen, although Poidebard's plan shows that the small fort (less than 10 000m^2) guarding a spring – which is not clearly visible on the satellite photo - did have such towers. Evidently, in the absence of any possibility for an excavation in the near future, a visit by a qualified archaeologist is necessary to verify the presence of any surface pottery. The absence of towers for the main structure may indicate a date either in the Hellenistic period or else in the early Islamic.

The wall of Jebel Cembe

Near the centre of the triangle formed by Batitas, Thannouris and Amostae (Tell Oumtariye) Poidebard found a long wall which he assumed was associated with the Roman frontier defences. It leads from a point near the abandoned town of Batitas, where the road coming from Singara splits into routes heading north-west to Thannouris, west to Amostae and south-west to join the Khabur at Shaddida (see discussion in Chapter 4). It leads from Batitas to the north-west and thus might have contributed to guarding the first of these routes towards Hassan Aga, although the SE-NW orientation seems wrong for defence of a frontier whose orientation was more likely SW-NE. (The road continues on to Thannouris.) However, as the study by Napoli has confirmed (1997), it can have had little to do with deterring enemy attacks

Figure 31. Extract from Poidebard's Plate CXLVII, oriented to the north and showing the course of the wall on the Jebel Cembe. The dashed yellow line is placed just to the south of the wall. The structure called by Poidebard 'ouvrage de défense indigène', visible to the south-west is now thought to have been a 'kite' or early animal trap.

because it is low and for the most part without ditches. Regrettably, the wall is not visible on the available satellite imagery, but Poidebard did publish an aerial photograph, reproduced above, as well as the details shown in Fig 13 above.

The wall of Jebel Cembe is the only 'long wall' known to exist in this region. Evidently, it is comparable neither to Hadrian's Wall nor to the enormous fortifications constructed by the Sasanians on their northern and north-eastern frontiers. Its alignment is also not what one might expect for a fortification guarding a frontier. But it does seem strangely long and important for a boundary wall, so more investigation is desirable.

The Khabur valley

To the south of Tell Tuneynir and Tell Oumtariye (Amostae), sites discussed above, the Khabur valley stretches for over 130 km to join the Euphrates at Circesium. The frontier between Rome and Persia lay along this valley from at least as early as he emperor Diocletian until it was lost first to the Persians in the early seventh century[66] and then to the Arabs following the battle of the Yarmouk in 636 CE.[67] The land to the east of the Khabur is arid and would have been extremely difficult for an army to cross – for example, from Hatra – because of the lack of water. One 'road' - or at least caravan route - is known south of the Jebel Sinjar heading east from Semsaniye (see map 2) but this is relatively far to the north.

Circesium (al-Qarqisiya in Arabic, but now known as al-Busayrah), at the most southern point of the Khabur where it joins the Euphrates, is known to have been a frontier post between Rome and Persia for centuries. It existed as a Roman post in the third century since, inter alia, Shapur I claimed to have captured it in about 256 CE.[68] It was apparently first fortified at the end of the third century CE by Diocletian, as Procopius informs us, and then restored by Justinian (*On buildings*, II.6.1). Julian's army crossed from here into Persian territory in 363 CE and the fortification is mentioned in the Notitia Dignitatum under the *Dux Osrhoenae* as the base of the Prefect of the Fourth Parthian Legion towards the end of the fourth century.[69] Its bishops attended three early Christian councils (Nicaea 325, Chalcedon 451 and Constantinople 536 CE), but nothing is to be seen of a church nor of the city and its fortifications today.[70] The site is thought to lie beneath the village of Al-Busayrah at the confluence of the Khabur and the Euphrates.

Poidebard published no photos and the Corona image for al-Busayrah, though clear, shows nothing of archaeological interest. However, when Herzfeld came through in 1907/8 he made two sketch maps reproduced here (Sarre and Herzfeld 1911-1920: vol1, 172 and 173):[71]

---

[66] Contrary to Streck's article on Karkasiya in the Enclyclopedia of Islam, New Edition. Circesium is not likely to have been one of the fortresses ceded to the Persians by Jovian in 363 CE since it figures in the Notitia Dignitatum, which is posterior to Julian's expedition.

[67] But only definitively towards 690 CE (Le Strange 1905: 105).

[68] Gordian died in 244 CE and was buried in a cenotaph 20 miles from Circesium according to Eutropius IX.2. See the ' Res gestae divi Saporis' or Shapur-KZ, where the Greek version of this inscription contains the name Κορκουσίουνα. amongst the cities conquered by Shapur I in 252-256 CE. Dillemann (1962: 203 n1) also cites the Chronicon Paschale of the reign of Decius (249-251), which states that the eastern frontier of the Roman Empire ran at that time *ab Arabia et Palaestina usque ad Circesium castrum*.

[69] This legion moved to Aleppo in the early fifth century according to Theophylact Simocatta (2.6.9). This historian also tells us (4.10.4) that Khosrow II when escaping to the Roman empire in 590 CE crossed the frontier here and found refuge with the commander of Circesium, Probus.

[70] But in the 10th century CE Qarqesiya was a thriving city with gardens and fields according to Istakhri and Ibn Hawqal (Le Strange 1905: 105).

[71] The accompanying text reads as follows. (trans. Google and AC): '*Busairah is the modern name of Circesium. The modern place, consisting of about 30 houses, lies on the Euphrates side of the old city. It is a raised military post overlooking the Euphrates Valley. We stayed in an empty house south of the main ruins. The old city, where the accumulation of rubble of which is very considerable, indicating a long duration of occupation, extends over a promontory of somewhat irregular shape. The Euphrates Valley forms two sides of it as a deep bay, while on the other side is the Khabur valley. The bank on which the old city lies is still today cut off by a ditch from the Khabur. The area of ruins thus forms a pronounced peninsula. Outside the ditch, however, there is a larger, flat and probably not long inhabited area covered with potsherds. The remains of various old buildings are still visible. Above all a kind of fort, Figure 79, of about 50 by 40 paces in area, with towers at the corners. The masonry consists of layers of rubble with brick trimmings. The bricks are Byzantine tiles with very thick layers of mortar. The entrance is through a gate on the east side. Best preserved is a domed building on the west side: an octagonal room fourteen paces in diameter, made almost square by apses in the corners. The apses each have 3 round niches, the straight sides have doors, the outside has a window. In the upper part of the wall there are two small windows above the doors. The dome vault begins above the octagon on curved pendentives. A*

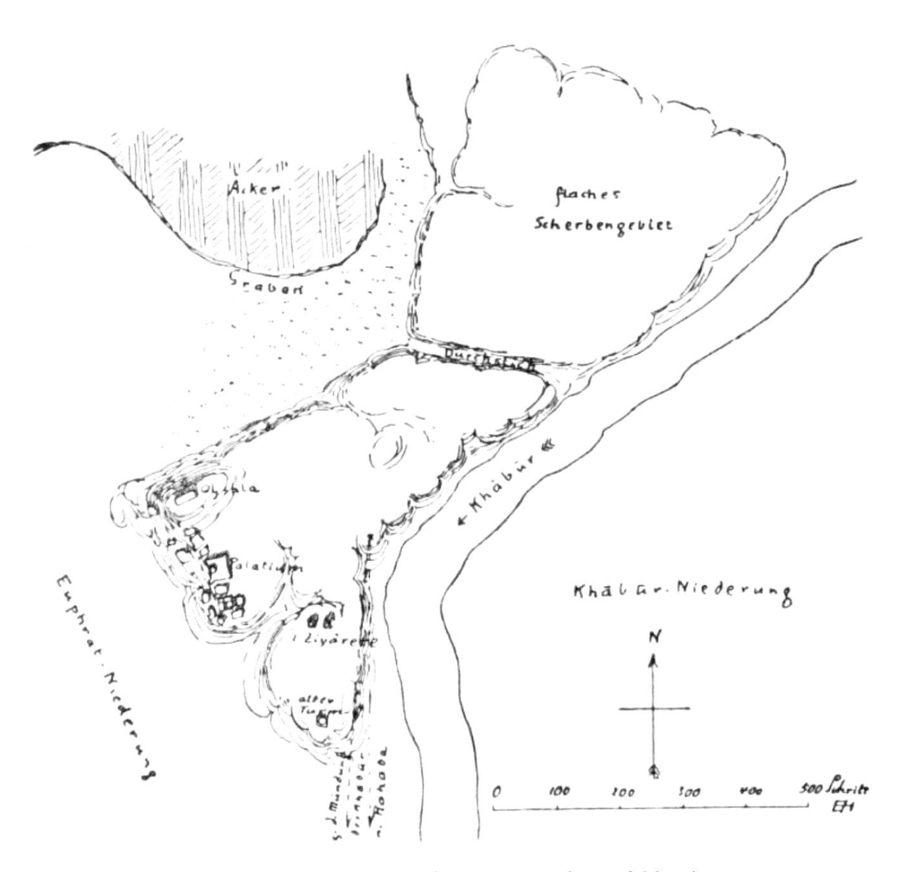

Figure 32. Circesium. Figure 78 from Sarre and Herzfeld Vol 1, p172

The handwritten text is difficult to make out.[72] The word 'palatium' is shown next to a square structure to which the plan below may correspond.

The scale bar is only legible in the original but according to this plan the outer dimensions of the fort, including towers, were 18x15m and the area within the walls was 15.4x12.4m or a bit less than 200m². Evidently, this seems small for such an important fortress. The outer fortifications were presumably much larger.

stairway lies to the north of this domed building. The whole building is not uniform, but repairs can be seen in several places. The inside was so incredibly dirty that the picture could only be taken very briefly. The ruins apparently lay with their west side on the city wall. A round tower of this city wall could be seen in the courtyard of the house where we stayed. Other remains of the city wall are still preserved on the Khabur side. I spied out a tall and strong round tower at the southern tip of the old city, but only from a distance. The pottery predominant in the ruins is Byzantine engraved glazed ware. There are also Islamic wares of the Raqqah type of pottery. Small illegal excavations had been carried out at the ditch opening, which had yielded mainly Raqqah pottery, said to have come from Dair'.

[72] The scanned version of the text available to the writer is taken from https://archive.org/.

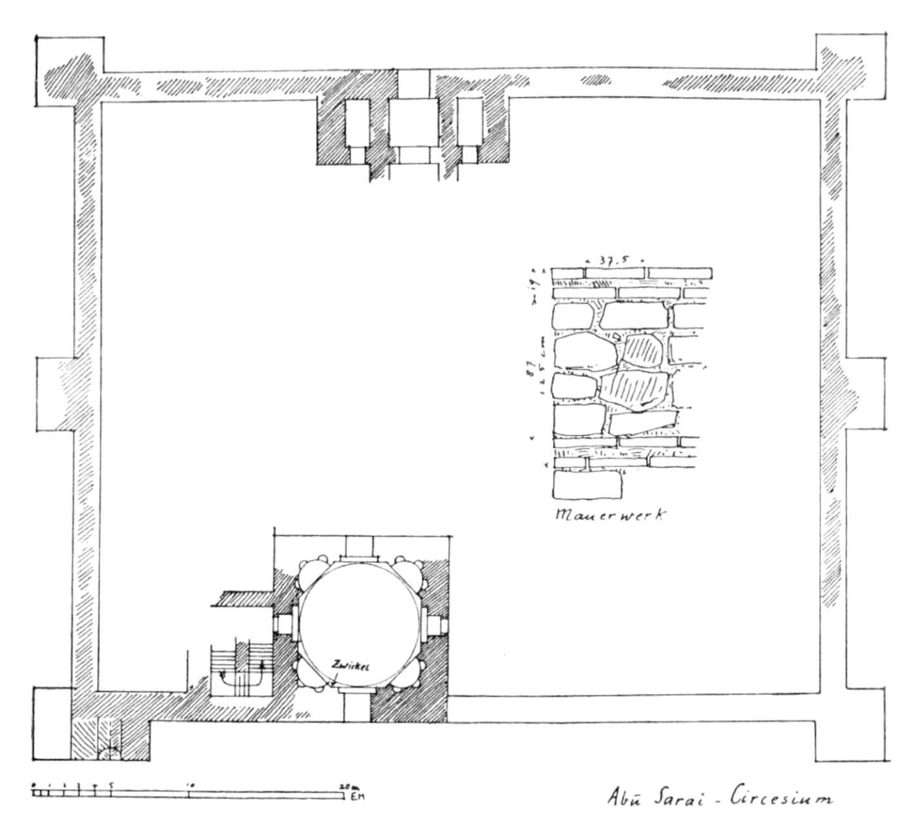

Figure 33. Circesium. Figure 79 from Sarre and Herzfeld Vol 1, p 173

North of Circesium

In the view of this writer the principal access to Singara from the west, for example in the time of Constantius II, was either down the Khabur from Resaina or from Nisibis or else down the Euphrates from Nikephorion via Circesium, where troops and messengers would have turned north along the Khabur. Routes across the desert, such as that shown on the PT from Carrhae to Amostae via the southern flanks of the Jebel al-Aziz, seem unlikely to have been much used - especially not by large groups - because of a lack of water (see also discussion in Chapter 4). In the Khabur valley there are at least two other sites known to have been occupied by Roman troops in the fourth century between Circesium and Thannuris: these are Apadna and Horaba. Both places were within the boundaries of the Roman province of Osrhoene. In the Notitia Dignitatum these apparently fortified sites are mentioned[73] after Circesium. 'Apadana' is also a city near the Khabur listed in Ptolemy's Geography as Ἀφφαδάνα.[74] Dillemann, following Herzfeld (1911-1920: 176-177 and 184-6) identifies it with 'Fedein', 26km upstream from

[73] In the case of Apatna the name of the unit is missing from the text; Horaba is mentioned because – as seen above - the '*Ala prima nova diocletiana*' was '*inter Thannurin et Horobam*'. Apatna or Appadana is now sometimes located opposite Circesium on the right bank of the Euphrates (see Edwell 2008: 68-70), although this seems incompatible with the Notitia Dignitatum which places it in Osrhoene.

[74] See Stückelberger and Grasshoff 2006: 582

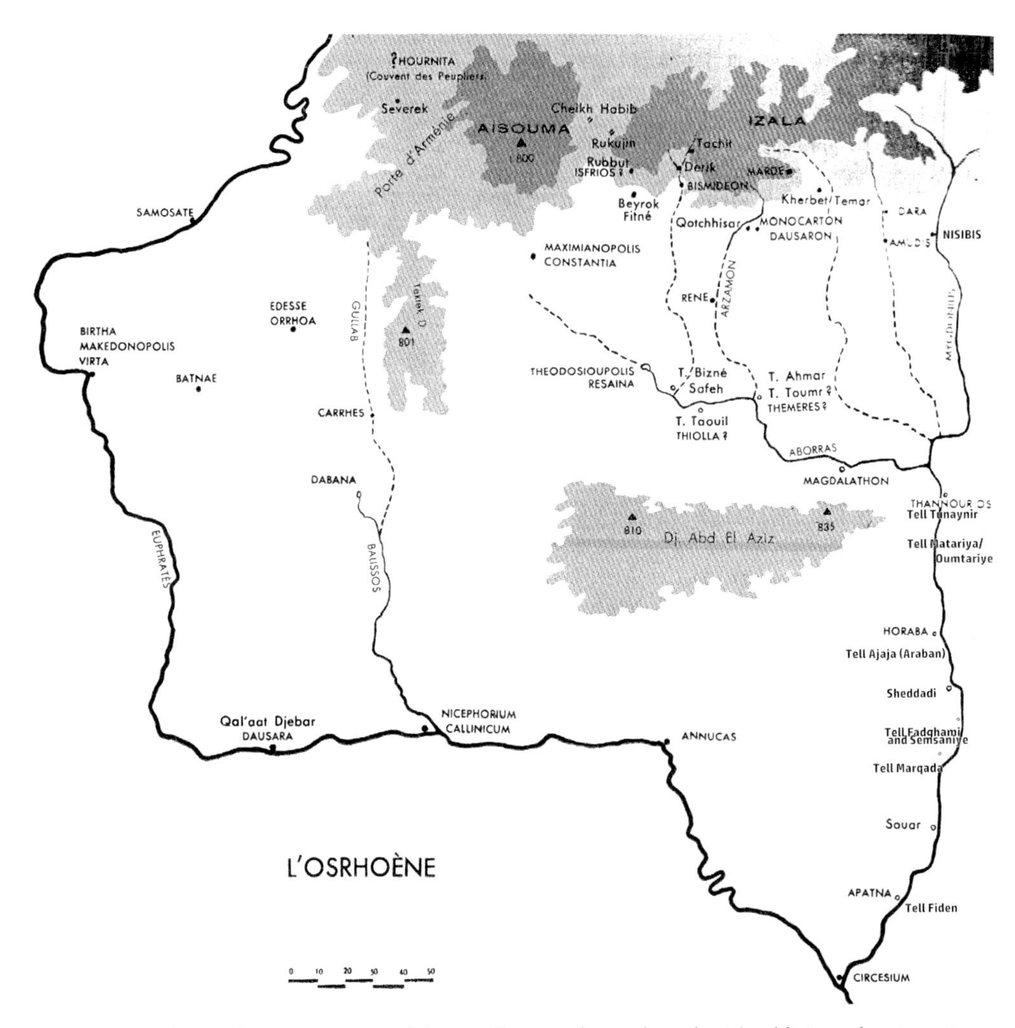

Figure 34. Osrhoene (NW Mesopotamia) from Dillemann (1962: fig. XI) with additions showing sites along the Khabur river ('Aborras')

Circesium, and Tell Arban with 'Horoba' (1926: 203).[75] Poidebard photographed several places along this valley and discusses them as '*postes du limes*' from p134 to 138 of 'La trace de Rome'.

Dillemann's map of Osrhoene and the Khabur valley is reproduced below so that readers may comprehend the distances involved and the position of some of the sites discussed in the valleys if the Khabur and Jaghjagh (*Mygdonius*).

Edwell is the most recent writer to discuss the Roman sites on the lower Khabur (2008: 76-81). He states that the Dura Papyri show the presence of at least one cohort in the mid-220s and

[75] This Apatna cannot be the same as the 'Apadna' near Mardin (Tell Harzem/Arcamo), which appears to have had a significant role as a place for collecting taxes under the Achaemenids (Dillemann 1962: 170). The name though appears in both cases to indicate a Persian royal palace.

probably two in the early 230s, The Barrington Atlas of the Greek and Roman World shows no less than fifteen sites between Circesium and Thannouris in the Khabur valley with occupation during the Hellenistic to Byzantine periods. Information concerning these sites comes from a survey conducted in preparation for a map in the TAVO series[76] by Röllig and Kühne (1977 and Kühne 1978). The reports concerned give little information about these sites[77] and the evidence shows potential Roman military bases only at Tell Fiden (Apatna?), Tell Seh Hamad and Tell Fadghami, where Musil had noted the terminus of a caravan route from Mosul (1927: 85).[78]

The many other sites showing signs of late Roman occupation are unsurprising since in late antiquity the whole Khabur valley appears to have been Roman territory right through to the conquests of Khosro II in the early seventh century CE. However, the valley did not play an important role in the wars between Rome and Persia, apart from the battle of Thannouris in 528 CE (see above). This may have been because of the difficulty of finding water for a large Persian army seeking to advance westwards from the Tigris via Hatra or Singara even by the northern route to Thannouris. Procopius says[79] that the tower built by Justinian at Thannouris was designed to keep out raiders and not to counter a major attack by the Sasanian army.

Even if Fedein was Apatna, as Herzfeld (who writes the name 'Fudain') and Dillemann supposed, neither Herzfeld's sketch (p. 177) nor the Corona image for this location[80] can offer details which might support an identification as a Roman fortification. A modern road has been built across it very recently.[81] The papyri from Dura discussed by Feissel and Gascou, also discussed by Edwell, mention an 'Appadana' which was an important centre but they show this site as being located on the Euphrates and not in the valley of the Khabur (1989: map on p543). Such a location is however incompatible with the fourth century Notitia Dignitatum which shows 'Apatna' as being in Osrhoene.[82]

Tell Ajaja/Arban/Horoba

The current name is Tell Ajaja. It is situated only 11km SSW of Tell Matariye (see above) and was the site occupied by Layard's expedition to the Khabur in about 1850, when it was known to him as 'Arban'[83] (1853: 272-284). He found there substantial sculptures of Assyrian winged bulls and a lion, as well as Egyptian scarabs and a medieval minaret, but mentions nothing of the Roman period. Nevertheless, according to Herzfeld (1911: 186) and Dillemann (1962: 203), Tell Arban/Ajaja is the 'Horaba' mentioned in the *Notitia Dignitatum*.[84] It was most

[76] Tübinger Atlas des Vorderen Orients.
[77] The authors appear to have been interested principally in the Assyrian period.
[78] Musil had visited the Khabur valley in the 1920s from the Euphrates and described some sites.
[79] As discussed above. Procopius, *On buildings*, 2.6.15
[80] 36°21'42"N, 40°33'46"E
[81] Fedein and the whole valley up to Haseké were the object of a survey by the university of Tübingen in the 1970s (Kühne 1977, Kühne 1978}. Very little is reported for the Roman and Islamic periods.
[82] That is on the north bank of the Euphrates and the west bank of the Khabur. A scribal error is however possible: Apatna, mentioned after Circesium, is shown in any case without indication of the military unit assigned to it and there is a gap in the text. The section on Syria Euphratensis shows no units on the Euphrates south bank other than Barbalissus, Neocaesarea, Rosafa, and Sura.
[83] Herzfeld gives both names and says that it was also known in common speech as 'Orban'. He noted four piles of a bridge in the river, which he describes on p187. Both the bridge and most of the ceramics he considered to be early Islamic.
[84] Oates states that Tell Ajaja was Assyrian Šadikannu, the destination of a march by Assurnasipal II from Nimrud to

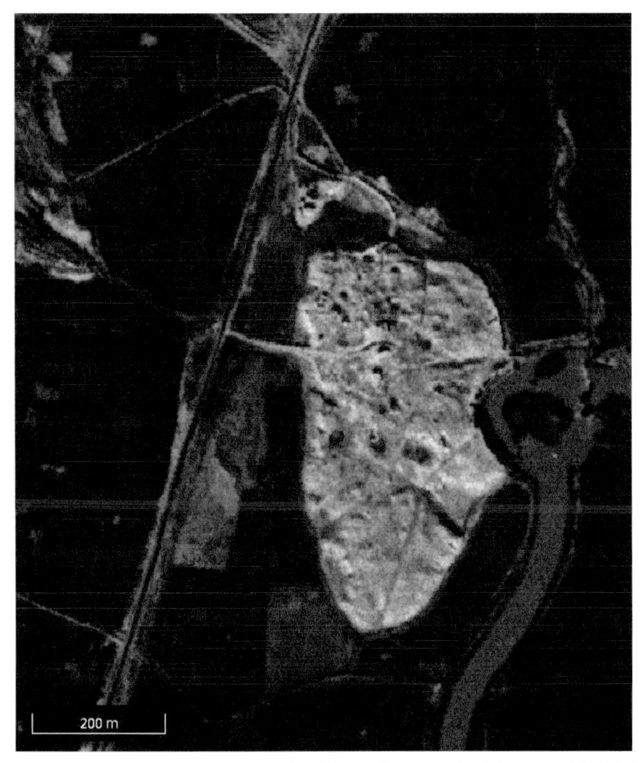

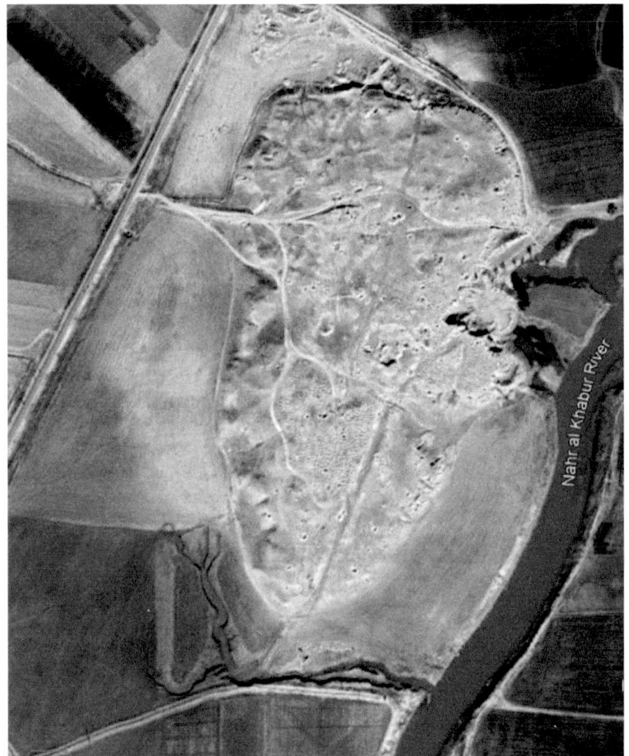

Figure 35. Tell Araban
a) Corona 5 Nov 1968
b) Google Earth 27 Feb 2021

recently investigated in 1982 but nothing of importance from the Roman period was found (Mahmound, Bernbeck et al. 1988).[85] The bridge found here by Sarre and Herzfeld (Herzfeld, Sarre and Berchem 1911-1920: 189) was dated by them to the 13th century.

The papyri from Dura of the early third century CE, discussed by Edwell (2008: 76-79), raise the possibility that Tell Araban/Ajaja was also the base of a Roman garrison called 'Castellum Arabum'. It may also have been known as 'Qatna', where *Cohors XII Palestinorum* was based in the 230s.[86]

Poidebard describes the site as follows (*La trace*, p137):

> A l'époque byzantine, [Arban] avait gardé sa place capitale dans le limes du Habour, comme l'indique la technique de certaines reconstructions des murs d'enceinte, de même type que les murs de Marqada.

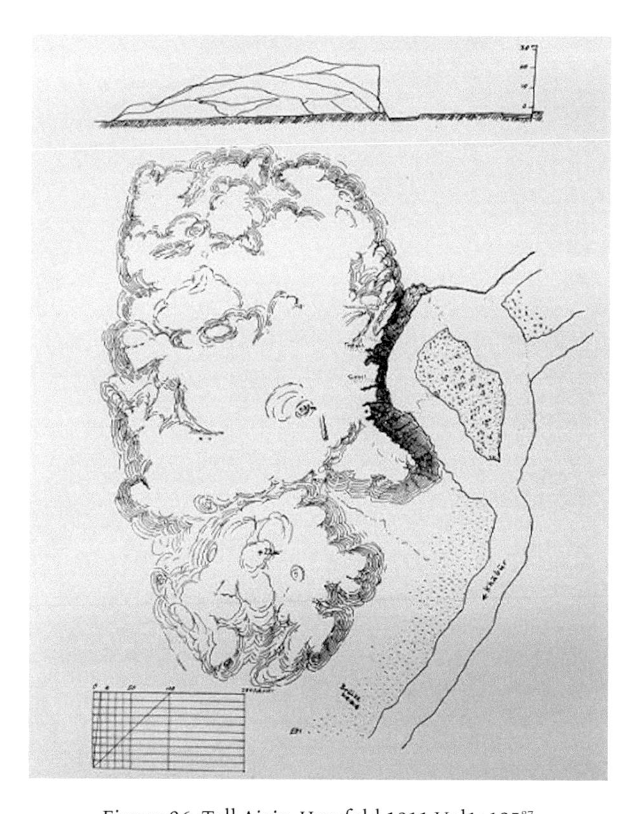

Figure 36. Tell Ajaja. Herzfeld 1911 Vol1: 185[87]

the Khabur via Tabite (Ta'idu?) and Magarisu (1990: 239).

[85] Although some Sasanian pottery was found.

[86] Edwell discusses also a papyrus from Dura concerning Cohors XX Palmyrenorum that show a detachment of soldiers at 'Magdala'. The site of Tell Megdel on the Khabur above Haseke probably corresponds to this place and to the 'Magdalathum', mentioned by Procopius as a fortress in Mesopotamia restored by Justininan (*On buildings*, II.4.5.6). It lies outside the area of NE Mesopotamia concerned in this book. Cf Chapot 1907: 303 and Poidebard's map 'Coude du Habour' reproduced at Figure above,

[87] Edwell states (2008: 79) that this plan shows a castellum in the middle of the site. But this writer is unable to

Figure 37. Tell Arban Poidebard Pl.CXIII. 36°05'26"N, 40°42'15"E

Once again there is nothing visible today at Arban in the satellite photographs which might indicate fortification by the Romans. There are other sites along the valley which may have been occupied in the Roman period, in particular the 'Marqada' mentioned by Poidebard.[88] This and other possible Roman posts are also discussed below in the chapter on roads. Dussaud shows on his map XV (*Haute Mésopotamie*) roads leading east from the Khabur valley from Marqada, Tell Arban and Thannouris, but indicates that the first two were medieval (Dussaud 1927: Chapter VII.6).

Tell Brak and the Jaghjagh

Continuing north beyond Thannouris along the post-363 CE frontier between Rome and Persia the Khabur river is joined by the Jaghjagh, flowing south from the Tur Abdin, at a point near the current major city of the area – Hasaké. The valley of the Khabur river turns west and continues up to Resaina, outside the purview of this book, which is limited to north-east Mesopotamia. The line of the Jaghjagh is north-south and close to where this river emerges from the escarpment of the Tur Abdin is situated the city of Nisibis.

There are many further tells between the fortress of Thannouris described above and the city of Nisibis. Several of these were thought by Poidebard to have constituted fortified posts on the frontier between Rome and Persia after 363 CE and indeed it would not be surprising to find such fortifications along the Jaghjagh line. Hasaké, the current major town of the area is

identify it.

[88] Sarre and Herzfeld 1911-1920: 18061, Poidebard 1934: 135. Poidebard's description : '*Tout autour de la plateforme : traces de murailles ; au N., restes de large fossé muni d'un talus extérieur élevé formant première enceinte. Murailles construites en technique byzantine : blocage de moellons de basalte, noyés dans abondant mortier très dur et alternant avec des lits de briques cuites*'. However Röllig and Kühne reported only pottery confirming occupation in the late classical and early Islamic periods (1977: 123)..

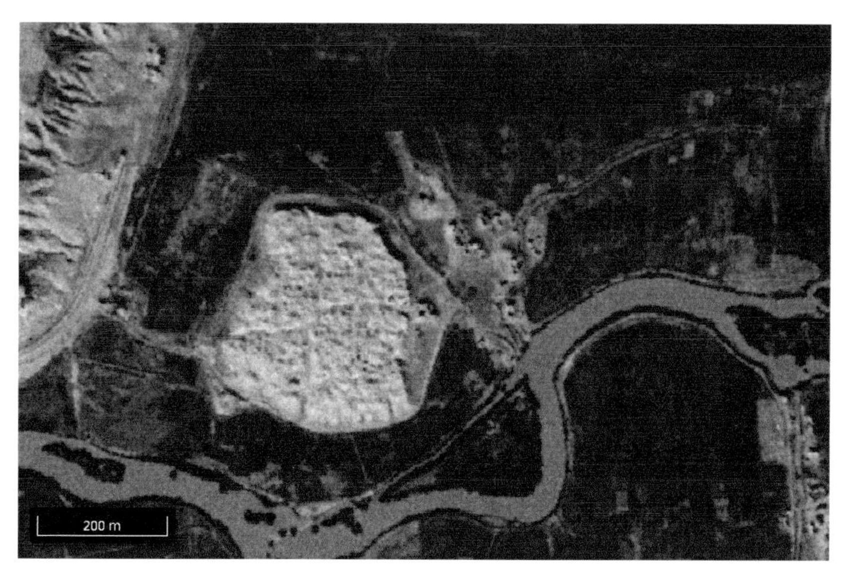

Figure 38. Marqada. Corona 5 Nov 1968. 35°44'38'' N, 40°46'00''E

largely a French colonial foundation but has some ancient antecedents. In the Roman period Poidebard said that the area was important because it lies on the junction of two Roman roads: north-south (Circesium to Nisibis) and east-west (Resaina to Singara).[89] 13km north of Thannouris on the Jaghjagh (known as the Mygdonius in antiquity) and to the north of its confluence with the Habour there was then a 'Roman' bridge at Soufeiyé (...*'gué de Soufeiyé (ou Soufaiyan) avec ruines d'un pont romain au pied d'une colline portant traces d'une ancienne ville'*. This bridge, according to Poidebard, carried a road from Mardin to Singara, but possibly also the north-south road from Nisibis to Circesium. It lies between two tells: 'Haséké' (left bank) and 'Gouweran' (right bank, i.e., nearer the modern town of Hasaké). Although he published some poor photos of a ruined pier of this bridge at Pls.CXVIII and CXIX, he states - without further evidence - that trial trenches at Tell Haséké revealed walls of baked bricks of the Roman fort,[90] while on the summit of Tell Gouweran there were still traces of an ancient square tower.[91]

For the ruins of the ancient town, Poidebard cites (p142, n2) Oppenheim and Herzfeld. The former's chapter ten (Oppenheim 1899, 1900) recounts a journey in 1893 from Deir es Zor to Nisibis; this journey was repeated in regard to its first part by Sarre and Herzfeld in 1907/8. At part II, p27 Oppenheim recounts his journey from Hasaké to Nisibis. Near a mound called Tell Barazé he reports the same ruins of the old stone bridge, which he believed was connected to the west-east Roman road shown in the Peutinger Table from Fons Scabore (Resaina) to Lake Khatuniye (Lacus Beberaci).

Herzfeld's account on pp189-191 of '*Archäologische Reise*' describes the ancient bridge as follows "*...The pillars of the bridge, four in number, still rise out of the water. The building materials*

[89] Poidebard 1934: 142. He also says here '*De Thannouris à Haseke les tells à distance régulière sur les deux rives, postes militaires ou fermes fortifiés gardant le Habour* .

[90] '*...les sondages ont permis de retrouver les murs en brique cuite du poste byzantin*'.

[91] '*...porte encore traces d'une ancienne tour carrée. La ville byzantine, comme la ville arabe, semble avoir été construite sur la plate-forme inférieure de Tell Gouweran.*'

are natural lava stones set in concrete mortar. The shape of the pillars has become unrecognizable. But the whole appearance of the bridge, in contrast to the Khabur bridge at Araban, leaves me accepting Oppenheim's supposition that it comes from antiquity" (translation Google and AC). However, although he remarks on the density of ancient occupation around the confluence (and the absence of modern houses), Herzfeld does not say anything about ruins of an ancient town near the bridge. Presumably Poidebard was referring to Tell Bizari (see next).

Only one of the tells between Hasaké and Nisibis was investigated thoroughly by Poidebard – Tell Brak, described below – but he does describe remains of Roman fortifications at others, in particular Tell Bizari. This tell is situated between Hasaké and Tell Brak in a stretch of the river where it flows east-west. Poidebard says (p.143) that it is located 1.5km upstream from the bridge at Soufeiyé on the left (here south) bank.[92] '*...This was a byzantine fortified town of the same type as Thannouris. A first platform surrounded by walls with square towers rises in tiers facing the SE, the direction from which enemies [would attack]: it was dominated by a tell or fortified redoubt whose platform was 20m above the plain. Same construction materials as Thannouris : blocks of calcareous stone or basalt pebbles set in a very hard lime mortar. On its SE face the wall is 300m long, 2m50 high and 1m50 thick*' (trans. AC). Two satellite images are provided at Figure 40.

We are fortunate to possess another view of the fortifications around Tell Brak dating from the Roman period. David and Joan Oates wrote a contribution to a 'Festschrift' for Adnan Bounni entitled 'Aspects of Hellenistic and Roman settlement in the Khabur basin' (1990). They visited this site (Tell Bizari) from Tell Brak, which they excavated in the 1980s. They suggest that it is Middle Assyrian Makrisu and Roman Magrus, the station mentioned in the Peutinger Table as that preceding Amostae for those coming from Hatra to Singara (Oates

Figure 39. Bridge at Soufeiyé Poidebard Pl. CXIX.3

[92] This would place it at a point before the Jaghjagh changes its course from E-W to N-S, but most maps show the position of the bridge as a a little further downstream, after the river has changed course.

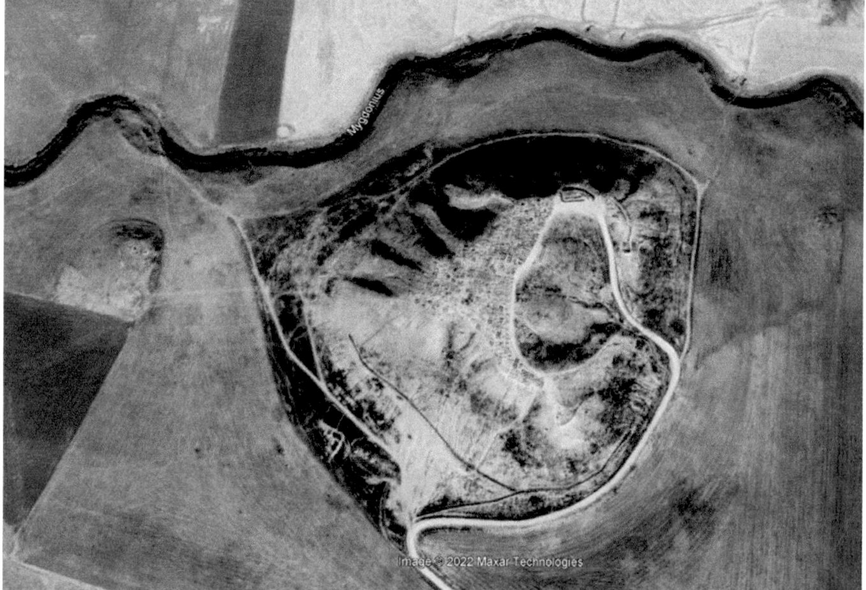

Figure 40. Tell Bizari. a) Corona 5 Nov 1968. b) Google Earth 24 Oct 2020 36°36'02"N, 40°47'09"E

Figure 41. Poidebard's post at Tell Zenbil (north bank). a) Pls. CXXI and b) CAST accessed 05/02/2022
36°38'18"N, 40°58'53"E

and Oates 1990: 238-9).[93] The Oates found a wall, possibly Roman, 300m long and 1m50 to 2m50 thick, together with 'a very large amount of Roman pottery', as well as sherds from pre-historic periods - especially Mitanni and Middle Assyria. Foundations of Roman buildings sealed the lower south-east side of the mound, which measures 480 by 379m and 20m high. It is said by them to command an important river crossing and to show evidence of extensive occupation in Roman and earlier periods.

Between Bizari and Brak, Poidebard found two promising sites for which his photos are reproduced at figures 41 and 42. He does not dwell on these in his text (p143), although both seem possibly to have been of Roman – or more likely Hellenistic[94] - origin. The camp at Tell Zenbil is described in the photo caption as a platform 96x96m; the 'post' at Tell al-Bab is said in the text and caption to have two towers with 'enceintes' of 40x40m and to be situated between two other posts.

Sadly, it has not proved possible to locate the 'post' of El Bab on the satellite imagery, possibly because of changes to the meanders of the Jaghjagh or the extension of cultivation.

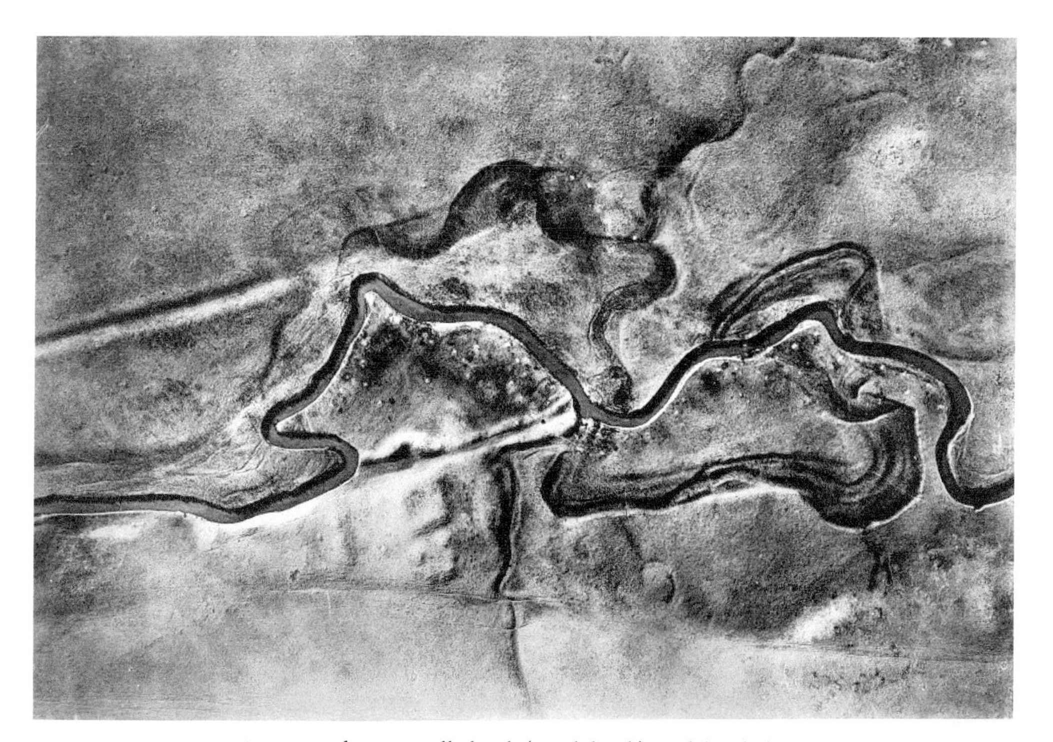

Figure 42. The post Tell el-Bab (south bank) Poidebard Pl.CXX

[93] This seems unlikely to this writer, who believes Magrus was to be found to the south below Thannouris and west of the river Khabur (see discussion below in 'roads')

[94] The Oates found two sites here: a mound 250x150m and the rectangular fortified enclosure of Poidebard where they found a large quantity of Hellenistic sherds but no others.

The river bends again, this time to the north as it approaches Tell Brak, a large mound now identified as the ancient city of Nagar.

Tell Brak

Dillemann published a map of Poidebard's claims for this valley of the Jaghjagh which is reproduced below.

Dillemann is extremely critical of Poidebard's methods and conclusions especially for this sector of the 'limes' (1962: 198-201). He notes in particular that Poidebard ascribed to the Roman period tells which lay both on west and east banks of the Jaghjagh. He also dismisses the second north-south fortified line described by Poidebard as lying some 30km to the west of Tell Brak and passing through Tell Bati (see below).

The one major site at which Poidebard conducted excavations was Tell Brak, whose position near the point at which the Jaghjagh turns from N-S to E-W and is joined by the river Radd coming from the east was thought by him to require a Roman post on the 'limes' (p143). Apart from the large Bronze Age tell at this site, which has been excavated over a long period by Oates and others, in 1927-8 Poidebard saw what he thought were three 'Roman' camps:

1. 8km to the south [in fact WSW) at Tell Zenbil (see figure 40 above and his Pl. CXXI)
2. 5km to the north, the triple camp of Tell Awan (Poidebard's Pls. I-III) – discussed below.
3. 5km to the east, across the Jaghjagh on its left (east) bank the bridgehead with a 'legionary camp', showing lines for tents (Pl. CXXII) – now known as Saibakh.

The square fortress at Tell Awan is large – about 270 by 280m when measured on the Corona image or over 75 000m^2. Corner towers are also visible. The site was investigated by the Oates who found very few sherds and no basis for dating the square enclosure, although they identified the circular enceinte as Late Assyrian from its plan (1990: 233).

Although Tell Zenbil (1 above) is still visible on satellite images of today, the triple enceinte at Tell Awan (2) is not. Fortunately, the Corona image of 1968 does reveal the exact position of all three and is shown above (figure 46). The fort at the bridge head opposite Tell Brak (3) is now under a village (Saibakh) and this was already true in the 1960s. It is now widely thought to be Sasanian and to have a twin at Ain Sinu (see figures 3a and b).

No ancient author refers to Roman fortifications at this point, but there are several unlocated toponyms in Procopius and in George of Cyprus.

For these fortifications, including that at Tell Brak itself, Poidebard states that he carried out a ground survey with rapid trial trenches ('sondages') at all three sites in 1927. Subsequently, he returned and found from the air a central 'castellum', some hundreds of metres to the north-east of the main tell, with a low platform, invisible at ground level, and with traces of corner towers. With the help of a battalion of French soldiers he excavated over a period of ten days the walls of a 'Byzantine' fort, in particular one of the corner towers in pentagonal form and part of an external wall.

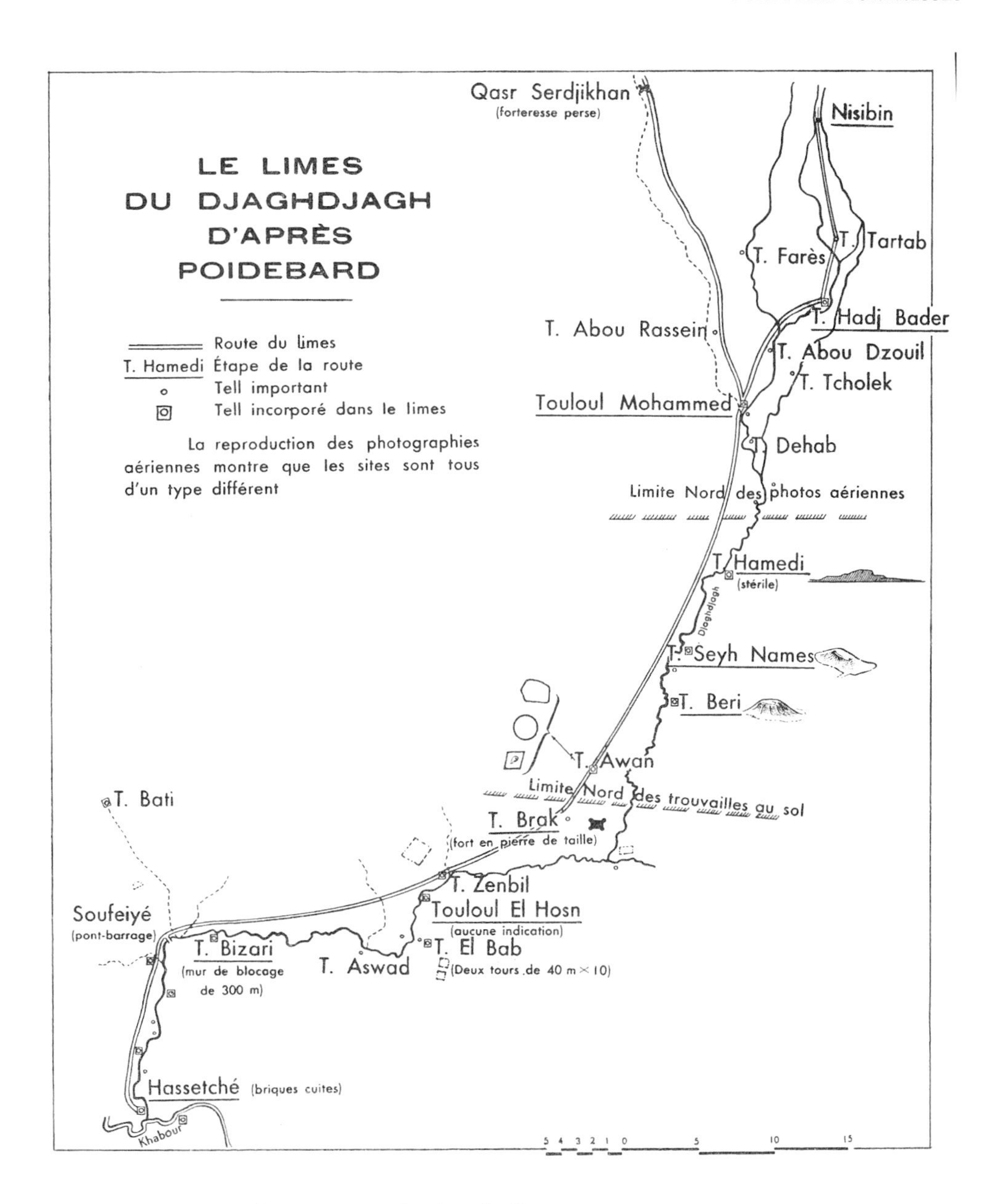

Figure 43. Reproduction of Dillemann 1962 Fig XXVI

In 1928 the work was continued and all the essential parts of the construction were uncovered. The 'castellum' measured 91x91m; apart from the four pentagonal corner towers, the fort had 24 circular side towers and a gate with drawbridge on the west side. Remains of a military chapel were revealed in the NE corner of the courtyard. He says (p144) that although no inscriptions were found the plan of the castellum, the nature of the materials used, the construction technique and a mason's mark on a pillar of the chapel confirmed the Byzantine origin of the chapel. (Poidebard uses the term 'Byzantine' where this writer would prefer to use 'Late Roman'; he states that this fort conforms to the principles of military construction from the period of Justinian, as used in north Africa, citing Diehl (1896 148ff).

Poidebard also drew parallels with the outlying forts of Dara, Serjihan and Qasr Curuk.[95] He says that the bricks used in construction are the same as those at Circesium, so this fort and those of Circesium and Serjihan could all be from the reign of Diocletian, rather than that of Justinian.

The castellum was surrounded by a pentagonal platform measuring 750x475m, with an external ditch 15 to 20m wide and a rampart. Poidebard thought that the town in the Roman period had been situated on the tell but that the inhabitants would have retreated to this fortified camp around the castellum in case of an attack (p145). Further aerial exploration by Poidebard revealed that outside this pentagonal platform and the enclosed late Roman town, there had once been

> ...an ancient rectangular compound with ditch, half erased. These were probably the remains of a legionary camp, placed in the centre of the external camps around. Quickly levelled to make room for the platforms of the Byzantine defences, it left behind in the steppe a few low mounds which were very visible from the air (trans. AC).

Figure 44. Tell Awan Poidebard Pl. I.1

[95] The first of these has been thought to be rather of Persian construction but this writer does believe it to be originally Roman (Comfort 2017: 219). It is situated on the north side of the modern border with Turkey 13km WNW of Nisibis/Nusaybin. The second, Qasr Curuk was near Amouda; it was seen by Poidebard in 1929 but seems to have since vanished; his Plate CXXXII.2, labelled as Qasr Curuk, in fact shows the tower of Serjihan (now Durukbaşı; see the same tower in Comfort, ibid, figure 48).

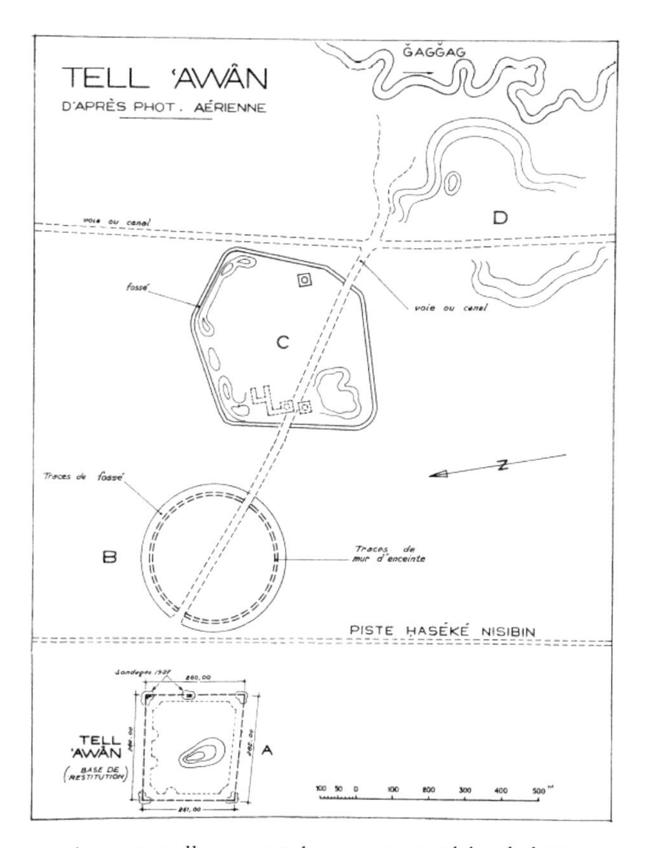

Figure 45. Tell Awan Triple enceinte. Poidebard Pl. III

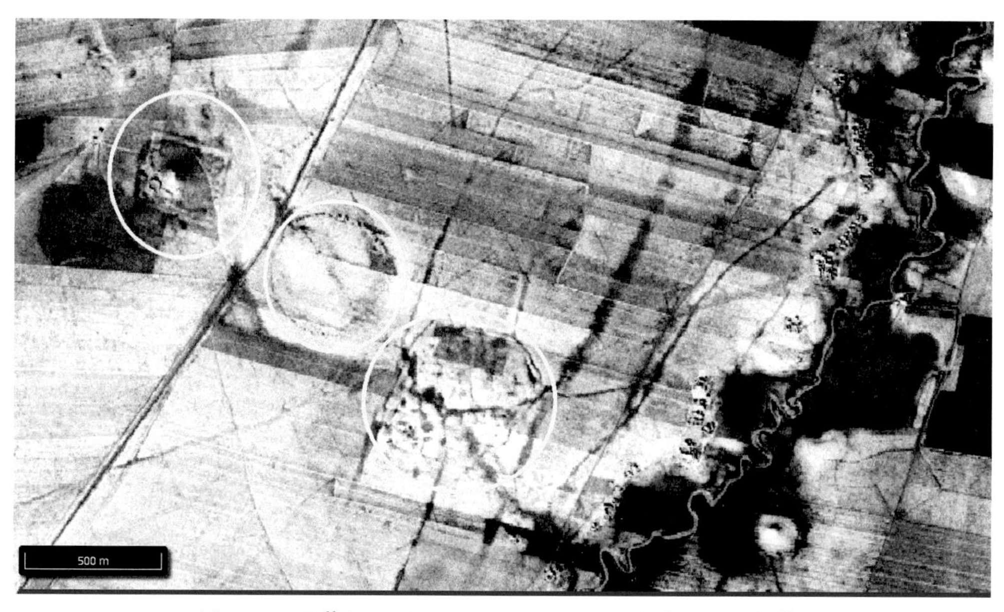

Figure 46. Tell Awan Corona 5 Nov 1968. 36°42'46"N, 41°04'59"E

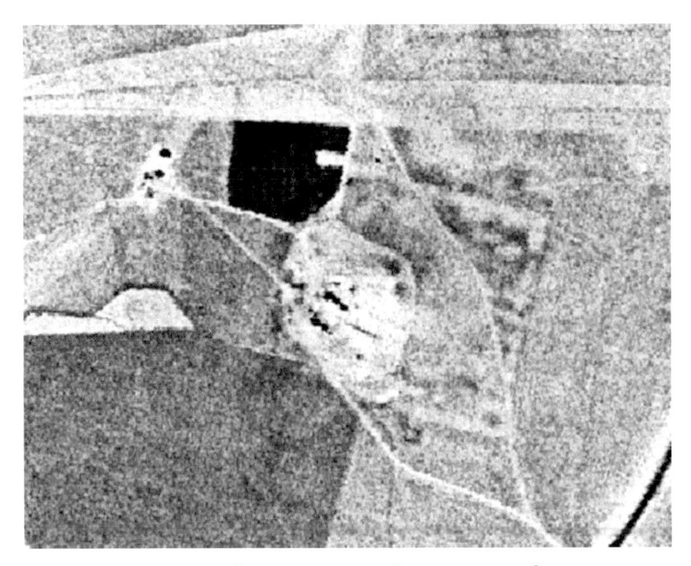

Figure 47. Tell Awan. Extract from previous figure

Figure 48. Tell Brak: Saibakh. a) Poidebard Pl. CXXII. b) Corona 5 Nov 1968. 36°39'39"N, 41°06'13"E

Most regrettably Poidebard published no other aerial photographs of the site. There is however evidence of his excavations on the Corona image of 5 November 1968, shown below. The 'platform' with remains of the Late Roman town is also visible.

His plans and photographs of the excavation are revealing but further data concerning the excavation, including the potsherds found at the site, were never published. Readers are urged to visit the online publication of Poidebard's 'atlas' (Vol 2 of '*La trace de Rome dans le désert*') for the complete collection of plans and photographs of the excavation, especially

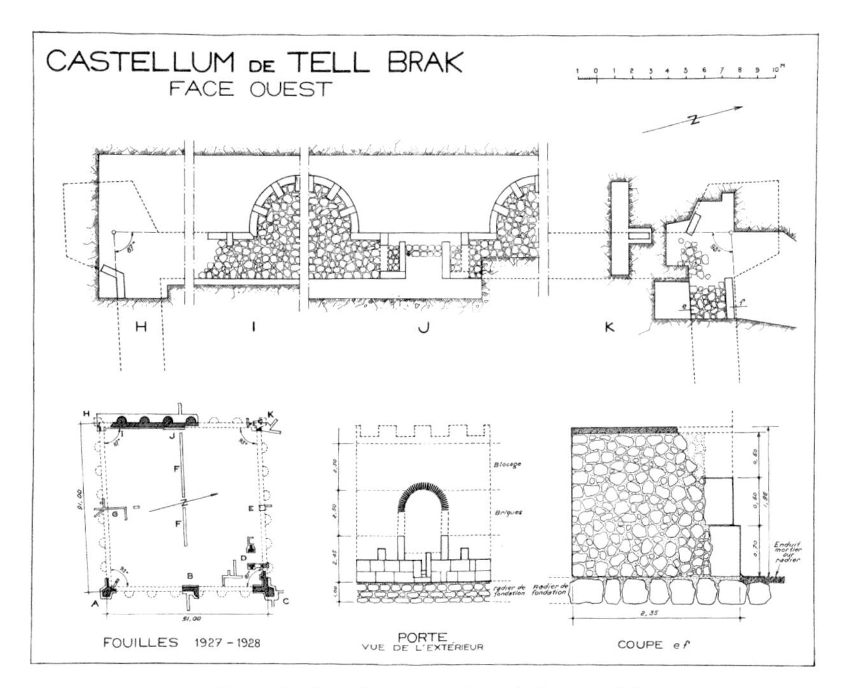

Figure 49a. Castellum of Tell Brak – west side and plan. Poidebard Plate CXXV

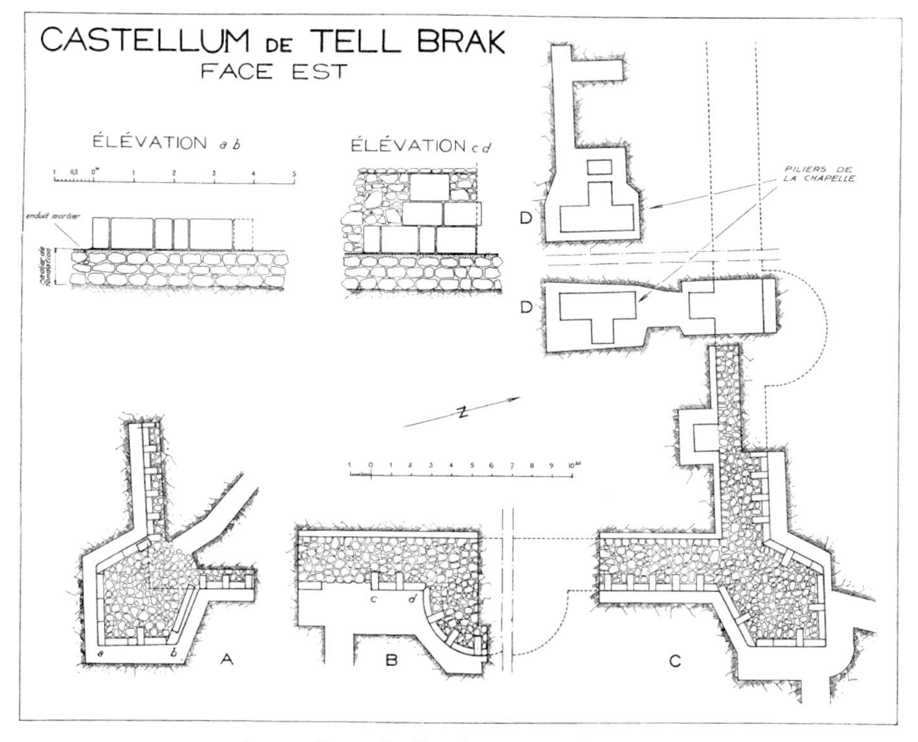

Figure 49b. Castellum of Tell Brak – east. Poidebard Plate CXXVI

Figure 50. Tell Brak Poidebard Plate CXXIII.

plates CXXVII and CXXVIII, since there is unfortunately insufficient space here for all.[96] Below are reproductions of Pls. CXXIV and CXXVIII.2 only – an aerial photograph of the excavation showing the walls and towers and a ground photo of a wall of the chapel.

It is evident from the photos that a large number of limestone blocks were used in the construction of the fort. These blocks would probably have been transported from the Tur Abdin to the north and are an indication that the fort is not Sasanian in origin (since their camps and fortresses were usually made of mud brick[97]). In the fourth century, at the time when the Peutinger Table was drawn up, it is possible that the site was known as 'Sihinnus'.[98] The likely period of construction would have been either the reign of Diocletian or that of Justinian. If the latter, then one of the unlocated toponyms for Mesopotamia in Procopius' *On Buildings* might also correspond to the site: Vimisdeon, Themeres, Vidamas, Thiolla, Phicas or Zamarthas (II.xi.14). Another possibility, perhaps specifically for Poidebard's triple enceintes at Tell Awan, would be Bebasa,[99] although Dillemann places this with Thilapsum at Tell Chaker Bazar (1962: 173), excavated by Mallowan[100] and situated 34km SSW of Dara, 27km NW of Tell Brak. (This site is outside the area covered by this book and Mallowan's report describes no finds from the period of classical or late antiquity.)

[96] https://repo.library.stonybrook.edu//xmlui/handle/11401/89118
[97] Although in the Caucasus the fortifications of Dariali and Derbend as well as the tower at Chirakh Qala are of stone (Sauer, Nokandeh et al. 2017).
[98] The PT shows a route from Edessa via Barbare, Chanmaudi and Thilapsum which seems to end at Sihinnus before – perhaps - continuing to Singara. Of these toponyms only Chanmaudi has been identified with any probability of success – it was very likely another name for Amouda (Dillemann's route no.4, 1962: 171-5).
[99] This was the site of a stop by the army of Shapur II during his campaign of 359 CE (Ammianus Marcellinus XVIII, 7.9). See Dillemann 1962: 290-297.
[100] Tell Chaker Bazar: Mallowan 1936a

Although a late Roman date was accepted for Tell Brak by Dillemann (1962: 199) and Isaac (1992: 256), Gregory rejected this (1996: 181-3).[101] The pentagonal corner towers have no parallel in Roman fortifications elsewhere. The small round towers shown on his plan (in Figure 49 above) do however seem reminiscent of those in the east wall of Dura Europos. In the absence of any other generally accepted proposal for the date of construction of this fort, this writer tends to the view that it is from the time of Diocletian and that the limestone blocks were brought from the Tur Abdin down the Jaghjagh, a feat requiring a solid implantation in the region which could have been acquired at the end of the third century by the Romans but perhaps neither by them nor the Sasanian Persians subsequently.

Oates, both in *'Studies in the ancient history of Northern Iraq'* and at the end of his report on excavations at Tell Brak for 1983/4, mentions this 'Roman' fort and that opposite to the east on the far side of the Jaghjagh. He draws attention to the similarity of the latter with Ain Sinu: (Oates 1968: 90-92 and Oates 1985: 171). In the article entitled *'Hellenistic and Roman settlement in the Khabur basin'* the Oates state that they found 'no evidence for a Byzantine date for the

[101] P.183: '...[Poidebard's] conclusions are completely unsubstantiated. On typological grounds alone, Poidebard's interpretation of Tell Brak as a 6th c. Roman fort should be viewed with extreme caution. It does not conform even to his own mistaken conception of what a 5th c. plan should be like and is completely unlike any other known or likely late Roman fort... In fact, in its proportions (if not its scale) it more closely resembles examples of Sassanian plans ... rather than the typical Islamic ones (believed by Poidebard to be 'post-Diocletianic'...'.

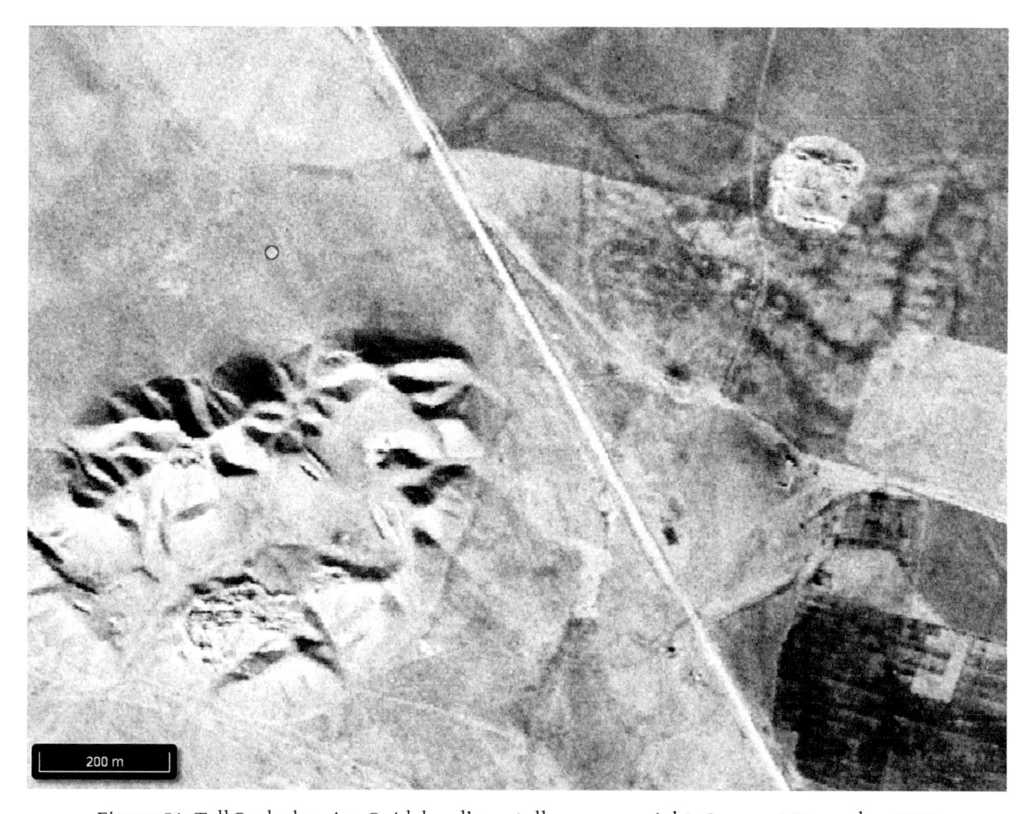

Figure 51. Tell Brak showing Poidebard's castellum upper right. Corona 5 November 1968

Figure 52. Tell Brak – castellum seen from above Poidebard Pl CXXIX

outer enceinte' nor for a legionary fortress other than the castellum itself. They note that no evidence was published by Poidebard other than the photos and plans of the castellum. But they also believed that the fort was probably of the fourth century CE and possibly associated with the re-fortification of the frontier following the loss of Nisibis in 363 CE (p228). The structural technique seemed to them to be similar to that of the walls of Singara – known to have been built before 363 – which they themselves had excavated and examined closely.

The Oates also reported that 1400m west of the castellum there was a low mound which did indeed show evidence of occupation in the Roman period in the form of diamond-shaped sherds found also at Hatra and Ain Sinu and dated to the first half of the third century.

In regard to Saibakh, the village east of the Jaghjagh and 3.5km SE of Brak, the aerial photograph shows a fort with four inner lines, apparently the remains of barracks blocks (Figure 48 above). Since Poidebard's day a village had been built on top of the fort, obscuring these lines, but the Oates noted an outer ditch 200m square and the faint traces of an inner roadway from north to south on the photograph. Poidebard had found bricks identical to those of the castellum but no evidence was found by the Oates of a 'praetorium' nor any surface pottery.[102] They state that the site of Saibakh is exactly parallel to, but slightly smaller than that of Ain Sinu. The only other example of such a site known to them is the 'fort' shown on Poidebard's aerial photograph of Tell Bati (30km WSW of Brak). This has now been destroyed but, in any case, the distinctive three inner rows of barracks blocks do not seem to this writer to be surrounded by any clear wall or ditch nor even properly aligned.

[102] A single bronze coin, coated with silver, was shown to them. *'Its size, average diameter c.23.5mm, might suggest an imitation of an early third century Antoninianus, a time when debasement of the cointage was particularly prevalent'* (p250).

Figure 53. Brak: Photo of gate. Poidebard Pl. CXXVII.2

The position of Tell Bati so far west of the assumed course of the frontier between Rome and Persia after 363 CE presents a serious conundrum for those who see in these three 'forts' Sasanian constructions, if indeed Tell Bati is such a fort. In any case,[103] Poidebard's conclusion that it formed a part of second defensive line to the west of the Jaghjagh must be dismissed, as Dillemann has already done (1962: 199).[104]

Going north of Tell Brak Poidebard mentions a Tell Beri, now called Tell Barri, (p147: '*...d'occupation byzantine*') and Tell Hmede. Even though he specifically states that excavations of the latter tell by Dunand did not reveal Roman fortifications, he nevertheless considered that it must have been a Roman post because a road, which he saw from the air, crossed the river here to continue east to another Roman bridge near Tell Garasa. He published a rather unprepossessing photo (Pl. CLXI,1) also of this bridge, which has now disappeared. There is no evidence to show that it was a Roman construction, although it is not all clear who else might have built this, nor indeed the bridge at Soufeiyé.

Italian excavations north of Tell Awan have taken place over many years at Tell Barri, now identified as ancient Kahat. Oates found to the north of this site two Attic sherds which may

[103] A fort 30km west of the line of the Jaghjagh is unlikely to have been Sasanian if the post-363 north-south frontier below Nisibis frontier was indeed along the river. The fort is also less clear in plan than that at Saibakh (figure 47).
[104] Poidebard posited a north-south inner frontier road west of the Jaghjagh from Thallaba to Mardin, which would have passed through this site (1934: 150).

Figure 54. Tell Bati. Poidebard's photograph (Pl. CXXXIX) re-oriented to show North at top and 'fort' circled in yellow.

be firmly dated to the second half of the fifth century BCE (p234); similar finds at Tell Barri confirm a connection with the Mediterranean in the Achaemenid and Hellenistic periods. For the first half of the first millennium CE some substantial traces including a defensive wall, large quantities of pottery and coins (Pierobon Benoit 2008). These indicate that Tell Barri was within the territory controlled by the Parthians but might also support Poidebard's assessment of Tell Barri as a late Roman settlement. Little clarity regarding its role in the Roman period has resulted[105] and there is no firm evidence from here that the Jaghjagh constituted the frontier between Rome and Persia after 363 CE. A single coin of Gordian III from the mint at Singara found in a ceramics workshop is insufficient to indicate with any certainty a role as a Roman station on the 'limes', although Pierobon Benoit does state that a late defensive wall in mudbrick on the summit may date from the period of conflict between Rome and the Sasanians. Lamps dated to the end of the eighth century CE indicate that the site continued to be occupied (2008: 193/4).

The last site mentioned by Poidebard before reaching the road from Resaina to Nisibis is Tell Hmede/Hamidi (possibly, ancient Taidu). Unfortunately the preliminary report includes only technical data without discussion (Eichler, Wäfler et al. 1990). There does not appear to be evidence of any military installation from the late Roman period.

[105] Rocco Palermo's book contains a chapter entitled 'Imperial Impact on a small scale: the site of Tell Barri between the 2nd and 4th century CE' (Palermo 2019: 164-187).

Dillemann's map (figure 43) shows how the road heading north along the Jaghjagh divided with one branch heading north-east to Nisibis and a second heading north-west to Amouda and Dara. The latter would have been the frontier road after 363 CE when Nisibis was ceded to the Persians and it would be of great interest to know how the Romans organised their frontier with Persia in the region after Nisibis was ceded in 363 CE. Regrettably no sites have been identified of forts north of Tell Hmede (also Hamedi or al-Hamadiya) until Serjihan.[106] It seems likely that this partly extant fort lay on the frontier, since Procopius specifically mentions in the sixth century that the frontier lay 28 *stades* from Dara towards Nisibis,[107] i.e. to the west of the latter city.

Serjihan, now called Durakbaşı, is right on the west-east line of the modern frontier between Turkey and Syria but on the Turkish side; it was visited by the writer in 2005 and was linked by Honigmann to a chapel dedicated to St Sergius.[108] Dillemann affirms the Persian identity of this fort, despite its evidently Roman style of construction (Comfort 2017: 219-220). It seems to this writer that, as for Tell Brak, it is likely to have been originally built for Diocletian, even if during the sixth century it was in Persian hands. Theophylact Simocatta tells us that Marcian, a general of the emperor Justin II, reconquered it in 573 CE but that he then went on to fail before Thebothon,[109] presumably Thebeta (see above).

Cizre and Bezabde

The northern limit of the region covered in this book (north-east Mesopotamia) is the Tur Abdin. The fortresses of the Tur Abdin, including those on its southern flank, are discussed in Comfort 2017. The roads are treated in the following chapter. The principal fortresses were Rhabdion (Hatem Tai kalesi) and Bezabde, now identified with Hendek, 13km NW of Cizre, but the principal crossing of the Tigris was probably at Cizre itself, even though the ancient name is unknown.[110]

Like Serjihan, Rhabdion, Cizre and Bezabde are situated north of the current border between Syria and Turkey. For a discussion, see Comfort 2017: 194-6 and Comfort and Marciak 2018: 87-9. The road from Nisibis to Cizre is however discussed below.

Castra Maurorum

The other major fortress on the northern part of the frontier between Rome and Persia in Mesopotamia is Castra Maurorum, mentioned by Ammianus Marcellinus as one of three fortresses handed over to the Persians in 363.[111]

[106] Meijer found a site with late Roman occupation halfway at Tell Muhammad Kebir but there are no details (1986: 26, site 231b)
[107] *History of the Wars* 1.10
[108] Honigmann 1929 who explains also the link with Sargathon. The saint apparently died here in 591 CE. Dillemann 1962: 192. See also Comfort 2017: 219-220.
[109] Theophylact Simocatta iii.10.4. This took place shortly before the Persians destroyed the outskirts of Antioch, sacked Apamea and took Dara itself. See also Whitby 1988: 256.
[110] See discussion in Comfort and Marciak 2018: 87-89. A further Roman fort, approx. 50x95m, was recently discovered at the site of the Ilısu Dam on the Tigris 24km north-west of Bezabde/Hendek (Tuba Ökse, Erdoğan et al. 2018; Comfort and Marciak 2018: 100-101).
[111] Ammianus Marcellinus XXV.7.9, where it is listed by name as one of three major fortresses surrendered, the other being Nisibis and Singara. 15 other forts ('castella') were also surrendered but are not mentioned by name. Castra

As discussed in Comfort and Marciak 2018: 69-71, this fortress may be Seh Qubba on the Tigris, a proposal made by the excavator Warwick Ball (1989). The difficulty with this identification lies principally in another reference in Ammianus Marcellinus where a raid by the Persians in 359 CE is described as follows (trans. Rolfe): '*...smoke and gleaming fires constantly shone from the Tigris on past Castra Maurorum and Sisara and all the neighbouring country as far as the city [Nisibis]*'.[112] This passage implies that Castra Maurorum was visible from Nisibis or at least from a point nearby, which is not the case for Seh Qubba, 115km distant on the Tigris. However, Cameron is perhaps correct in saying that this is more a flight of 'imagined vision' than a report of a real event (2018: 190).

There is no other known large fortification of the Roman period immediately to the south of the Tur Abdin and situated between Nisibis and the Tigris - except possibly the town of Babil, now Kebeli, just on the Turkish side of the frontier with Syria and known to have been an important Assyrian settlement. Poidebard states[113] that this was a military post in the Roman period and that its four gates indicated that it was an important crossroads. Dillemann (p213) believed that the town plan drawn by Poidebard (Plate CLIX) was weak proof of its status and that the traces found by Poidebard were probably of a much older town. Its great size (460x610m) for the north and west walls visible in the Corona photograph below) is larger than one might expect of a Roman military camp and might indeed correspond to the fortress of Castra Maurorum, but possibly also to another Sasanian camp. Honigmann, a notable expert on the Rome's eastern frontier, did in fact already confirm this identification with Castra Maurorum in his review of Poidebard's '*La Trace de Rome dans le désert*',[114] apparently dismissing the other possible identifications proposed by Poidebard. A visit by the writer in 2007 confirmed the existence of an important site at this village and the outline of Poidebard's plan but did not provide evidence of Roman occupation.

As alternative sites for Castra Maurorum Poidebard mentioned specifically '*le poste-observatoire de l'Izeddin Dag, le castellum de 'Abra et le camp de Lelan*' (p160), but he also said that several other camps were found controlling wadis that led to the east-west road between Nisibis and the Tigris. (Unfortunately, examination of the satellite photographs for the area has not revealed these.) Poidebard's plan of 'Abra El Foqani (also Plate CLIX) shows a large Assyrian circular fortress with a diameter of 450m - which he compares to Arslan Tash (near Kobane and south of Sürüç), excavated in the 1930s by Thureau-Dangin - and a small Roman (?) fort; for Izeddin Dağ he published no plan of the observatory mentioned above; for Lelan the satellite imagery reveals no walls which might correspond to a Roman fortress (see figs. 62 and 63 below), although this seems like a good candidate for the *Thilsaphata* of Ammianus' report concerning the retreat of the Roman army to Nisibis under Jovian in 363.[115] The position of Lelan is well-known, that of Izeddin Dag is shown by Poidebard on his map published in '*La Trace de Rome*'

Maurorum is described here as 'munimentum perquam opportunum', translated by Rolfe as '*a very important stronghold*'.

[112] XVIII 6.9 '...fumus micantesque ignes assidue a Tigride per CM et Sisara et perlucebant, solito crebriores, erupisse hostium vastatorias manus superato flumine permonstrantes.' Sisara is usually identified with Sisauranon (Comfort 2017 : 219).

[113] La trace de Rome, p160.

[114] Honigmann 1934: 478

[115] Dillemann discusses the location of Thilsaphata, notes the likely links with Ur and Thebeta, but arrives at no conclusion concerning its position (1962: 312).

as being about 20km south-west of Babil on the south side of the current border between Syria and Turkey.

This writer has located 'Abra El Foqani (now Abira, according to Google Earth) at a position 28km SW of Kebeli on the satellite imagery, but not Izzedin Dag. The 'castellum' which he shows at figure 55 below is 51x43.5m, far smaller than the adjacent '*enceinte assyrienne*' and presumably too small to be a serious candidate for Castra Maurorum. In contrast the site of Seh Qubba, excavated by Oates, comprises 25 hectares for the summit alone (figs.58 and 59), while an alternative proposal (Qubur al-Bid, a site 25km ESE of Nisibis and 23km west of Abra) shows a fort of 95x150m (Wood 2004)[116] but is probably also too small for serious consideration (figure 57).

Although the fortifications of Seh Qubba are large, it should be noted that their irregular form is very different from that of the squared-off fortifications of Hendek (37°24'07"N, 42°04'00"E), which this writer believes to be Bezabde, although Ammianus Marcellinus mentions them both in the same context of major fortresses surrendered to the Persians in 363 CE (see Comfort 2017: 194-6 and Comfort and Marciak 2018: 95-97). This leaves Babil/Kebeli as the best option for Castra Maurorum in the eyes of this writer, despite the negative view of Dillemann.

Tell Lelan was a city of the third millennium BCE known as Shekhna and later as Shubat-Enlil, abandoned around 1700 BCE; although the excavators do not mention Roman levels it could be a strong possibility for Castra Maurorum for two reasons: it is located only 28km SW of Nisibis; and Fiey mentions a possible identification of this site with 'Adhrama' a way-station between Mosul and Nisibis on the Abbasid road (Fiey, 1964, citing the translator of Ibn Khordadbeh, De Goeje, although his article is primarily concerned with stations on the Iraqi side of the modern border). In Poidebard's photo (Pl CLX.1) he describes it as a '*Tell Assyrien et camp romain (invisible de terre)*', but without providing further details in his text. It is clear from the 1967 Corona image that the camp must be the feature to the north of the tell, but there is no available confirmation of its date which seems to this writer quite possibly Sasanian. Neither Roman, nor Sasanian nor Islamic levels are mentioned in the publications of the Tell Lelan excavations,[117] but - as mentioned above – its position may correspond to the *Thilsaphata* mentioned by Ammianus Marcellinus as the point at which Julian's army regained Roman territory in 363 (XXV.8.16).

Eski Mosul and the Tigris

The eastern limits of the region under review are those bordering on the Tigris and below the modern town of Cizre. As discussed above, Balad/Sharabadh, now Eski Mosul, may have been the most south-eastern point of Roman control, but we know almost nothing about its Roman history and if it had a name this may have been just the other '*ad flumen Tigrim*' mentioned

[116] Wood's proposal is briefly discussed in Comfort and Marciak 2018: 69-71. Examination of the Corona and Google Earth imagery has allowed the writer to identify the site at 37°00'42"N, 41°31'38'E. The Corona photos available from the CAST website and recent imagery from Google Earth show less detail than the image which Wood obtained, apparently from military sources, and published in JRA 2004. It is not possible to confirm his analysis of the ditches around the structure and the internal arrangement of the fort. Wood died as a result of a roadside bomb in Iraq in 2003.
[117] Especially, Weiss 1983

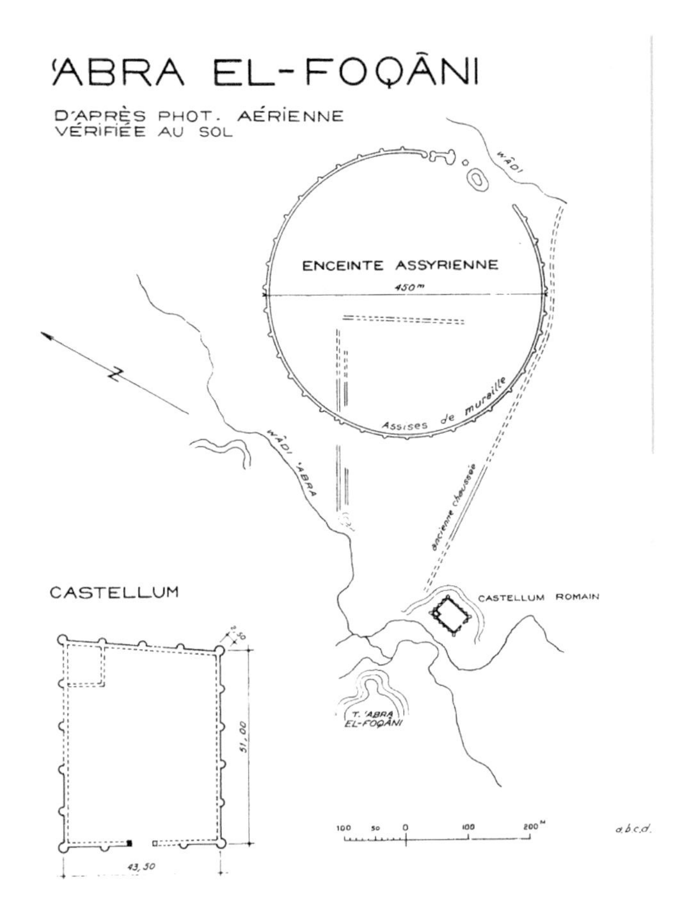

Figure 55. Abra Extract from Poidebard's Plate CLIX

in the Peutinger Table.[118] It is the object of a long article by Fiey, but little is known about its history in the pre-Islamic periods other than the Sasanian name of Sharabadh.[119] Between Bezabde and Mosul/Nineveh there are no sites along the Tigris known from ancient authors, although during the survey excavations conducted by Warwick Ball in association with the Mosul dam (Ball 2003) he did find the fortified site with Roman occupation at Seh Qubba - which he thought was '*Castra Maurorum*' (see above).

Mosul itself was mentioned by Oates as a possible site for '*ad flumen Tigrim*' (Oates 1968: 77) but there can be no certainty of this.[120] Kennedy published a report of an inscription, now

[118] Stein discusses the site of Eski Mosul on pp 95-102 of his report. He was convinced that at least the bridge near Eski Mosul on the Wadi al-Murr was Roman; but Reitlinger believed it to be medieval because of an Arabic inscription (1938: 147-8). (In regard to the nearby bridge at Kısık Köprü, however, Reitlinger agreed with Stein that the lower courses are Roman.) Dillemann must surely be wrong in placing 'ad Tigrim' much further south at the confluence of the Tigris with the Great Zab (1962: 167). Oates confirmed that by the 1960s no material trace of Roman occupation had yet been found at Eski Mosul (1968: 77).
[119] Oates states (1968: 54) that it was a Late Assyrian town called Balata. Fiey's study of Balad and the surrounding region concentrates on its later history as a Christian bishopric (Fiey 1964a). He states (p192) that the Sasanian name of Sharabadh was indicated only by Hamza and Yaqut, while Christian writers always referred to it as Balat.
[120] See also Oates, 1968: 80. He points out that the identification of 'ad flumen Tigrim' with Eski Mosul (rather than a bridge opposite Niniveh at Mosul itself) and the choice of the line Tell Afar to Eski Mosul via Tell Abu Marya (the Assyrian town of Apqum) would involve changing the distances indicated in the PT.

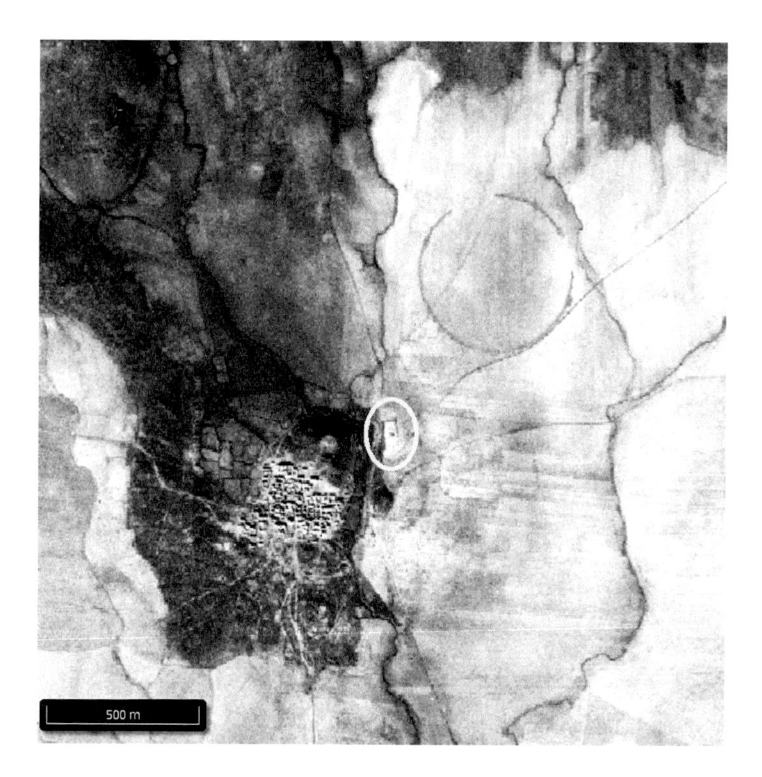

Figure 56. Abra Corona 2 Aug 1969. 37°01'40"N, 41°47'15"E. Poidebard's 'castellum' circled in yellow.

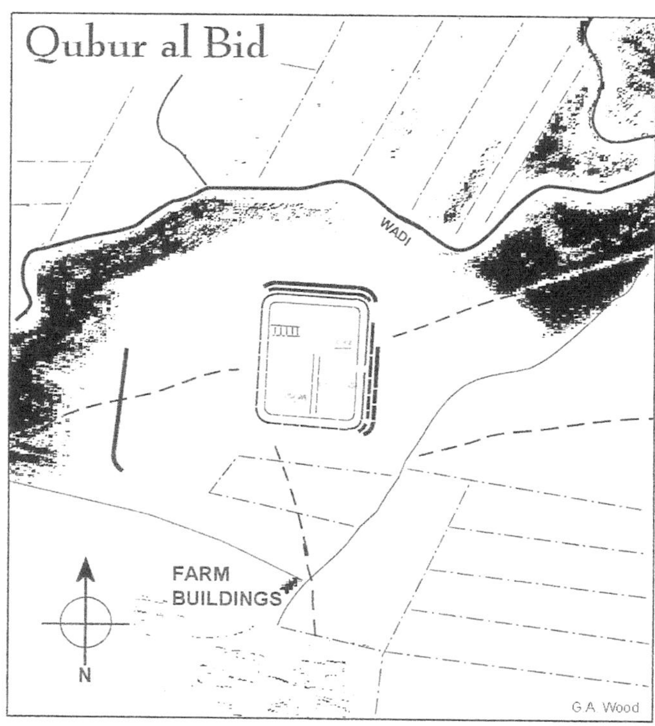

Figure 57. Qubur al-Bid. Copied from Wood (2004: 400). 37°24'07"N, 42°04'00"E.

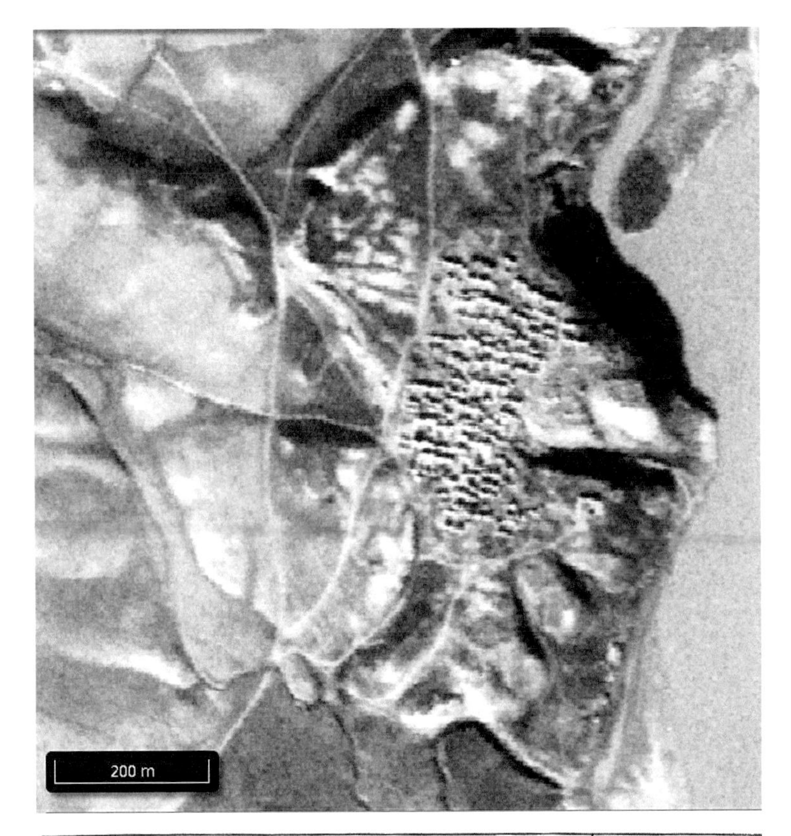

Figure 58. Seh Qubba. Corona 11 Dec 1967 36°51'32"N, 42°29'30"E

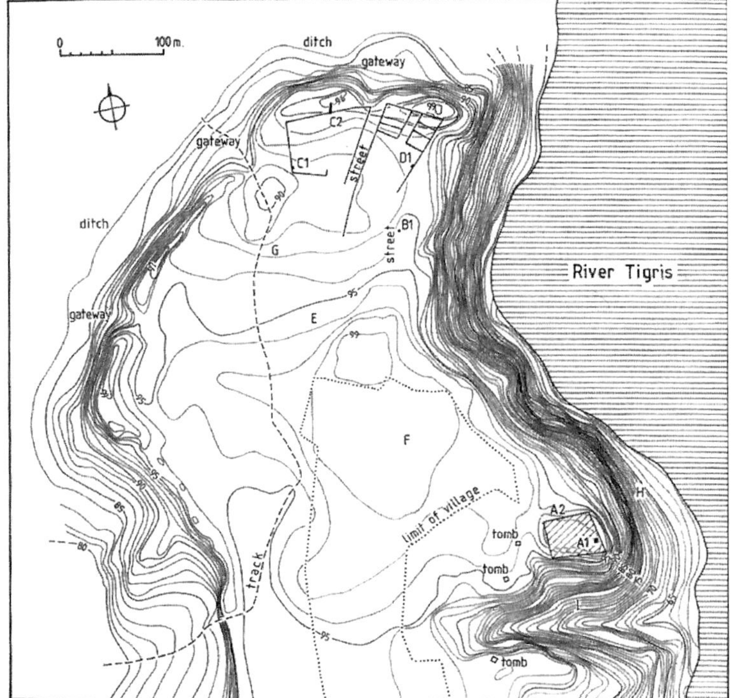

Figure 59. Seh Qubba Ball 2003. 64

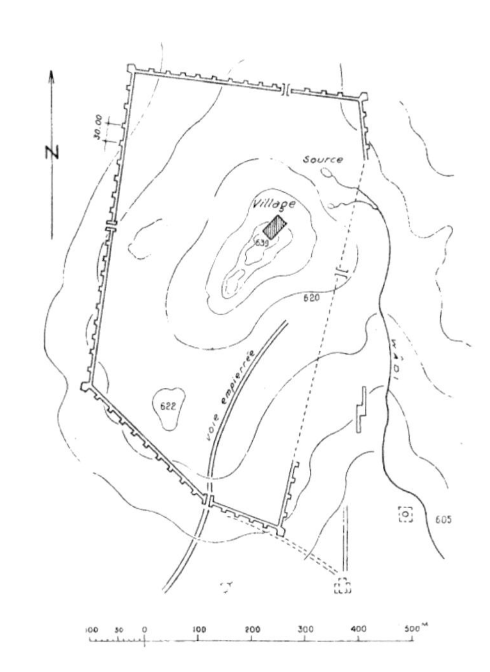

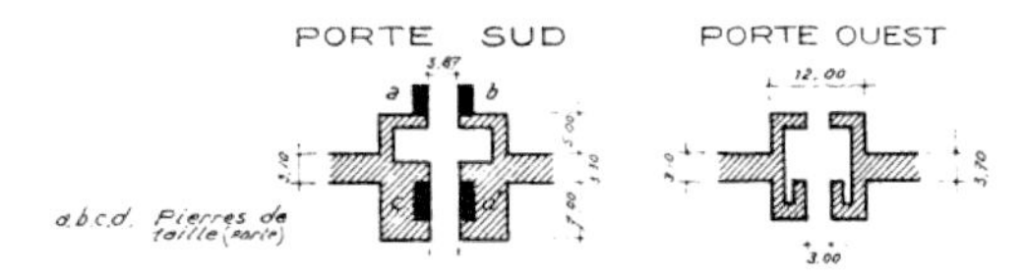

Figure 60. Babil. Extract from Poidebard's Pl. CLIX

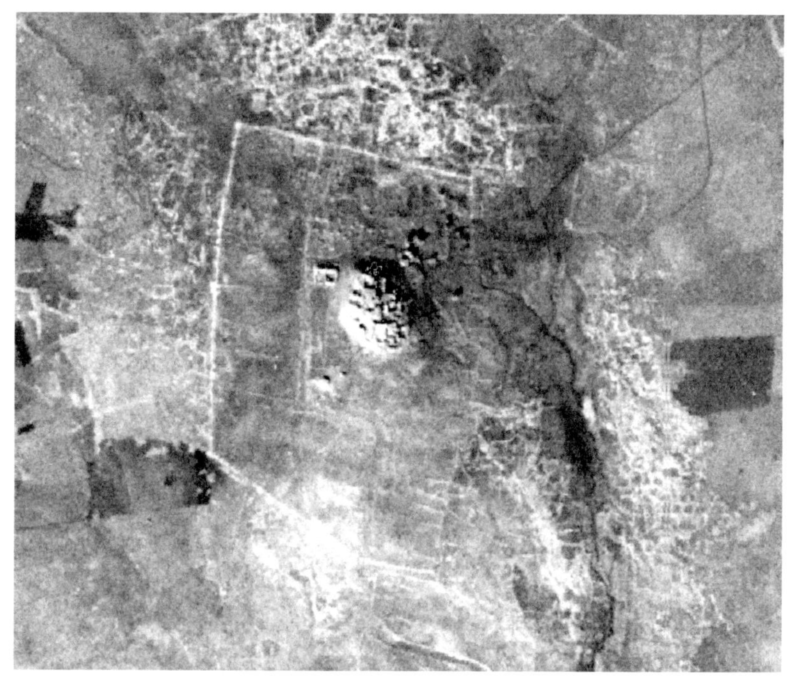

Figure 61. Babil/ Kebeli Corona 11 Dec 1967. 37°11'12"N, 42°01'41"E

Figure 62. Tell Lelan. Poidebard Pl. CIX.1 '

Figure 63. Tell Lelan. Corona 11 Dec 1967. 36°57'26"N, 41°30'18"E

disappeared, found on a bend of the Tigris below Mosul. The inscription bore an image of an eagle and referred to '*Occuli legionum*' (Kennedy 1988). Regrettably, no Roman outpost such as Kennedy postulated is visible in the Corona imagery for the banks of the Tigris south of Mosul. But it must remain a possibility that the ancient road heading east from Singara reached the Tigris at a crossing point here at Mosul rather than at Eski Mosul (Sharabadh) 40km to the north-west. The antiquity of Mosul is discussed in Comfort and Marciak 2018: 59-65.

On the east bank of the Tigris remains from antiquity include the wall at Feshkhabur known as the 'Roman bridge' (although it is not a bridge at all), the inland walled site of Zaferan, Zakho and remains of two bridges and, perhaps, two castella (Comfort and Marciak 2018: 75-81). At Zakho Maunsell saw and drew an octagonal fort which has now disappeared (1890). Its dating is most uncertain.[121] On the north side of Iraqi Kurdistan's border with Turkey are the remains at Basorin and the archaeologically unexplored site of Shakh (ibid: 81-87).

Although not shown on the Peutinger Table, it seems probable that the 'Abbasid road' from Mosul to Nisibis was also used to some extent in antiquity. Certain named sites are known from the early Islamic period[122] but none from the classical or late antique periods have yet been fully investigated. Stein found some square 'castella' which he ascribed to the Roman period, which may have been posts along this road, but it now seems probable that at least some these are of the early Islamic period.[123] Stein's description of the area is included in his report (Gregory and Kennedy 1985: 102-118). Further work needs to be done to revisit the forts which he mentions but none can yet warrant inclusion in a review of fortifications such as this. In his discussion of the Partho-Roman period in the area of the Mosul Dam (then known as the 'Saddam Dam'), Ball indicates that – apart from Seh Qubba – '*it is impossible to tell anything about the nature of settlements in this period for much the same reasons as in the Hellenistic period: the material was from disturbed surface contexts and no architecture or occupation deposits survived*' (2003: 18). His bibliography does not even mention Stein's report.

Fortunately, Wilkinson and Tucker (1995) did find a few sites in this region which seem likely to have been forts or camps guarding the route. In particular, their site 54 is especially striking and shows up remarkably well on a Corona photograph of 1967 even though on recent satellite images it is hardly visible. This pentagonal construction, reminiscent of the 'Castellum' at Ain Sinu/Zagurae but much larger, has a total area of 250 000m^2 with the west side measuring 440m and the south side about 570m.[124] It is thus also comparable to the Sasanian camp at Qohbol 50km to the west. The finders described it as follows (Wilkinson 1995: 128):

> 54) 3km ESE of Gar Sur (92). Extensive pentagonal enclosure formed of low earthen bank. Gap in W bank (? gate) aligned on hollow way. 2 minor gaps in N bank and one in S bank may also have been gates. Mounded area in SE covers 5.9 ha is 2.5m high; includes 3 enclosed depressions. Hassuna[125] pottery (and some bitumen lumps) found around central depression (K) and on areas D to N and C to S. Remainder of mounding

[121] See also Gertrude Bell's photo reproduced in Comfort and Marciak 2018 : 79.
[122] Le Strange 1905 99-100; Fiey 1964b
[123] See the brief discussion in Comfort and Marciak 2018 : 74. As mentioned above, Oates in his unpublished report to the British Academy of November 1953 states that several of Stein's castella along caravan routes are 'undoubtedly medieval khans'.
[124] Compared to 37 000m^2 for the area of AS2 at Ain Sinu (see above).
[125] 'Hassuna' is a period in the Late Neolithic.

> Sasanian/Early Islamic (dominant to W) and M[idle]/L[ate] Islamic (dominant to E). Periods: standard Hassuna (2.5ha); L3rd (trace); Sasanian/Early Islamic (3.1ha); M/L Islamic (4.2ha). The enclosure was not dated directly but probably dates from first major phase of occupation; i.e. Sasanian/Early Islamic.

Apart from some much smaller enclosures which Wilkinson and Tucker identified as possible road-side forts, they also mention (pp70-71) three similarly large enclosures to the north of their survey area which were apparently seen on Iraqi aerial photos: Chilparat,[126] Bir Uqla (or Ugla) and Jazruniya.[127] These are not now visible on the satellite imagery. They speculate that such walled enclosures served either to police the desert and control nomadic tribes or else to defend the Sasanian frontier against the Roman empire. However, the 'low earthen bank' surrounding site 54 near the village of Gar Sur seems a weak fortification compared to the Sasanian Empire's huge constructions elsewhere (in particular, the Gorgan Wall) and to the Roman fortifications of Singara.

The largest site of this area is however Tell el-Hawa. Although the Barrington Atlas shows this site as having late Roman occupation, nothing substantial is said about this period in the excavation reports (especially Ball, Tucker et al. 1989 and Ball 1990). In his article for the 1996 book edited by Bartl and Hauser, Ball remarks that '*It was not until the stability of a Mesopotamian renaissance was established with the advent of the Abbasid Empire that the area was able to flourish once more*' (Ball 1996). He noted in particular that the 'Abbasid road' from Mosul to Nisibis, discussed by Fiey (1964), was guarded by a new town at Tell el-Hawa. No such town existed in the Roman/Parthian or Byzantine/Sasanian periods. The later survey of the north Jazira by Wilkinson and Tucker also failed to find military sites which could be ascribed to the Roman or Byzantine periods of occupation and confirmed that many of Stein's Roman 'castella' were in fact Sasanian or early Islamic (1995: 68-9).

[126] Referred to by Oates (1968: 54) as a station on the Assyrian road from Nisibis to Niniveh, the others being Tells Roumeilan, Hawa, Iweinat and Hugna

[127] Jazruniya was investigated by the team excavating in the Zammar region in connection with the construction of the Saddam Dam, now known as the Mosul Dam (Ball 2003: 175 and plates 57/58). They found an essentially Middle Islamic ruined town, which would have been controlled in this period by the Atabegs of Mosul. In the review of this period on p19 Ball speculates that it was 'Bashazza', a minor regional centre that displaced Barqa'id (Fiey, 1964: 115-116). A single Byzantine coin may be an indication of earlier occupation, but no walled enclosure is mentioned in this report. Bir Uqla (or Ugla) was identified by Fiey with the important medieval site mentioned by several Arab geographers as Barqa'id. There is no information available concerning the Roman/Sasanian period for these three sites. All three have been located on the satellite imagery and no fortifications are apparent.

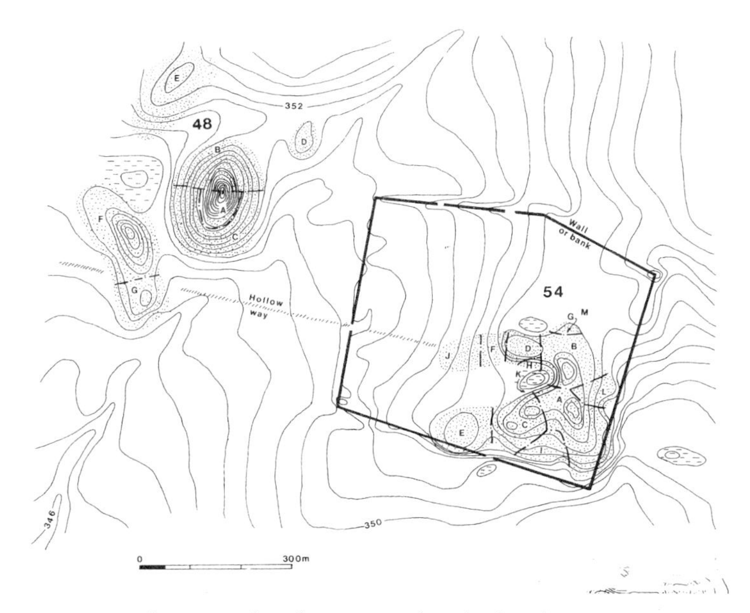

Figure 64. Wilkinson and Tucker's site 54 (1995). The adjacent site 48 is a prominent tell with occupation from the Assyrian to the Parthian periods but not Sasanian.

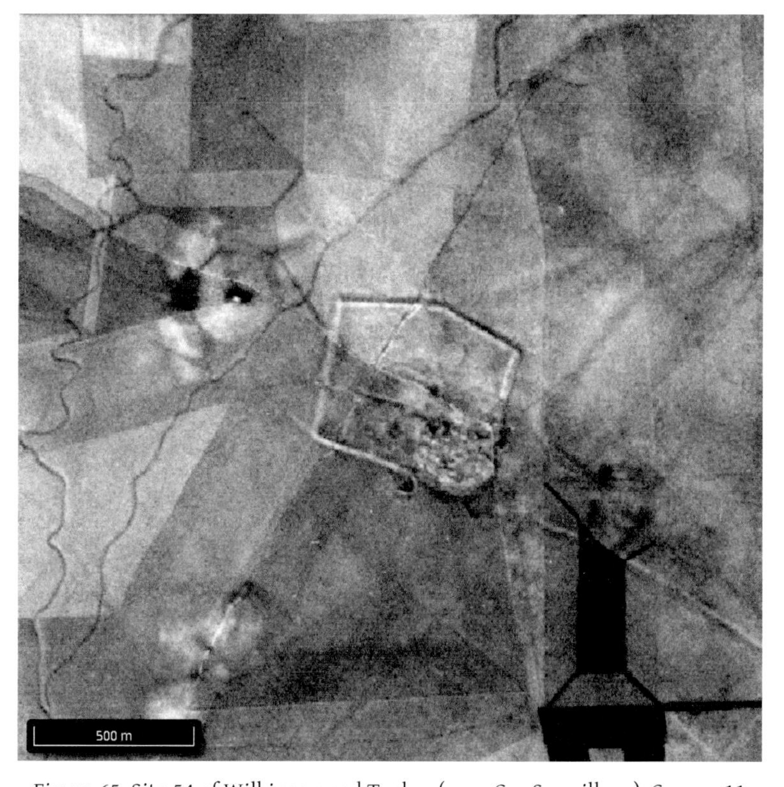

Figure 65. Site 54 of Wilkinson and Tucker (near Gar Sur village). Corona 11 Dec 1967 36°43'03"N, 42°25'17"E

Chapter 4

The roads

Ancient roads have often been identified in the Near East as 'hollow ways', eroded by the passage of animals over centuries, which can be seen as dark lines spreading out from ancient settlements on the satellite imagery and particularly the Corona images of the 1960s (Wilkinson 1995: 24-28, Wilkinson 2003, Ur 2003). In many cases such lines terminate close to the 'tell' concerned, but occasionally they continue for great distances and provide good evidence of major roadways. However, for the roads studied here such hollow ways are rarely the main evidence.[1] In certain cases, there is evidence of construction as well as erosion, especially around the crossings of water courses or 'wadis'. Since such construction would need to be verified on the ground, this section of the book can only be considered as preliminary.

Like the fortifications described above, the roads discussed here are situated in eastern Syria and northern Iraq (west of the Tigris), regions not directly known to this writer who has not been able to visit them in person. Publicly available mapping of this region is sadly incomplete and placenames for many sites discovered on the imagery are often difficult to identify, but one source for current village and site names not otherwise available is the MapCarta website for which local people are able to introduce names themselves.

Inter alia, this chapter seeks to locate some of the placenames known from the Peutinger Table.

The first person interested in the archaeology of this region was Layard (1853: 234-336), who travelled with a large caravan from Mosul to the river Khabur via Singara in the middle of the 19th century; Layard had found much of interest for archaeology but unfortunately the placenames he provides around Singara are often difficult to track down because the population of the plains was then largely nomadic. On Mount Sinjar itself the situation was different: both then and today the villages were and are occupied by Yezidis. He does mention several sites along the Khabur river which can be clearly identified, although on territory then controlled by nomads, but he does not refer to any Roman road and his caravan appears to have avoided roads altogether.

Yet the Roman south gate of Singara was the point of arrival of a road coming east from the Middle Khabur. This Roman road can still be easily traced on Google Earth and on other satellite images[2] along the foothills of the Sinjar mountain range heading west. It joins the Khabur some way south of the fortress of *Thannouris* (see above and Comfort 2009: 326-7), probably at the station marked on the Peutinger Table as *Amostae*.

The routes around Singara are described briefly by Oates. Figures 1 and 2 from his article of 1956 are reproduced below.

[1] For an apparently ancient road that is certainly not a hollow way see, for example, figure 83 below.
[2] Especially Microsoft Bing on the website 'Zoom Earth'.

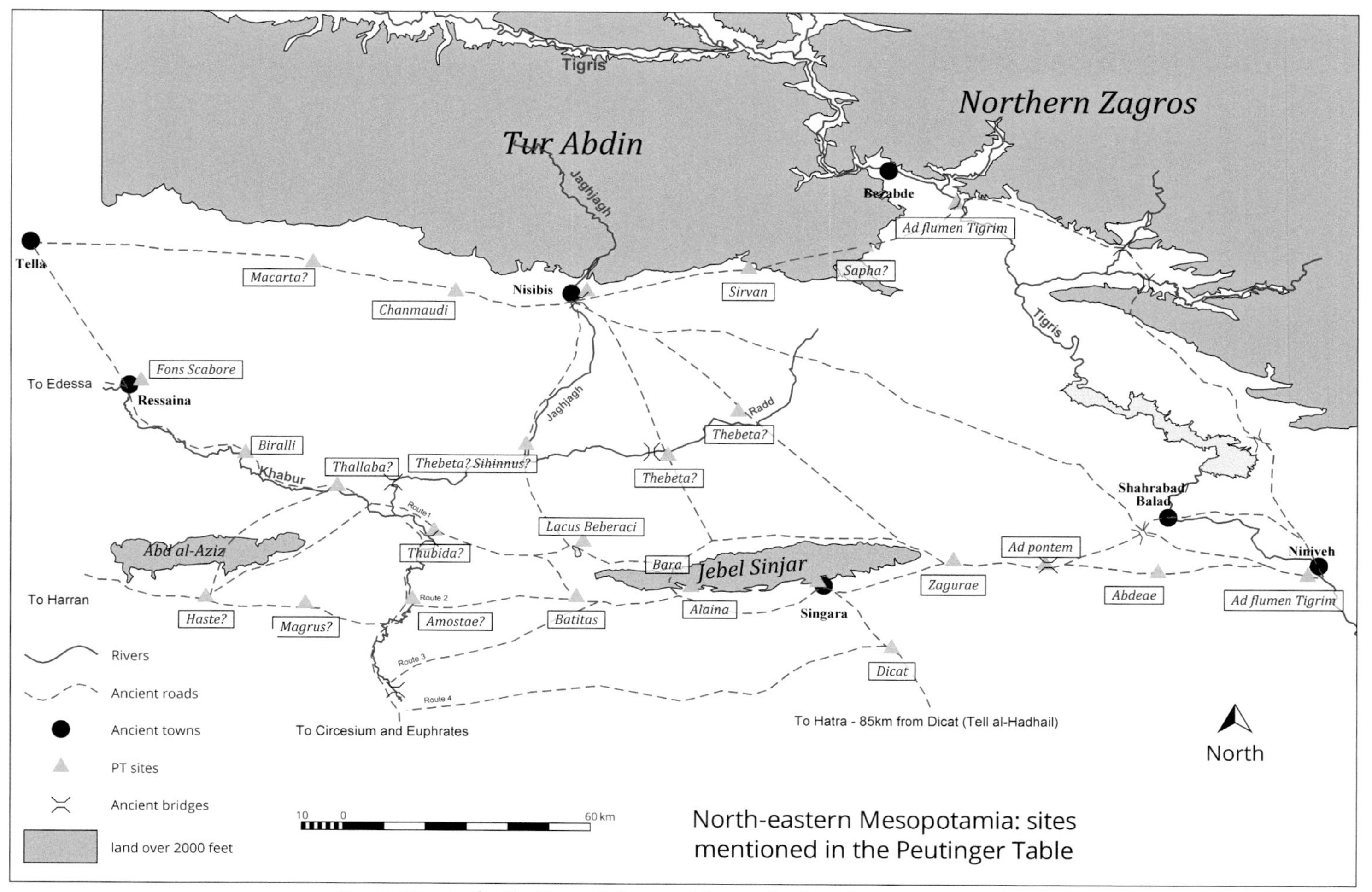

Map 3. Sites in the Peutinger Tables and the roads of north-east Mesopotamia

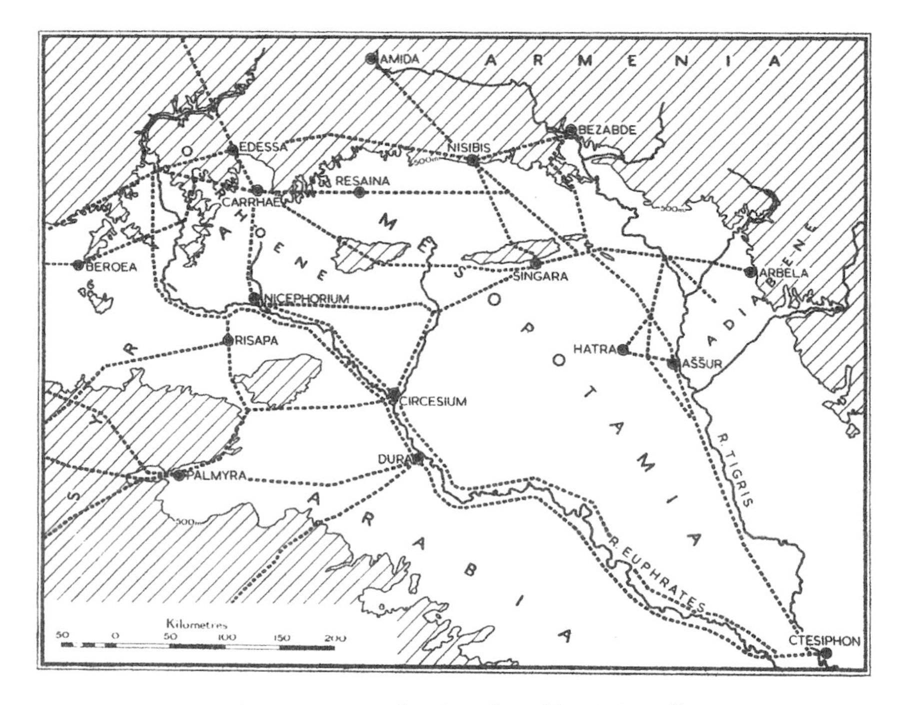

Figure 66. Oates 1 “Syria and Parthia c A.D. 200”

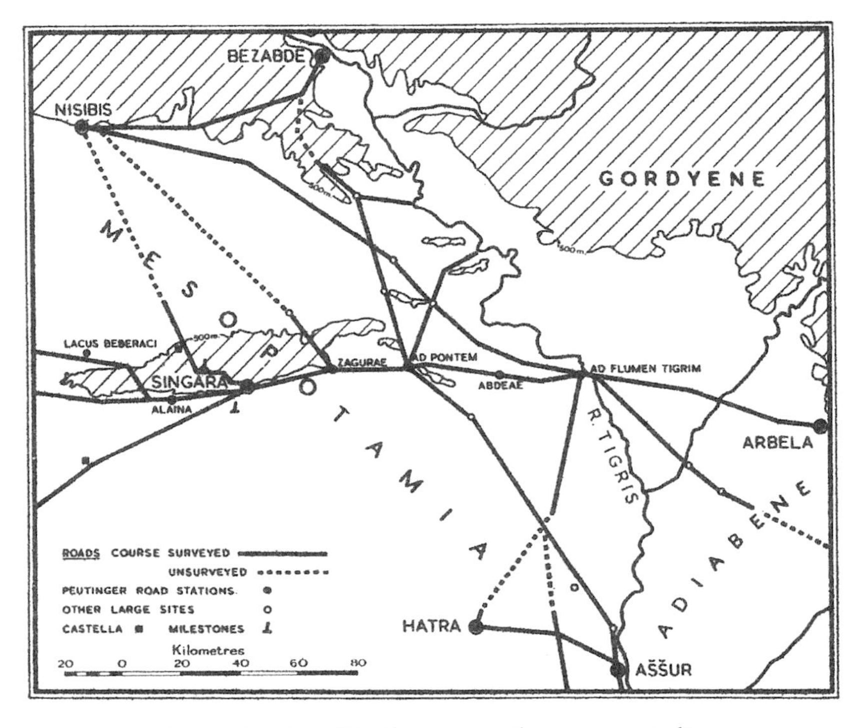

Figure 67. Oates 2 “Northern Iraq in the Roman period”

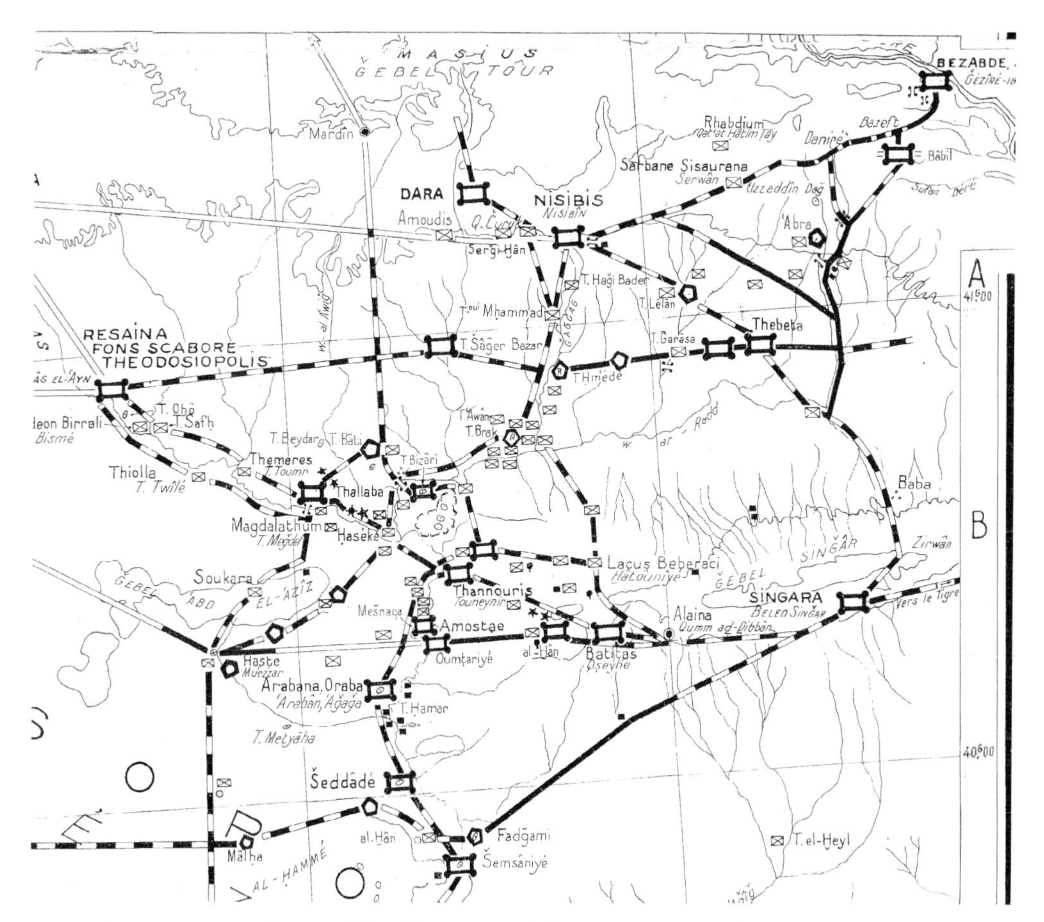

Figure 68. Extract from Poidebard's map entitled 'Le Limes romain dans le désert de Syrie : observations aériennes et vérifications au sol (1925-1932) (map drawn at scale 1/1 000 000 by 'la Compagnie Aérienne Française', Suresnes 1933). Large rectangles indicate fortified towns; small ones = Roman posts (castellum/castrum); pentangles = ancient cities; solid lines = Roman roads visible from the air or on the ground; dashed lines = routes of Roman roads indicated by waystations and watering points.

These maps do not correspond in all respects to that drawn up by Poidebard and published in 'La trace de Rome dans le désert' (1934) – see Figure 68 above. The three maps created to accompany this book (Maps 2, 3 and 4) include the results of recent research and also differ from those of Oates in significant respects.

The placement of some of the roads in Poidebard's map above is doubtful, as will be seen below. It is also now believed that *Bezabde* (top right on the map extract) was situated 16km to the west of where it is here placed both by Poidebard and Oates (at the position of modern Cizre; see Comfort, 2017: 194-6), while the position of *Thebeta* is also doubtful (see above). However, Poidebard, like Stein, was able to visit both by air and often also on the ground many roads and sites which have since become inaccessible or have simply disappeared; their information is therefore invaluable. Aurel Stein was also concerned with the Roman road network and examined in particular the roads between Nisibis and Singara and those heading south to Hatra.

Roads north of Singara[3]

The Habur plains to the north of Mount Sinjar have been the object of several archaeological surveys in recent years.[4] None of these were especially interested in the roads, nor in the period of confrontation between Rome and Persia. Nisibis and its links with the Tigris valley, sometimes via Singara, have remained of importance for the history of the region from very early times and it seems probable that the road followed by early Assyrian merchants heading for Kültepe in Anatolia passed through the area.

During the period 100 to 600 CE, several roads existed to the north-west leading from Singara in the direction of Nisibis, the first capital of the Roman province of Mesopotamia. They passed on either side of the mountain ridge, the Jebel Sinjar, which rises from 500m just north of Singara to over 1100m. That to the west of the mountain passed through the village of *Baba* (now Bara), where remains of abandoned settlements are visible on Corona imagery at several locations around the northern end of the pass, and continued north (or north-west) to Nisibis, possibly via *Thebeta*, with a branch heading west via the *Lacus Beberaci*, now lake Khatuniye, and then on to *Ressaina* (Ras el-Ayn) along the north bank of the western Khabur river.

Poidebard mentions a second possible route from Nisibis to Singara further to the east via a site at Lelan, nearer Nisibis, where he found a fortified town (see discussion of Castra Maurorum above; for the pre-history of this important site see for example Weiss 1983);[5] it may then have passed through Thebeta, although the PT implies a direct route from Nisibis to Thebeta and then to the western end of the Jebel Sinjar (the Baba pass). He had heard of another such site along this more eastern route to the north-west of the 'Zerwan pass', also with fortifications (which must have been the 'Ghobal' discussed above). This route appears to correspond to that followed by the Roman army in their retreat to Nisibis following the death of Julian.

Poidebard correctly indicates in his text that Bara/*Baba* is at the western end of the Jebel Sinjar at the foot of a pass (which he here calls 'Samouka'). However, his map reproduced at Figure 68 places *Baba* at the eastern end, where a pass crosses to Ain Sinu. This must be the Gaulat pass mentioned by Oates (1968: 80; 'Qaulat' in Stein), but Poidebard calls it the 'Zerwan - or Zirwan - pass'. (His positioning of *Baba* on the map is apparently offered as an alternative possibility to the Bara at the western end of the chain, which would render it more compatible with the PT.) It should be noted that the route from Nisibis represented by these sites lies

[3] This paper does not discuss all possible routes to Bezabde. Poidebard describes two such routes: firstly, from Nisibis (see Comfort 2009: 111-113 and below) and secondly north-east from Singara, but it is only in the more northern section of the latter route that he found physical evidence (La Trace, p.166 and Pl CLXI.2). This road has not yet been identified in the satellite imagery and may not be Roman.

[4] See the discussion of the 'Khabur triangle' in Palmisano 2018: 85ff.

[5] The site was first occupied in the 5th millennium. In the third millennium, it was known to the Akkadians as as Shekhna. Around 1800 BCE, the site was renamed "Shubat-Enlil" by the Assyrian king, Shamshi-Adad I and it became the capital of Assyria in northern Mesopotamia. Shubat-Enlil was abandoned around 1700 BCE.

several kilometres to the east of the straight line between Nisibis and the next PT station of *Baba*, generally considered to be Bara at the western end of the Jebel Sinjar.

Unfortunately, the possible site of Thebeta seen by Poidebard (figure 8 above) lay just to the south of the survey area examined by Meijer (1986). It is also 25 kilometres to the north-west of the border of Syria with Iraq. The survey of Wilkinson and Tucker (Wilkinson 1995) was confined to the Iraqi side of the border and centred on Tell al-Samir and Tell al-Hawa to the north-east of the area surrounding Mount Sinjar.

The first option for Thebeta proposed by Poidebard was at Tell Hader, south of Tell Garasa, but this site has not yet been found on the satellite imagery. Regrettably cultivation of the ground between Nisibis and Mount Sinjar was already well advanced by 1967, date of the first Corona photographs, and much that was seen by Poidebard in the 1920s and 30s has since disappeared, in particular the roads.

Aurel Stein also investigated roads heading north from Jebel Sinjar and was informed by an aged Yazidi of another old road running east-west along the northern flanks of the mountain (p34). He investigated two small sites, which he believed to be Roman 'castra', near 'Khan as-Sur',[6] which lies 34km west-south-west of Kohbol/Ghobal[7] and 9km south of the border between Syria and Iraq. 2km further north he identified a larger 'castellum' forming a square with each side 105m long (plate 10). Local people confirmed that this lay on a route to Nisibis. A further 18kms to the north, on the Syrian side of the border, Stein found another fort at 'Khan ad-Deim' on a line leading north to Tell Garasa via the ruined bridge (no longer extant).[8] He thought that the identification of this route as a Roman road was proved by the Karsi milestone (see discussion below). However, this road seems now more likely to have turned south-west from Khan as-Sur and crossed the western end of the Jebel Sinjar via the Bara pass. Most regrettably, it has not yet proved possible to identify on the satellite imagery the sites along this route found by Stein. Nor is there a clear line visible for the road itself, since it passes through the damp ground of the Radd valley and even in the 1960s the surrounding ground was intensively cultivated.

The Wilkinson and Tucker site mentioned above and here shown in Figs.64 and 65 appears to have been located on the old road from Mosul/Nineveh to Nisibis. This road is likely always to have been an important trading route, but perhaps less so during the confrontation in late antiquity between Rome and Persia, especially since the roads between Nisibis and Singara may have replaced it, even for commercial caravans continuing down to Hatra and lower Mesopotamia; it does not appear in the Peutinger Table. Its course during the Abbasid period is discussed by Fiey (1964b), who mentions on page 115 a 'Roman' bridge at Kisik, 8km south-west of Balad (Eski Mosul). He provided no further details, but the bridge is also mentioned by Aurel Stein who published two aerial photographs, although none of the bridge at ground level[9] (see discussion below with two satellite images from 1967 and 2014). The bridge was investigated by Reitlinger during his collaboration with Seton Lloyd's survey of mounds

[6] See plates 9a and b and the description on page 37 of his report.
[7] According to Google Maps, this is now spelt 'Khana Sor'
[8] According to Meijer (1986: 14), who mentions the site at 'Tell Qarasa' (no.98), the remains of the Roman bridge to the south have completely disappeared and none are visible on the satellite imagery.
[9] Stein in Gregory and Kennedy 1985, p93, Plate 21.

Figure 69. a) and b) The probable site of the 'Roman' bridge at Kisik 36°28'6"N, 42°40'19"E
Corona December 1967 and Zoom Earth January 2014

south of Singara (1938: 144-5); he ascribed the ruined bridge to the thirteenth century CE but seems to have thought the piers were Roman Evidently, the remains of the bridge need to be investigated further.

Fiey also mentioned a 'Roman camp' (p115) located 3.5km north-east of Tell al-Uwaynat. He had already said on p111 that the old track passed through a Roman fort 'recognized by a Professor Palgen of Baghdad University'. Details of the camp/fort were not published by either Fiey or Palgen, to this writer's knowledge, but it was possibly the same as the pentagonal structure found by Wilkinson and Tucker. The latter suggested a 'Late Sasanian/Early Islamic date' and discounted the attribution to the Roman period made by Fiey (and Palgen) 'owing to the total absence of Parthian-Roman pottery' (1995: 70).

The course of the road between Nisibis and Mosul during the Roman period was discussed by Stein (1985: 102-118). His research was conducted before World War II and before that of Fiey. Apart from the two aerial photographs mentioned above, he describes the bridge at Kisik Kupri in detail on pp94-5. Two arches were then (and possibly still are) extant which, because they are pointed, Stein ascribed to a later period while indicating 'reconstruction of a bridge originally Roman'. Other bridges of the late Roman period also have pointed arches (see, for example, the Antağ bridge, probably built for Justinian and also called Gömey Perdı, described in Comfort 2009: 67, which is located north-west of Silvan (once Martyropolis). However, it is evident that such a 'Roman' bridge could not have been built on Persian territory after CE363, unless by captured Roman engineers.

Stein mentions the journey from Mosul to Nisibis of Karsten Niebuhr in 1766 (1778 and c.1992); Fiey mentions that of James Silk Buckingham in 1816 (1827: I, 448-475; II, 1-19); to these should be added the travels of Jean Otter (Otter 1748: 149), a Swede sent by Louis XV of France to open negotiations with Persia. All three mention that their caravans passed through the area in fear of raids by Yezidi bandits based on Mount Sinjar and that there were then no villages along the route, even though in the Abbasid period there had been at least one flourishing town at Barqa'id (south-east of the current Syria/Iraq frontier) and possibly another nearer Eski Mosul at Ba'aynatha (Fiey 1964).

Balad, also known in the Sasanian period as Sharabadh, and now Eski Mosul, lies some 7.5km north-east from the obvious course for the Mosul/Nisibis road. It is discussed briefly in Chapter 3 above and is likely to have been an important crossing point of the Tigris but the archaeological reports concerning Roman and Sasanian levels of the town have not yet been translated from Arabic.[10] According to Fiey, the town was an important Christian bishopric in the fifth century and was very prosperous in the eighth (1964a). For general discussions, see Stein in Gregory and Kennedy 1985: 95-102 and Comfort and Marciak 2018: 65-68.

Following his description of Eski Mosul, Stein included a chapter in his report entitled 'Towards Nisibis: a corridor for trade and invasion'.[11] This paper does not address all his 'Roman' finds, some of which have been described by others as being from later periods. Stein had noted Poidebard's Roman road heading east from his suggested site of Thebeta (see above) and confirmed its continuation towards the Tigris. He identified various structures near the Tigris

[10] 1999 'Recent excavations in Iraq', *Iraq* 61 : 200

[11] Gregory and Kennedy 1985: 102-118.

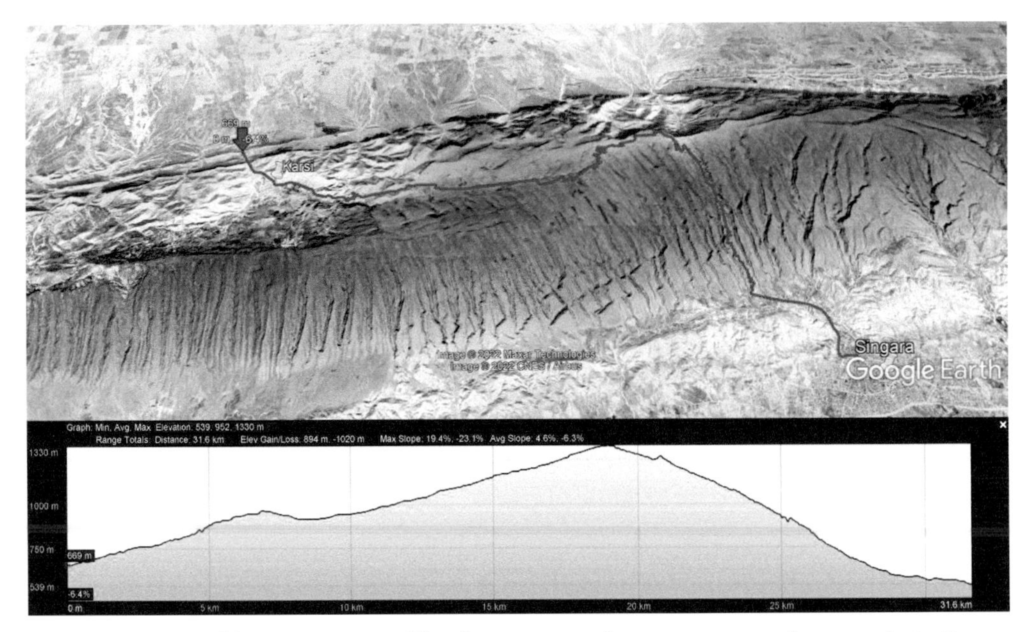

Figure 70. Possible route across middle of Mount Sinjar from Karsi. Extract from Google Earth

valley as being possibly of Roman origin, but in 1985/6 the British Archaeological Expedition for the Saddam Dam Salvage Project found no evidence to support this claim (Ball 2003).

Returning to the roads from Nisibis to Singara, apart from the north/south route passing west of Jebel Sinjar via Lake Khatuniye and Bara/*Baba*[12] and that to the east which came down via the Gaulat pass to *Zagurae*/Ain Sinu, some people, including Oates, have proposed a third route directly over the top of the range. An inscription, possibly from a milestone, was found in the village of Karsi at the northern foot of the chain before 1927 (Cagnat 1927; Comfort 2018 (Kolb): 118, n26).[13] This route is highly unlikely because of the steepness of the descent on the southern flank. The milestone was perhaps displaced – from Khan as-Sur? See extract from Google Earth with elevations shown below. The modern road from Singara to the summit has 81 hairpin bends.

Roads east of Singara

The road from Nisibis to the east of the Sinjar mountain chain led to the Tigris crossings at either Eski Mosul or Mosul/Niniveh, which are not shown as such on the PT; this route has been briefly discussed above and would have passed through the fort at Ain Sinu, the *Zagurae*

[12] Poidebard's map shows - probably wrongly - *Baba* at the north-eastern end of Mount Sinjar. In fact, it lies near the north-western corner and must have been a crossroads with one road heading west to *Lacus Beberaci*/Lake Khatuniye and a second going north towards Nisibis.

[13] AE 1927, 151: Imp(erator) Caes(ar) [di]vi / Nervae f[i]l(ius) Nerva / Traianus Optimus / Aug(ustus) G[er]manicus / Dacicus [Pa]rthicus / pontif(ex) [max(imus) t]rib(unicia) [potes]/[tate]. Cagnat published no photo (although one was taken by Mouterde and apparently seen by Cagnat) but he states that it was found on a column fragment. He ascribes it to 116/7 CE, that is, just before Trajan's death.

of the Peutinger Table (above and Oates 1968), but now believed to have been at least in part a Sasanian fortification from some time in the third century. Oates mentions (p197) that the east-west highway from Nineveh to the Khabur was used by the Romans as their frontier road. The Peutinger Table shows a road as follows (north-west to east):

> Nisibi XXXIII, Thebeta XVIIII, Baba XXXIII, Singara XXI, Zagurae XVIII, ad Pontem XVIII, Abdeae XX, ad Flumen Tigrim XX.

The road is shown as continuing from Mosul (possibly to be identified with '*ad flumen Tigrim*' – see Chapter 3 above) to Hatra, which would have involved a sharp turn to the south after arriving at the Tigris. It seems probable that a road also linked Tell Afar (*ad Pontem*) to the Tigris crossing at the Sasanian settlement of *Shahrabad/Balad* (now 'Eski Mosul') as well as to Mosul itself, although this is not shown clearly on the PT.

Oates also says that '*The course of this road can be traced on the ground ..., as a trough up to 20m wide and 5 metres deep along the southern foothills of the Sinjar range, rounding the northern edge of Jebel Ibrahim above Tell Afar, and thence running straight across the plain and over Jebel Atshan to the Tigris crossing opposite Nineveh.*' He draws attention to the fact that the route was important long before the arrival of the Romans. It has not yet proved possible to inspect the road on the ground in order to assess the nature of the Roman element in its construction, but it is apparent from the satellite imagery that at least in part it is well-preserved (figs.71 and 72). Occasional deviations from the main, early modern, route tend in this writer's view to confirm the antiquity of this road. The crossroads visible in figure 72 has one branch heading north-east to Ain Sinu and a second due east which rejoins this route near Vicat (shown as 'Hajji Yunus' on the Arkansas CAST Corona atlas).

Figure 71. The road 14km east of Sinjar. Corona 11 Dec 1967

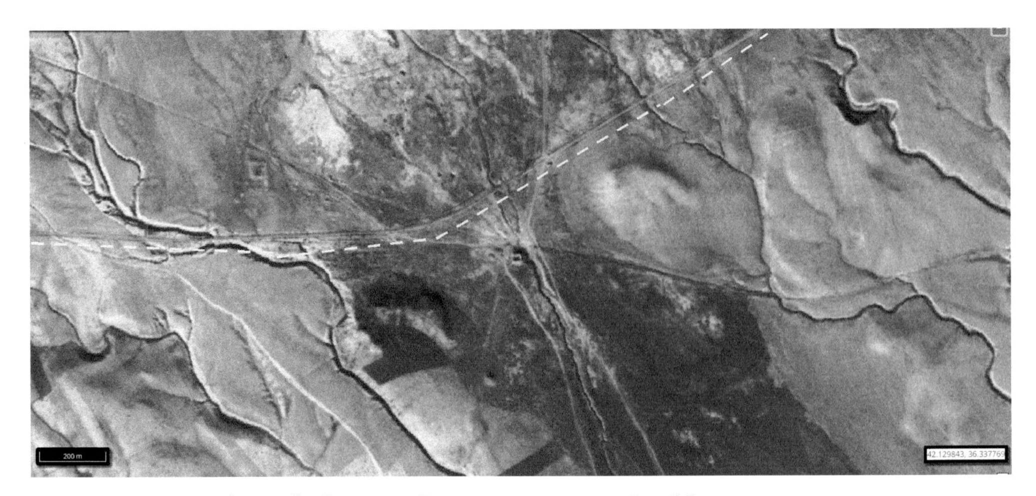

Figure 72. The road 28km east of Sinjar. Note crossroad and forts. Corona 11 Dec 1967

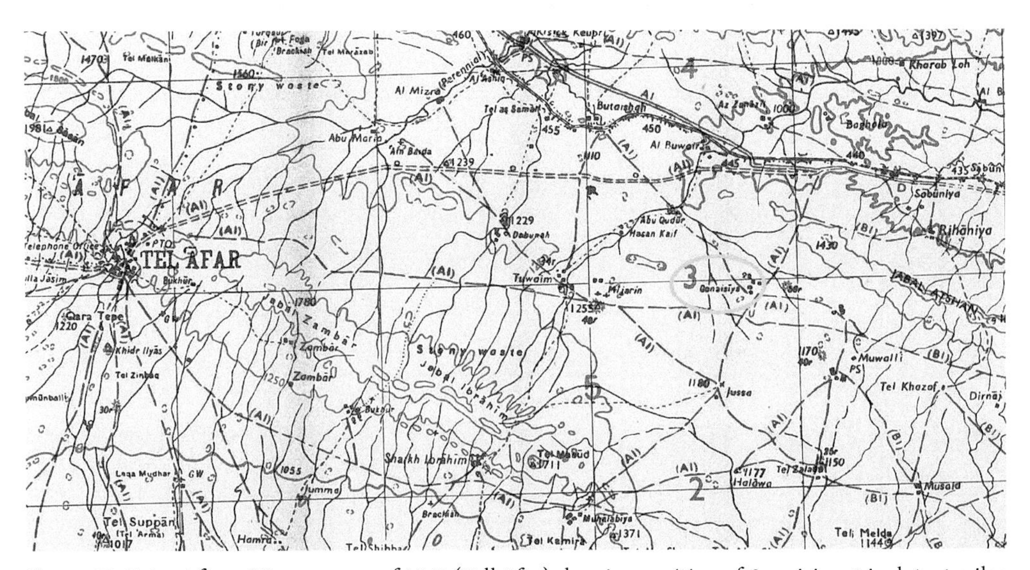

Figure 73. Extract from US army map of 1942 (Tell Afar) showing position of Gonaisiya; 1 inch to 4 miles

Oates was surely right in identifying, already in his article of 1956, at least two of those stations shown in the PT which are mentioned above: *Zagurae*=Ain Sinu ; *Ad Pontem*=Tell Afar.[14] He identified *Abdeae* with Gonaisiya (where he saw a large medieval fortified khan and red burnished pottery of the fourth century CE), which is situated 30km east of Tell Afar, see Figure 10 below; but this is dependent on his fourth identification of *ad Flumen Tigrim* with Mosul. No doubt the Tigris crossings changed in importance over time but it now seems

[14] Tell Afar was identified by Ritter 1854: XI 453 et seq) with the 'Thilsaphata' of Ammianus Marcellinus (XXV, 8.16) It was visited by Sachau (1883: 337) and Layard (1853: I, 312). It is also described by Stein (Gregory and Kennedy 1985: 92 and 139). It lay on the route from Hatra to Nisibis followed by the army of Jovian after the death of Julian. But Dillemann considered that Thilsaphata was probably another form of the name Thebeta (1962: 312).

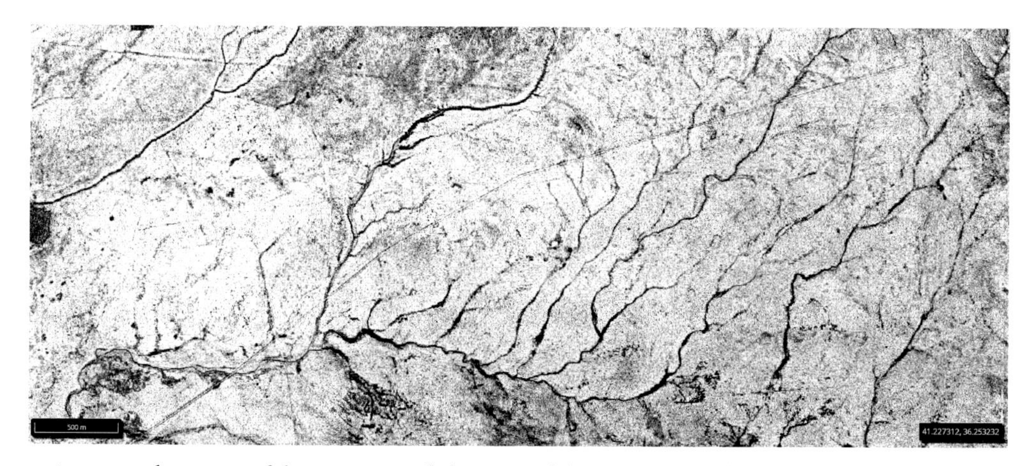

Figure 74. The course of the ancient road 8km west of the current Syria/Iraq frontier. Corona 11 Dec 1967 (see also figure 71 above)

possible that *ad flumen Tigrim* should be placed at Eski Mosul, 40km to the north-west. He was also perhaps wrong in assuming that the second PT road via Singara followed the same route as the first (see discussion below in regard to routes to the south of Singara).

Roads to the west of Singara and to the Khabur valley

Near Bara/*Baba* but on the southern side of Jebel Sinjar, this road joins with two or three others coming from the west and the river Khabur. These roads and their continuation below the mountain chain's southern flanks as far as Tell Afar are for the most part clearly visible on Corona imagery of 1967/1968 and, less so, on recent imagery available from Google Earth and Microsoft/Bing (Zoom Earth); the course of the southern road has been partly re-used by the early modern road preceding the current highway in Iraq (highway 47) and for the section west of the modern border – probably by highway 715 in Syria, planned but not yet built (?). This latter road and its 'antiquity' are discussed below (route 3). In some sections the Roman surface seems to be in a pristine state, at least as seen in the images of 1967/68. A Roman milestone from the reign of Alexander Severus (AD 222-235) was found 5km SW of Sinjar in around 1950 (anonymous report in Sumer 8, 1952, p229) and confirms its course.

The Peutinger Table, last revised towards the end of the fourth century CE (at least for this area), shows Singara twice: as a station on the road from the Khabur (discussed by Oates in 1956) and then as part of a route from *Tharrana* (probably a place south of Harran and Edessa) to Ctesiphon via Hatra, which would have followed a route south of the west-east portion of the Habur river valley, with a crossing point somewhere to the south of *Thannouris*. Oates did also address much of the latter route in 'Studies in the ancient history of Northern Iraq' (1968:78-80).

This second road is shown on the PT with the following stations: *Tharrana 18, Roschirea 17, Tigubis 16, Hadia 15, Themessata 8, Haste 20, Magrus 20, Amostae 20, Batitas 20?, Alaina 20, Sirgora (Singara) 12, Zagora (Zagurae) 10, Dicat (or 'Vicat') 12, Ad Herculem 22, Hatra 28, Sabbin 28, Phalcara 20,*

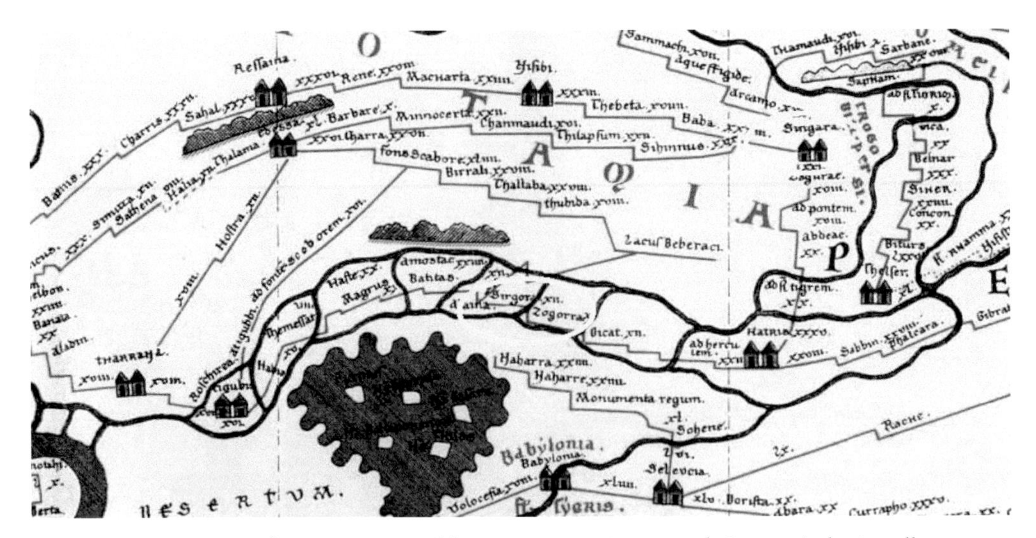

Figure 75. Extract from Peutinger Table, Segment XI: Singara and Sirgora circles in yellow.

Gibrata, Peloriaca 20, Thanna 28, Artemisia 31, Cesiphum (Ctesiphon). This route appears to start in reality at Edessa and is likely to have been the main link between there and Hatra until the latter's demise.[15]

Many of the places along the route have not been convincingly identified, although Konrad Miller and Louis Dillemann attempted this (1916: 742-3 and 778-9; 1962: 185-190). The road system around Hatra is discussed in Altaweel and Hauser (2004) and is not addressed here in any detail. The route from *Tharrana* as far as *Singara* is presented as number 6 in the writer's doctoral thesis (Comfort 2009) and is the least clear of all those discussed therein. This second Peutinger route overlaps with the first around *Singara*, which – together with the variant spellings - raises interesting questions about a possible second source for the compiler of the PT in regard to this section of the map.

The names provided are sometimes difficult to read. The spelling which Oates used for ancient place-names shown on the PT sometimes differs from that used by Miller in his 'Itineraria Romana' (Miller 1916). The distances between stations are indicated in Roman miles for this

[15] Most of this route is in north-western Mesopotamia (Osrhoene) and therefore outside the limits set for this book. Although the course of the second route is not always certain, it was discussed by Dillemann in his major work entitled 'Haute Mésopotamie orientale'. Heading from west to east, Tharrana has been identified by many with Harran, despite the fact that this place appears elsewhere in the PT as 'Charran' (for example, Miller, 1916: 778 and Honigmann, 1934: 477), but Tharrana is stated by Dillemann to be Ain el-Arous, source of the Balikh river (1962: 177), that is, Dabana in the ancient world. Tigubis is mentioned by Ptolemy as 'Thengoubis' and is perhaps to be associated with the later site of Kharab Sayyar (early Islamic) visible on satellite imagery at 36°35'27"N, 39°33'50"E. Dillemann places Tigubis at Ain el-Beida (1962: 185), where von Oppenheim found a Roman camp and settlement ('Tell Halaf', 1943-2010: chapter VIII). Haste was identified by Poidebard (1934: map at end) with a site called Tell Muezzar south of the Jebel abd el-Aziz, a mountain chain lower than the Jebel Sinjar and situated to the west on the same latitude. (The course of the road would therefore have been at least some 25kms south of the west-east course of the upper Khabur river and would have passed through what is now mostly desert but may once have been more fertile. The PT stations Roschirea, Hadia and Themessata are not known, although Miller and Dillemann did make suggestions (1916: 778; 1962: 184-6). To the south-east it is not evident that the principal road to Ctesiphon would have passed through Hatra, which lies west of the direct line.

region, but these are also difficult to read in several cases and have often been shown to be simply wrong, usually because of errors by copyists. In general, this paper uses the spelling and figures of Miller rather than Oates (e.g. 'Amostae' and not 'Amostat', as used by Oates - and by Dillemann). Comprehension of this section of the book will be aided by consultation of Poidebard's map ('*Coude du Habur - Défense du Limes*'), reproduced at Figure 13 above.

The Khabur river after leaving its source near Ressaina (Ras el-Ain), on the existing border between Turkey and Syria, flows for about 80km east-south-east to the current regional capital of Hasaké (which is at the confluence with the Jaghjagh river, descending south from Nisibis). After a further 15km it changes direction near the site of the Roman fortress of *Thannouris* (Chapter 3 above) and heads due south for nearly 200km to the confluence with the Euphrates at *Circesium* (now al-Busayrah). When Layard visited in about 1850 there was no permanent habitation at all between Ras-el-Ain and the confluence with the Euphrates, but only the tents of nomads (1853: 284).

Entering the Khabur valley and the area of main concern for this book, Poidebard placed the PT station of *Amostae* 15 km south of *Thannouris* at a crossing of the Khabur and then another 'Roman fortified town', called *Batitas* on the PT, located 15km south of Lake Khatuniye (*Lacus Beberaci*) at 'Qseibe' (mentioned as 'Kseybe' on a French map of 1938[16]). *Alaina* is discussed in Chapter 3 above and was about 32km east of Qseibe.

The Roman frontier road ran west-east about 5km to the south of the settlement of Sikaniyeh, identified here with Alaina. The ruined fort some 5.5km to the west at the foot of the Bara pass (see Chapter 3 above) appears also be of ancient origin and would have guarded the pass leaving the east west-road to Singara for another heading north-west to Lake Khatuniyeh – and perhaps to Nisibis.

There are several routes from the Khabur heading east towards Singara; three join near the current border between Syria and Iraq (see Map 2). The most northern of these (route 1) leaves the Khabur from a point near *Thannouris* ('Tell Tuneynir' ;[17] see Chapter 3 and Fuller and Fuller 1998). Route 1 is also shown on Poidebard's maps and has been traced on the satellite imagery. It passes not far from a fort identified by Poidebard at 'Touloul Mougayir' (*La Trace*, p156 – also visible on the satellite images) and it arrives at Qseybe/*Batitas* from the north-west, with a branch continuing direct to Lake Khatuniye (*Lacus Berberaci*).

The next route from the Khabur (route 2) is shown by Poidebard as leaving from *Amostae* and passing after 27km by a first Roman fortress at a place not named on the PT which he calls 'al-Han' (see Chapter 3 above). The Roman nature of this fortress remains to be confirmed.[18] After a further 14.5km like route 1 it then passes the 'town' called by Poidebard 'Qseybe' which he identified with *Batitas*, name of a site shown on the PT and discussed in Chapter 3. A suitable place has been identified at 36°17'21"N, 41°13'59"E, where ruined houses are visible on the Corona image of 1968 (figure 17), but the village of Qseybe no longer exists. The road

[16] 'Qamichliye-Sinjar', 1:200 000, Service géographique du Levant, Beyrouth. Consulted in the British Library.
[17] Strangely, *Thannouris* does not appear on the PT but it could correspond to *Thubida*, although Poidebard places this a little further east at 'Sheikh Mansour', which I have been unable to identify. Thannourios is also likely to have become important after the work carried out under Justinian and therefore substantially later than the PT.
[18]

continues beyond Batitas (and the junction with route 1 coming from *Thannouris/Thubida*), crosses the modern frontier between Syria and Iraq to Alaina and then continues to Singara.

The position of *Amostae*, also discussed in Chapter 3 above, is the subject of disagreement between Poidebard and Dillemann. Poidebard indicates a crossing of the Khabur via a site which he called Oumtariye (currently shown on the University of Arkansas's Corona website as 'Tell Matariye', which now rises as an island from the South Hasaké reservoir). The fortified town of *Amostae* is shown on his map (figs.20 and 21 above) as being a little to the north-west - possibly situated on a bluff overlooking the river at 36°19'10"N, 40°46'24"E. There are clear signs on the satellite imagery, Corona, Google Earth and Bing Microsoft (Zoom Earth) of the ancient road heading west to the fort 'al-Han' (shown on Poidebard's map) and then continuing east to *Singara* via the presumed site of *Batitas*. This road leaves the banks of the Khabur river at 36°17'40"N, 40°44'58"E.

As mentioned above, according to Poidebard (*La Trace*, p156) *Haste* was located at Tell Muezzar and *Magrus* at an intermediate station he calls 'Tell Touwenan' and *Amostae* at Mesnaqa-Oumtariye. But Dillemann had already expressed doubt about the crossing point of the Khabur. There is a fairly clear indication on the satellite imagery of an ancient road heading north-east from *Haste*, joining the Khabur near the modern town of Hasaké, which could be an indication that *Magrus* and the Khabur crossing lay further north, but this seems unlikely to this writer: a location for *Magrus* near the confluence of the Khabur and the Jaghjagh – as proposed by Oates - implies that the route described in the PT was more likely to have followed the north bank of the Habur to Ressaina, rather than passing south of the mountain range now called the Jebel abd-al Aziz. The PT already shows another such route from *Ressaina/Fons Scabore* via *Thallaba* and *Thubida* to *Lacus Beberaci* , although the location of these toponyms is also uncertain – see also route 5 in Comfort 2009: 138-140.

The relevant section of the PT is as follows:

Fons Scabore (Resaina) 44, Birrali 28, Thallaba 28, Thubida 18, Lacus Beberaci.

This route follows the north bank of the Khabur river as far as the confluence with the Jaghjagh near the modern city of Hasaké. The ruins of a bridge at Soufeiyé some 11kms north of the confluence, described above, had led Dillemann and others to propose a diversion towards the north but a crossing nearer the confluence seems perfectly possible. For the purpose of this paper the main place of interest is *Thubida*, which was placed by Herzfeld at the site of 'Shaikh Mansur' (Sarre and Herzfeld 1911-1920: Vol1, 196). This writer has not been able to identify convincingly this place on the satellite imagery; but *Thubida* must in any case have been near the confluence and the site of the fortress of Tunaynir/*Thannouris.*[19] It was at the beginning of the road to Batitas named here as route 1, as well as of a route continuing on to *Lacus Beberaci*/ Lake Khatuniye.

The problem with the identifications made by Poidebard turns on the position of *Magrus* and *Haste*; although Poidebard indicates the course of a Roman road on the west bank of the Khabur heading west to the next PT station but one, called *Haste*, none is visible on the satellite

[19] see discussion in Chapter 3.

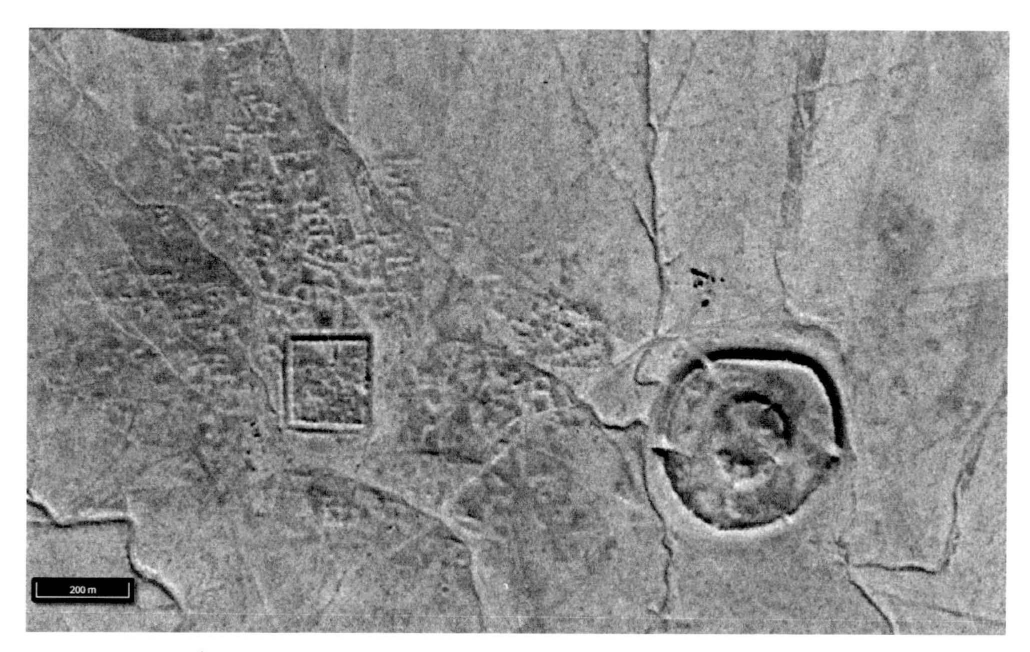

Figure 76. Haste/Muezzar Corona 1968. 36°15'26"N, 40°19'49"E (Poidebard 'La Trace' Pls.CXXXIII-IV)

imagery. Poidebard himself shows it only in white on the map reproduced here as figure 68 above, i.e. as '*non-étudié au cours des recherches*'. *Haste* itself could indeed be 'Muezzar' as he indicates, since there is a small square fort here visible on the satellite imagery to the west of an Assyrian (?) round fortress,[20] which might be a Roman construction; but the absence of an east-west route visible as a 'hollow way' on the satellite imagery raises questions about the identifications for all of this section of the PT route between *Haste* and *Singara.*

A site with many ruined buildings visible on the Corona imagery is situated 11.5km to the south-west of Tell Muezzar (possibly a village now called 'Manajid Fawqani', figure 77 below). This seems to be a stronger possibility for the location of Haste since it is situated on an ancient road visible on the satellite imagery. This road heads east to the Khabur, arriving at Tell Arban (Horobam? Now known as Ajaja – see Chapter 3 above), which was said by Herzfeld to be the most important tell in the lower Khabur valley (Herzfeld, Sarre and Berchem 1911-1920: 184).[21] Along this road and very visible on the Corona imagery, there are two tells and

[20] A road shown by Poidebard heads north from this site across the crest of the Jebel abd-al Aziz to join the Habur west of the modern regional capital of Hasaké near a site called *Thallaba* on the Peutinger Table. This road passes what must be a magnificent castle at 'Soukara' (which is probably of a later date, although Poidebard states on p150 that it seems to be of 'Byzantine' origin – 36°25'37"N, 40°23'55"E) and another Assyrian or Mitanni round fortress at 36°30'24"N, 40°27'23"E, about 25km due west of Hasaké. A site near here is named 'Siha' on the Mapcarta website. No images are provided here because these sites lie outside the main lines of communication discussed in this article, but Poidebard's map shows another 'Roman' road passing nearby from *Haste*/Muezzar north towards Hasaké and the Khabur valley in its west-east portion. The Assyrian site has recently been the object of scientific excavations, visible on Google Earth, but the writer has not discovered its name.

[21] The road heading west from this site is likely to have reached the valley of the Balikh some way south of Ain al-Arous, supposed by Dillemann to be the site of the *Tharrana* of the PT and therefore even further south of Harran. No old road is visible on the satellite imagery between either of these places and the south of the Jebel abd-al Aziz

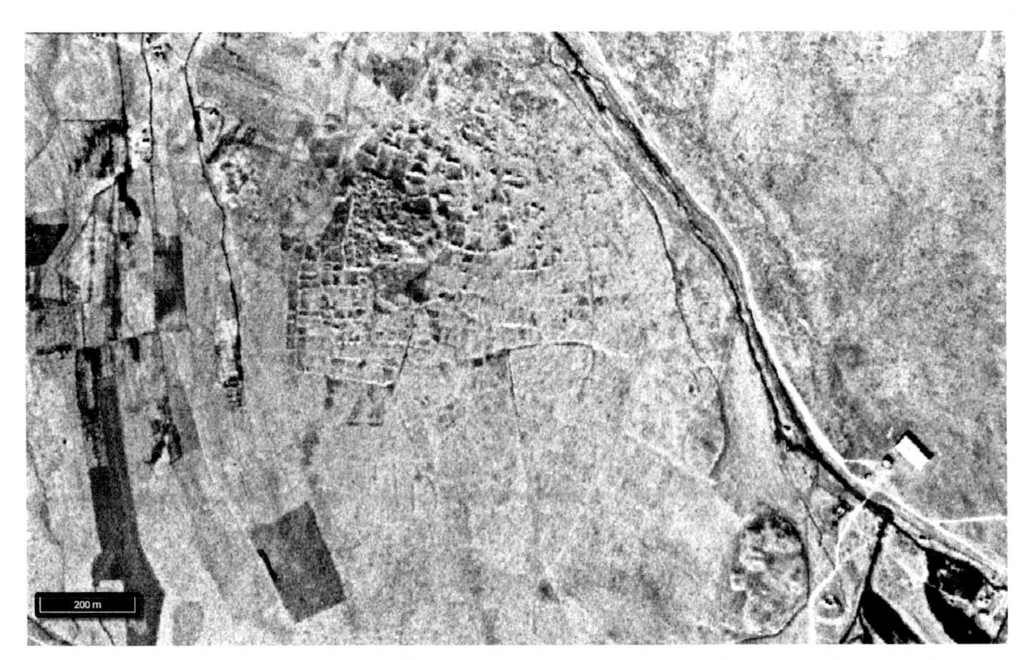

Figure 77. Site 11.5 km SW of Tell Muezzar at 36°10'02"N, 40°16'02"E - Manajid Fawqani?

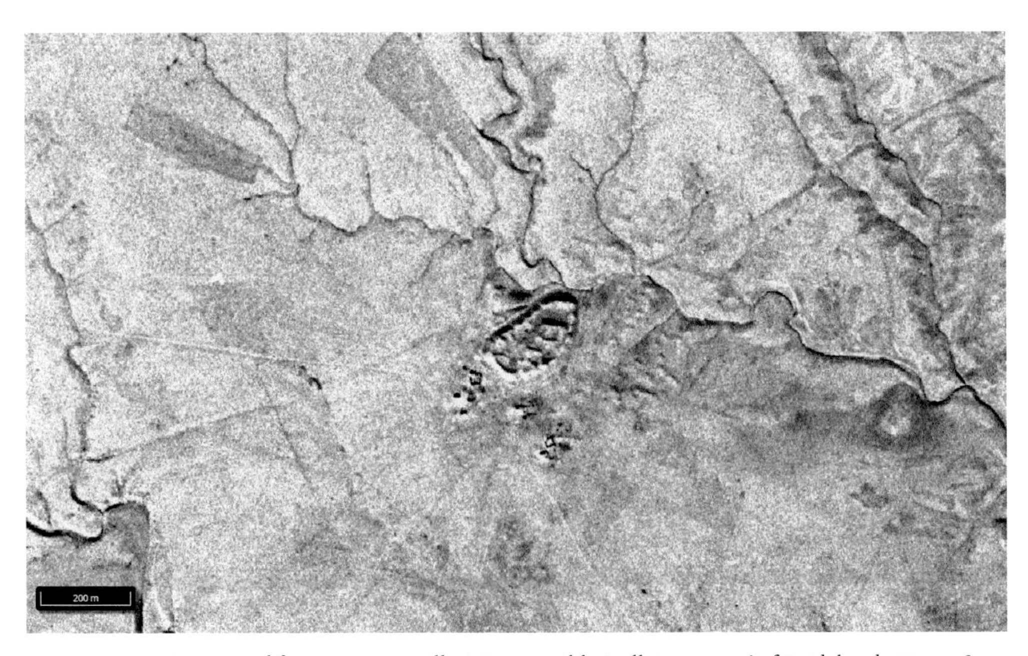

Figure 78. Site on road from Haste to Tell Ajaja – possibly 'Tell Touwenan' of Poidebard *Magrus?*
Corona 1967 36°11'26"N, 40°27'30"E

the structure shown below, which could be the Tell Touwenan mentioned by Poidebard (p156; figure 78 below) and the intermediate station on the PT called *Magrus.*[22] It is therefore possible that the main crossing of the Khabur was at Tell Ajaja and not at Tell Matariye (although the Roman road could also have simply continued up the Khabur valley as far as Tell Matariye before turning to the east).

The route coming from the west via Haste seems more in the nature of a trail for camel caravans than a route constructed by the military for carts suitable for supplying the garrison of *Singara*. It therefore seems probable to this writer that the main Roman road to *Singara* from the west came via *Callinicum* (also known as *Nikephorion* and now Raqqa) down the Euphrates to the confluence with the Khabur at *Circesium* (now al-Busayrah). It would then have turned north along the west bank of the Khabur to a crossing of the river. This could have been located either at Semsaniye/Fadgami - south of Tell Ajaja - from where, as Poidebard says, it continued north-east to *Singara*, or else at Sheddadi, a little to the north.

The road leaving Sheddadi would constitute the third route leaving the Khabur towards Singara and would have linked with routes 1 and 2 near *Batitas* and the current border between Syria and Iraq. That leaving from Semsaniye/Fadghami would be the fourth but this – if it existed in antiquity - would have headed either direct to Singara or else to Hatra on a line some 25km to the south of route 3.

Sheddadi was visited by Layard (1853: 297). He described it as a

> ...lofty platform, nearly square, from the centre of which springs a cone. On the top are the tombs of several Jebour chiefs [the Jebour tribe being the group of Bedouins then controlling the Khabur valley], marked by the raised earth, and by small trees now dry, fixed upright in the graves. I found fragments of pottery and bricks, but no trace of inscriptions. Between Sheddadi and Arban we saw several ruined bridges, probably of the time of the caliphs...

On the following day Layard accompanied a plundering expedition 'as far as a large ruin called Shemshani' (1853: 298). This place is evidently the 'Semsaniye' of Poidebard, from which point the latter saw the beginning of the road heading north-east to *Singara*. Layard states (1853: 299) that after the large mound of 'Fedghami' he reached after a further hour and three quarters (on horseback) 'Shemshani', which he described as

> ...a considerable ruin on the Khabour ... consisting of one lofty mound, surrounded on the desert side by smaller mounds and heaps of rubbish. It abounds in fragments of glazed and painted pottery, bricks, and black basaltic stone, but I could find no traces of sculpture or inscription. The remains of walls protrude in many places from the soil. Above the ancient ruins once stood a castle, the foundations of which may still be seen.

where Haste is most likely to have been situated. So, it is likely that the 'Route des Nomades' between *Tharrana* and the Khabur river which is discussed by Dillemann did indeed pass by this site but that it started somewhere near *Nicephorium* (Raqqa).

[22] *Magrus* is identified by Oates with Assyrian Magarisu and modern Tell Bezari (1985: 169-170 and 1990: 239), but this is north-east of Haseke and difficult to reconcile with the other stations along the route in the Peutinger Table. The word Magdalu (and variations) is simply a Semitic toponym meaning 'tower'.

Figure 79. Possibly, Hirbet al-Han with a Roman (?) fort (36°03'36"N, 41°15'19"E) – 40km NE of Semsaniye, near current Syria/Iraq frontier Zoom Earth © ESRI, HERE, Garmin

One difficulty with identifying either or both of these routes leaving Sheddadi and Semsaniye as part of the frontier road linking *Callinicum* with *Singara* is the scarcity of possible forts of the Roman period. Their relative absence along the route may be an indication that the road was not long in use - if indeed it is of Roman origin at all.

Poidebard states that the road from Semsaniye to *Singara* had existed before the Roman period and that its course was marked by the presence of a 'post' at Hirbet Gelawi after 26km, by numerous ancient wells and by a 'castellum' 14 km beyond Hirbet Gelawi, called by the Bedouin 'Hirbet or Bir al-Han' (*La Trace*, p156). This appears to have been situated on a prominent mound situated on the current Syria-Iraq border and an image is shown at Figure 79 which may correspond to this site.

Poidebard's map shows two fortresses in this part of the Khabur valley, one to the north at Sheddadi (which corresponds to the modern name of Ash Shaddida) and one to the south at Semsaniye. He describes the most southerly route (4) leaving the Khabur in the direction of Nisibis as follows (pp156-7) of 'La trace de Rome dans le désert', trans AC):

> A road from the Khabur to Semsaniye/Fadghami and arriving at Singara was found during a flight piloted by the commandant Ruby. We overflew it together in 1930 and I

> followed it on the ground on the right bank from Semsaniye as far as Malha. This was the last section of a road from Callinicum to Singara.
> The ancient mounds which mark the route indicate that it existed before its use in the Roman period.
> Between Malha and Semsaniye (52km), the road follows the very flat steppe of the Wadi Gahid which leads from Malha, opposite Fadghami on the Khabur and avoids the basalt range of Al-Hammé. On the way lies Hirbet Gelawi (26km), a post from a period before the Roman and by numerous ancient wells and then at 14km from Hirbet Gelawi,by a castellum of the same type as Touloul Mougayir to the east of Thannouris.[23]

It has to be said that this road heading north-east from Semsaniye, proposed by Poidebard as the main route from *Callinicum* to *Singara*, is less impressive – when seen from space - than the road just 20km to the north between Sheddadi and a point near Qseybe/*Batitas* (see below). Since he does not mention route 3, it seems possible that Poidebard's pilot saw both 3 and 4 and then confused them. The direct route from Semsaniye/Fedgami to *Singara* (4) seems to peter out some way before it reaches this destination, although there are various potential tracks visible on the satellite imagery.

A possible explanation for the existence of route 4, the most southerly of the possible links between the Khabur and Singara, is that this route was not originally intended to serve the needs of Singara at all but was rather the main link between Hatra and the west via the Euphrates valley. Evidently, the route would have fallen into disuse after the abandonment of Hatra following the great siege of Ardashir in CE 240/1. It would not have needed to go so far north as Singara but could have reached Hatra from Tell al-Hadhail (see below and Figure 34).[24]

In contrast, the more northerly route (3) from Sheddadi to *Batitas* is remarkably clear and seems to continue without interruption all the way to *Singara*. It is mentioned by Herzfeld, although he does not seem to have travelled along it (Sarre and Herzfeld 1911-1920: vol1, 201). He says that a direct route from Singara to the Khabur (i.e. the route 4 described by Poidebard) did not exist, but that there was an important caravan station at 'al-Qusaibah', which must be the Qseybe of Poidebard, here identified with the *Batitas* of the PT.

However, it is strange that there are not only no obvious forts visible along this stretch of road, despite its very clear appearance on the satellite imagery; neither is any ancient name known for the crossing of the Khabur at Ash Shaddida nor of settlements along the route. An extract from a modern Zoom Earth image is attached below (figure 80) of the latter site, for which a plan was drawn by Herzfeld when he visited the Khabur (Sarre and Herzfeld 1911-1920: 183). At maximum enlargement of the satellite image the foundations of various ruined buildings become visible.

The question also has to be considered whether the 'ancient' roadway found between Ash Shaddida (Sheddadi) and Singara which shows up so clearly on the Corona imagery is not

[23] A fortification corresponding to Touloul Mougayir has been located on the satellite imagery and will be included in the forthcoming article on fortifications.
[24] Foietta (2018: 151-2) indicates that the probable western border of Hatra in the second and third centuries was the Khabur, although there were no known settlements of the Parthian period between Hatra and the Khabur.

Figure 80. The crossing of the Khabur at Ash Shaddadi ('Sheddadi' - Corona 1968) – 36°04'00"N, 40°29'20"E

Figure 81. Sheddadi Zoom Earth. The mound is 3km south of the crossing.

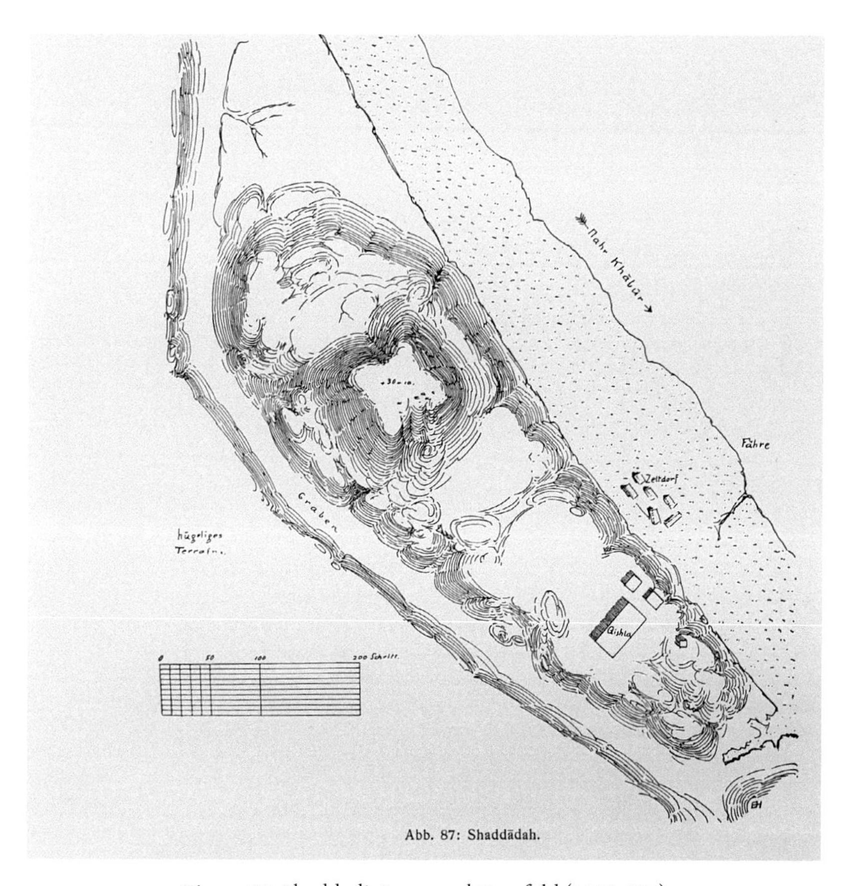

Abb. 87: Shaddādah.

Figure 82. Sheddadi. Sarre and Herzfeld (1911: 183)

perhaps something else much more recent, for example an oil pipeline, despite its mention by Herzfeld. Its course is more strikingly visible on the 1967/1968 Corona images than any other ancient road in the region and could therefore have been confused with a buried pipeline. There was indeed an oil pipeline constructed between 1932 and 1934 between Kirkuk and Haifa, but its course lay much further to the south and no other such early oil pipeline is mentioned on Wikipedia. Another explanation of this linear feature seen on the Corona images, other than the Roman road suggested here, has not been found. The road also links in very satisfactorily with the old road continuing east to Mosul from the Syrian/Iraqi frontier and for the moment this is the route of choice for the main frontier road between Circesium and Singara. A line corresponding to the course of the road west of the frontier is also shown on the French map of 1938, mentioned above (see note 35).

But this 'Roman road' was not one seen and described by Poidebard in the 1930s. It seems not to have been in use as a modern road in 1967 when the Corona images were made, although the line of the route has apparently been chosen for a modern highway linking Syria with Iraq in the future. The old road on the Syrian side approaching the border certainly existed on

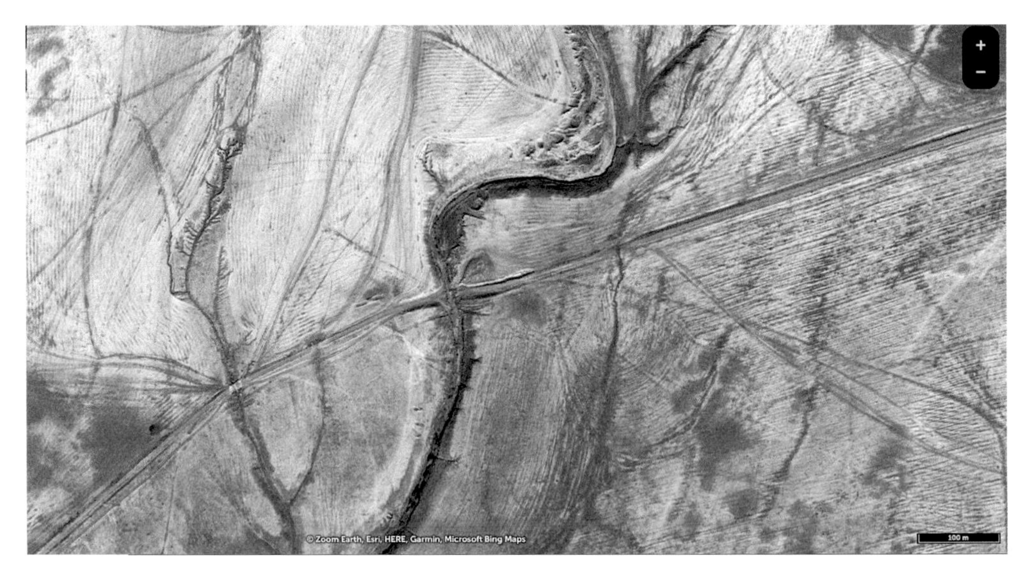

Figure 83. The road near 'Qseybe' (route 3 - see also fig 11 above) 36°15'58"N, 41°15'3"E. Zoom Earth August 2012

the Corona images of 1967 even though it was not mentioned by Poidebard, who was working there in the 1930s. The conclusion must be that it is either the Roman frontier road - not identified by him - or possibly an otherwise unknown route constructed between 1935 and 1967 but never put into use. Only a visit on the ground can resolve this.

Roads south-east of Singara

Altaweel and Hauser have examined the Corona imagery and discussed the possible routes between Singara and Hatra in detail (2004). An important conclusion concerns the site of Dicat, shown on the Peutinger Table as lying between Ain Sinu/*Zagurae* and *Ad Herculem*. The complete series of toponyms for this stretch is *Sirgora (Singara) 12, Zagora (Zagurae) 10, Dicat 12, Ad Herculem 22, Hatra.*

It is evident that until its capture by Shapur I in CE 240[25] Hatra was the most important city of the region south-east of Singara and perhaps of all north-east Mesopotamia. Its relationship with the Parthian court is unclear but seems to have changed over time (Sommer 2004). As the centre for a kingdom of Arab tribes both nomadic and settled it appears until its capture and abandonment to have controlled all the land between the Khabur and the Tigris. However, the relationship with Rome after the conquests of Severus also remains unclear. The Romans notoriously failed to capture the city on three occasions - in CE 117 (Trajan); in 197 and in 199 (Septimius Severus).[26] Three Latin inscriptions have been found in the city (Oates 1955). In his discussion of these Oates states that the expression '*domita Media*' in one inscription is

[25] Year 551 of the Babylonian Seleucid calendar, that is between April 240 and April 241. For the dates of the sieges see Hauser 2009: 121. Hauser emphasizes that after its capture by Shapur the city was not razed but simply abandoned.
[26]

likely to refer to a victory of Gordian. If Roman troops were then stationed there the known predilection of the last king of Hatra for a Roman alliance may have been the 'casus belli' which led to Shapur I's siege and the fall of the city. But Hauser found no evidence that the siege walls were designed to cope with the threat of Roman troops coming to relieve the siege. Singara lies 110 km north-west of Hatra, possibly too far for the available Roman troops to have been of any use.

A major site on the route linking the two cities is Tell al-Hadhail (Figure 84a). Hollow ways described by Hauser and Altaweel do show an important route linking Hatra and Singara directly, without passing by Ain Sinu.[27] Tell al-Hadhail is first discussed by Ibrahim (1986: 72, site no. 205) and then by Hauser (1995: 230-232). Ibrahim found evidence of both Parthian and Sasanian occupation. Hauser's conclusions concerning the identification of this site with *Dicat* are repeated in the article of 2004 (Altaweel and Hauser, 2004: 75-77) and the satellite images do indeed indicate that this was the main route. Why then does the Peutinger Table show the road as passing through *Zagurae*, which would involve an unnecessary dogleg to the east? There may be an explanation in that the route from Hatra to Nisibis followed by Jovian in CE363 would have gone via Zagurae and not Singara, captured by the Persians in 360.

Oates, on the other hand, placed *Dicat* (also spelt 'Vicat') at Tell Ibra, 'a mound 14km east of Ain Sinu (Oates, 1968: 79; see image below). Only further research on the ground can resolve the problem definitively but Hauser seems to the present writer more likely to be right about a direct route to Hatra from Singara, rather than one continuing all the way to the Tigris before doubling back to the south-west, which is what Oates seems to propose.

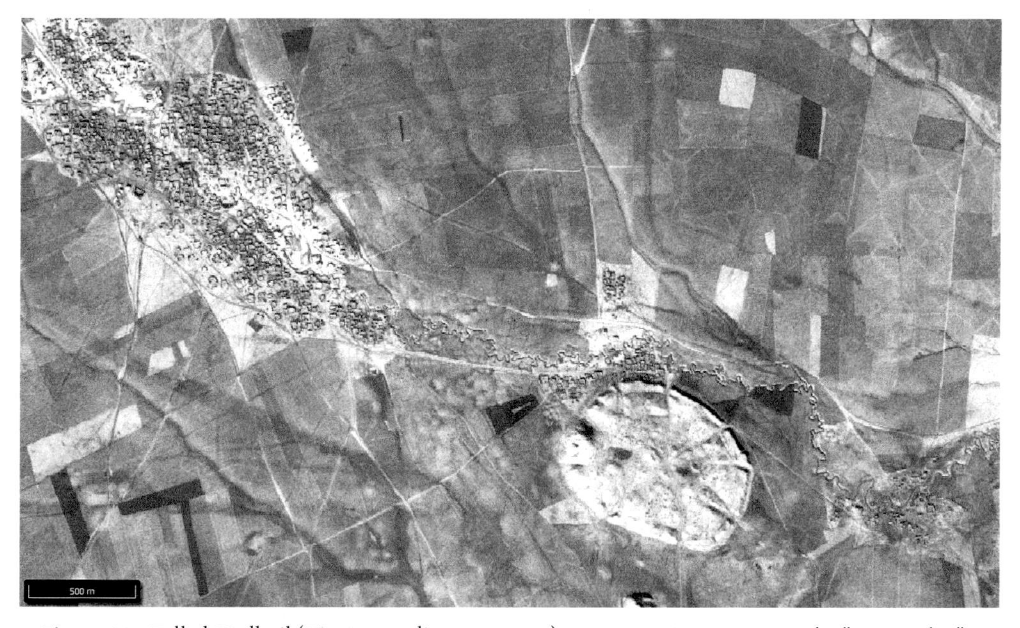

Figure 84a. Tell al-Hadhail (Vicat according to Hauser). Corona 11 Dec 1967. 36°08'56"N, 42°03'16"E

[27] See also Foietta 2018: 121 and Fig.73 on p130.

Figure 84b. Ibrat as-Sagira (Vicat according to Oates). Corona 11 Dec 1967. 36°22'28"N, 42°19"53"E Corona 11 December 1967. 36°22'28"N, 42°19'53"E

The northern road from Nisibis east to the Tigris

The route along the foothills of the Tur Abdin led from Nisibis to a Tigris crossing which may have been at modern Cizre (see Comfort, 2018: 87-9). It therefore ran on a track nearly one hundred kilometres north of but parallel to that between the Khabur, Singara and the Tigris crossings to the south at Nineveh or Sharabadh (Eski Mosul), which is discussed above. It is somewhat far from Singara but is included here because it lies within our definition of north-east Mesopotamia. It is mentioned by Procopius in a most interesting passage discussed also below in Chapter 5 concerning the frontier. It is evident from this passage that Procopius himself had travelled along it (perhaps around 550 CE) and that it was then in regular use – presumably by traders travelling to Arbela and Ctesiphon.

Poidebard discusses this route on pp158 to 161 of '*La Trace de Rome*'; apparently it was chosen in 1921 as the line of the Turco-Syrian frontier between Nisibis and Cizre by a 'Commission Internationale' whose report provided '*précisions archéologiques importantes*'.[28] The current frontier in fact must lie for the most part a little to the south of the ancient road since

[28] This writer has been unable to locate the report concerned.

Figure 85. Uğur. Corona 11 Dec 1967. 37°10'59"N, 41°57'00"E

Procopius implies the latter was close to the foothills of the Tur Abdin and Rhabdion. The modern road was not finished at the time of the Corona satellite photographs (1967/8); 35 kms to the east of Nisibis the link with Cizre north of the frontier did then appear to have followed an old route passing through Sirvan rather than a narrow road actually along the frontier 2.5km to the south.

Substantial ancient remains are visible at Uğur, 8km west of Kebeli (figure 80 below; for Kebeli, see Chapter 3 (Castra Maurorum) and figure 57). No ancient name is known for Uğur, but it seems probable from the visible remains that it was an important stop on the road between Nisibis and the Tigris.

The road is mentioned in the PT (see extract at figure 75, top right-hand corner, and below) as follows: *Nisibis 10 - Sarbane 28 - Sapha - ad flumen Tigrim* (a second time). Dillemann (1962: 83) locates *Sarbane* at Sirvan/Sisarbanon and *Sapha* on the Safan Chai or Sufan Dere, a small tributary of the Tigris which joins the main river near Feshkhabur (p160). Despite the missing distance figure in this section of the PT, he believed that *Sapha* and 'ad flumen Tigrim' were two distinct locations. To this writer it appears more probable that, while there may indeed have been two distinct stopping points, the Tigris crossing for the road from Nisibis (and then

Figure 86. Extract from the Peutinger Table (see also figure 75 above) showing the road from Amouda (Thamaudi) and Nisibis to the Tigris

Figure 87. The road west of Cizre (Bazeft on the horizon). Poidebard PL CLVIII.3

descending on the east bank of the Tigris to Arbela) was at Cizre rather than Feshkhabur, but there can be no proof of this because of changes in the course of the river (Comfort and Marciak 2018: 73-78 and 87-89).

If the crossing was at Cizre, as Poidebard thought (p159), then either the ancient name of Cizre was indeed 'Sapha' (and the separation from a place known as "ad flumen Tigrim" was non-existent) or else Sapha must have been located to the west of Cizre.[29] No suitable location is visible on the satellite photos, but an old road can indeed be traced leaving Cizre for 20km in a south-westerly direction as far as Kebeli, which is in this book thought to be the most likely location for Castra Maurorum (*pace* Dillemann). Kebeli is in fact situated close to the headwaters of the Sufan Dere so perhaps 'Sapha' was just another name for 'Castra Maurorum'.

The extract from Conrad Miller's facsimile[30] of the Peutinger Table shown above is not helpful other than providing the names 'Sapham' and 'ad flumen Tigrim'. It wrongly shows the road from Nisibis with the long ridge of the Tur Abdin (?) to the south and not to the north, as it is in reality, and it is not explicit in placing the site of Sapha in regard to the Tigris.

Poidebard says that local people used the name 'Darb al-Antik' for the road from Nisibis to Cizre (p159) and it was known as an important trade route. According to him it passed from Nisibis along the foothills of the Tur Abdin via Sirvan (the Sarbane of the PT),Tell Ibel, Sirigor, Bazeft (Katran köy) and then Cizre. Unfortunately, not all the old names have been identified by this writer. Remains of the road were apparently visible at the villages of Ayn Ser (now Pınarbaşı) and Danire (Uğur? Cığır?), but these remains are not now visible on the satellite images. He published a photo of this road shortly before it arrives in Cizre (Plate CLVIII, 3).

[29] Ptolemy's 'Sapphe'appears to correspond to this 'Sapha' and his coordinates place it near the Tigris. The editors also consider that it corresponds to modern Cizre (Stückelberger, 2006: 583)
[30] http://www.fh-augsburg.de/~harsch/Chronologia/Lspost03/Tabula/tab_pe13.html

Chapter 5

The frontier in north-eastern Mesopotamia

This chapter seeks to address the nature of this frontier in the light of the foregoing chapters on fortresses and roads. It does not refer to the very copious existing literature on Roman frontiers, except insofar as north-eastern Mesopotamia is directly concerned. Elton warns us against the exclusive use of fortifications for identifying frontiers (1996: viii), but for this region other information concerning language and culture is often lacking. In any case the use of Aramaic and Greek was common on both sides of the political frontier between Rome and Persia and religion in late antiquity, whether Jewish, Christian or Manichaean, also respected no political boundaries.

Whittaker is one writer on the Roman frontiers who does specifically address the frontier in northern Mesopotamia (1994: especially 139-141). His book is associated with the idea that the '*limes*' was a zone and not a line, a view which is not accepted here – at least for the region concerned. In regard to the reign of Septimius Severus he states that: 'The cities of Mesopotamia continued to be the keys to Roman power without there being any sense of new frontier' (p58). It is evident that control of cities was essential in this area which had been - relatively speaking - urbanised for centuries. But the cities possessed defined territories, which often had to be defended.

Whittaker also discusses also the Diocletianic 'limes' in Syria from Damascus to the Euphrates. He notes rightly that the forts constructed by Diocletian did not constitute a serious barrier for an army and that Roman control depended largely on arrangements with local Arab tribes (p136). In northern Mesopotamia there was even less physical presence and nothing at all comparable to the Gorgan Wall on the north-east frontier of the Sasanian empire. But there still seems to have been a line separating the empires even if it was defended for the most part not by a continuously manned series of fortifications, but rather by mobile field armies based in or near cities.

The nature of the Roman frontier in the east, especially in late antiquity, as a demarcated line rather than a zone has been convincingly addressed by Greatrex (Greatrex 2007).[1] He cites in particular the point between Dara and Nisibis mentioned in *De Ceremoniis* as that where Roman dignitaries had to meet a Persian ambassador on the frontier.[2] It seems evident that both sides knew where the border lay.

It might be expected that many fortifications on both Persian and Roman sides of the frontier would have existed in view of the conflict lasting centuries. However, the line of the frontier seems to have fluctuated and not just after 363 CE. Many forts described above seem to have existed not as frontier defences but as small road-side garrisons. It also seems possible that

[1] Although the long wall in the Jenel Cembe as described by Poidebard and Joelle Napoli, discussed above, has to be rejected as part of a demarcation of the frontier.

[2] See Greatrex and Lieu 2002: 124-8. This point is specified by Procopius (Wars 5I.1014) as lying 28 stades to the east of Dara.

even larger fortifications were frequently not manned except when needed as campaign bases. Isaac's view expressed in the '*Limits of Empire*' (1992: especially 257-260) was that the line of the frontier was irrelevant as a military concept in the area of north-east Mesopotamia.

Nevertheless, the frontier was policed, if permeable. The episode involving John of Tella on Mount Sinjar in the sixth century CE required soldiers on both sides of this frontier to collaborate in apprehending him (see footnote 18 above; also discussed in Greatrex 2007: 111, who cites the interrogation of John by the marzban recounted in the '*Life of John of Tella*' by Elias[3]). Furthermore, a 'frontier commission' composed of Barsauma (then bishop of Nisibis), the Persian marzban, the Roman dux and the king of the 'Arabs' met in 484 to define the frontier around Nisibis, possibly in the context of raiding by Arab tribes (Labourt 1904: 139, Dillemann 1962: 223). Sadly, there is no information available concerning the methods and results of this commission.[4]

In the writer's doctoral thesis the nature of the frontier between Rome and Persia was discussed in broad terms (Comfort 2009: 229-244, Chapter 6-i) 'Frontiers and defence'). Amongst other considerations this chapter addressed the issue of land taxes. It seems evident that, for two empires with developed bureaucracies and state revenues dependent largely on taxes on land, those individuals cultivating land in the countryside must have known to whom their taxes should be paid. This implies that this frontier was indeed a line and not a zone, at least for those regions where land was owned and cultivated.

At the northern edge of the region discussed in the book, just below the fortress of Rhabdion (Comfort 2017: 215-7), there was in the sixth century CE, according to Procopius,[5] an area of cultivated land that belonged to and was worked by Roman farmers, but which was surrounded by Persian territory – the *Romaion agron* in Greek or 'Field of the Romans'; the Roman farmers paid a tax of 50 staters annually to the Persians. In exchange, the Persians were allowed to continue in possession of a village producing grapes near Martyropolis. There was a road used – and apparently 'owned' and therefore maintained - by the Romans which headed east from Dara and Nisibis to the Tigris. This road passed through this territory below Rhabdion and near the adjacent Persian fortress of Sisauranon, sacked by Justinian's general Belisarius in 541 CE and later the site of a battle in 591 in which the Romans were victorious (59: 219-220). The passage in Procopius – and in particular the reference to a vineyard - is discussed at the beginning of the book about the upper Tigris in antiquity, written by this author with Michal Marciak, entitled '*How did the Persian King of Kings get his wine?*' (Archaeopress 2018). What Procopius tells us is also relevant to the discussion of the frontier since it confirms – at least for the sixth century CE - both that the boundary between specific agricultural areas was clearly demarcated and that the road going through the area towards the Tigris continued in use.

[3] Greatrex and Lieu 2002: 98.

[4] This episode is also discussed in Fiey 1977. The information comes from two letters from Barsauma to his metropolitan Acacius published in the 'Recueil des Actes synodaux de l'église de Perse' ed; J-B Chabot in 'Actes et extraits des manuscrits' vol 37: 532. Barsauma mentions that in response to a serious drought the tribesmen had begun to cross the frontier to Roman territory on raids for animals, people and supplies. The marzban in Nisibis, Qardag Nakoran, took back the captives and arranged an exchange but negotiations with the Roman dux inside Nisibis, where the Romans were received with honour, failed because of a further such raid which took place while they were talking. Eventually a treaty was signed with the help of Barsauma who, because of his special knowledge , was retained for this purpose in Nisibis despite an order that he go to the royal court in Ctesiphon.

[5] Procopius, Buildings II.iv

In north-eastern Mesopotamia there had been a very long history of occupation of the land before the period discussed here and the land between Singara and Nisibis in particular seems likely to have remained under continuous cultivation because of the rich soil and the presence of water suitable for irrigation from the Radd river (a tributary of the Jaghjagh and Khabur). But in times of war such as the periods of armed conflict between Rome and Persia it seems likely that the rural population suffered from the depredations of the armies concerned and that actual numbers of people present on the land may have much diminished.[6] It is also likely that countrymen fled in some cases to cities for protection. Thus, we know that during the sieges of Amida in 359 and 505 CE the urban population was substantially increased and that of Edessa also grew in a period of poor harvests and famine (Trombley and Watt 2000: 41).

Nevertheless, it seems probable that then – as now - much of the population continued to cultivate the land and normally lived in villages outside the main cities. When the frontier between Rome and Persia changed, the population of such villages must necessarily have transferred from one tax area to another. But there is no clear information available for this period about when and how such frontier changes took place, nor indeed about the nature of the relations between the settled population of the countryside and nomadic pastoralists. Raids on settled areas by nomadic tribesmen certainly took place and we know that Justinian fortified Thannouris in the sixth century CE specifically to deter such raids.

The Roman frontier is likely to have included Singara from as early as the conquests of Avidius Cassius, acting for Lucius Verus during his campaign of 165 CE during which he captured Ctesiphon.[7] But it does not seem to have reached the Tigris opposite Nineveh, except perhaps for a short period during Parthian control of the east bank. Until further excavations have been carried out no clear indication can be provided of the extent of Roman control down the Tigris below Seh Qubba (see discussion of Castra Maurorum above).

Other than Singara itself – and perhaps the Sasanian camp at Qohbol - the various fortresses described here probably had as much importance for controlling raids by nomads and protecting trade routes as in deterring organised aggression by the other 'super-power'.[8] No long walls existed in this region, possibly for the reasons discussed below; major campaign bases for large armies outside the main towns of Nisibis, Singara, Bezabde and – perhaps - Eski Mosul are also missing. From 507 Dara constituted a very important Roman fortress near Nisibis, which had been surrendered to the Persians in 363, but Dara is a late addition to the region's fortifications and outside the artificial geographical limits set for this book. There are however at least two other important exceptions – Circesium for the Romans and now Qohbol for the Persians. The former was an essential starting point for the Roman frontier heading north from the Euphrates and also an important border crossing fortified by Diocletian (see above). Qohbol appears also to have been an important bridgehead for the Persians, at least until they recovered Nisibis in 363. This seems to indicate that under the Sasanians the frontier was pushed back from the region of what is now Mosul towards Nisibis.

[6] Lyonnet's survey of the upper Khabur region found the area south of the road from Resaina to Nisibis 'astonishingly empty' of settlement in the Byzantine-Sasanian period (5th to 7th centuries CE) (Lyonnet 1996353).

[7] See note 22 above.

[8] In this respect it differs from the situation a little further north where a rather dense network of forts existed in and around the Tur Abdin (see {Comfort 2017) . This network did slow down substantially the Persian attacks under Khosrow II in the early seventh century CE.

A further exception concerning the absence of major fortresses is once again 'Castra Maurorum'. This Roman military base was one of the three named fortresses transferred to the Persians by Jovian in 363/4. It is referred to by Ammianus Marcellinus as a 'very important stronghold' (XXV.7.9; see note 129 above). Warwick Ball, who placed it at Seh Qubba, treats the Partho-Roman period in detail and has this to say in his 'Discussion' concerning the Sasano-Byzantine period[9] of the history of the site (Ball 2003: 79-81):

> The history of this border area indicates an extremely fluid political situation at this time. The area remained a frontier zone, and we can assume that the area around Seh Qubba continued as a battleground between the rival Byzantine and Sasanian empires, since the ramparts continued in use and may even have been restored in this period. It is a moot point whether the Roman connection could have been politically sustained by the Byzantine empire which inherited the problems of this frontier region (Oates 1968) but military activity undoubtedly continued in the north of Iraq and was accompanied by a period of brief hegemony. This sort of political see-saw is extremely difficult, if not impossible, to trace in the archaeological record...

In fact, Oates does not refer to any period of 'brief hegemony' after 363 and it is unclear what Ball was thinking of, but it is interesting that he apparently found evidence of late Roman occupation at Seh Qubba, even if 'Castra Maurorum' was in fact at Babil/Kebeli, which has not been excavated.

Regrettably, no markers of the frontier north and east of Singara are yet known. The roads and trade routes seem likely to have been of importance to both Rome and Persia but we do not know who was responsible for road maintenance nor do we know anything about the nature of the garrisons of the forts, beyond that information provided in the *Notitia Dignitatum* for the Roman side of the frontier and a few papyrus fragments from Dura Europos.

Both Rome and Persia, especially the latter, displayed outside Mesopotamia the capacity to construct long linear fortifications. The reasons for the absence of long walls marking this frontier are not known for certain but may have included the following:

a. A reluctance by both Rome and Persia to accept the prevailing boundaries of the third to the sixth centuries CE as permanent. Both sides at different moments wished to extend the frontier into the territory of the other.
b. An acknowledgement by both powers that the geographical conditions and difficulty of maintaining and supplying large garrisons rendered impossible construction and manning of a major fortification between the Euphrates and the Tigris outside the existing main cities – other than the specific case of Dara, constructed by Anastasius in 505 CE.
c. A recognition that long walls, while a good deterrent for nomadic tribes without siege technology, could not stop a determined attack by an army accustomed to taking cities.

In Syria Diocletian is known to have constructed a *'limes'* consisting of a line of forts and a military road from near Damascus heading past Palmyra to join the Euphrates near Resafa at

[9] Ball gives the following rough dates for these periods: Partho-Roman - early 1st millennium AD; Sasano-Byzantine - mid 1st millennium AD (2003: 5).

Soura.[10] In Mesopotamia no such organised 'limes' appears to have existed and the frontier followed the course of the rivers Khabur and Jaghjagh, although there was a large salient before 363 to include Nisibis, Bezabde and Singara. It is this salient which is the main object of concern in this book, but it has to be said that neither the salient nor the later frontier along the Jaghjagh appear to have been seriously fortified by the Romans to a level sufficient to deter Persian invasion. It is unclear why Diocletian strongly fortified the line from Palmyra to the Euphrates and Circesium itself but did not build in stone a line of forts to Singara.[11] The garrisons known to have existed during the third century in the Khabur valley must have occupied fortifications built of mudbrick and, until excavations are conducted which are directed specifically at identifying these, Poidebard's findings for the '*limes*' up the Khabur and the Jaghjagh cannot be verified. Even the Italian excavations at Tell Barri produced only doubtful results in this regard (Pierobon Benoit 2008: see above).

In 363 Jovian surrendered Nisibis, Singara, Bezabde and Castra Maurorum, together with 15 other fortresses.[12] For Castra Maurorum its position is disputed and for the fifteen fortresses we do not know their locations; one is likely to have been Bezabde but others may have been on the eastern and northern sides of the Tigris. It now seems likely that up to the fall of Hatra the line of the frontier lay to the south of Eski Mosul/Sharabadh but probably did not include the Tigris banks opposite Nineveh. Hatra seems to have been at least in alliance with Rome, if not actually occupied by Roman troops prior to its fall to Shapur I in 240/241; the Sasanians may have constructed Qohbol soon after this date after pushing back the frontier from Sharabadh in the direction of Nisibis.[13] But a 'screen of forts' consisting of Ain Sinu, Qhobol and 'Site 54' cannot be said to constitute a defended line comparable to the Roman 'Strata Diocletiana' between Damascus and the Euphrates.

The declaration of Isaac that a fortified line in Mesopotamia did not exist (1992: 257) may therefore be correct despite the curtain of forts suggested by Howard-Johnston. There are many known strongpoints, but these seem not to have constituted a defended line for either side; the fact that Persian Ur (=Qohbol?) lay to the north of Roman Singara in 363 CE shows a bewildering lack of consistency that must handicap any study of the 'limes' in Mesopotamia.[14] This also appears to be incompatible, of course, with the idea of a frontier with firmly identified tax districts on each side.[15]

After 363, when it must be assumed that the south-north frontier lay along the line of the Khabur and Jaghjagh starting at Circesium, any remains of a fortified 'limes' are indeed disappointing, despite the reports of Poidebard. However, it should be noted that Procopius gives the names

[10] See Barrington Atlas of the Greek and Roman World, maps 68 and 69.
[11] Although it is suggested above that both the fort at Tell Brak and that at Serjihan were of Diocletianic origin.
[12] Ammianus Marcellinus, XXV, 7.9
[13] However, the closest parallels date to the late 4th to 6th centuries (Sauer, pers. comm.).
[14] As discussed above, Ammianus states that Constantius II fled after a defeat (near Alaina?) to Thebeta (which he calls Hibita) in about 343 (XXV.9.3). He refers to it as a 'stationem intutam' i.e. not fortified – but possibly 'unguarded ' or'unsafe'. Nevertheless it was apparently under Roman control. Yet he also says (XXV.8.7) that Ur was a Persian fortress ('Persicum castellum') in 363. The term 'castellum' may indicate a structure too small for the huge campaign base at Qohbol but if Ur was Qohbol and Thebeta/Hibita was close to Ur on the road from Hatra to Nisibis, as this writer believes is most likely (see discussion of Thebeta above), then either Ur changed hands during the 20 years separating these events or at that time the frontier lay between the two.
[15] The situation for the period from 240 to 360 is comparable to the placement of the bastides of the Hundred Years' War in the writer's own region of Aquitaine, with English foundations in the 1260s to the east of contemporary French foundations despite an apparent north-south boundary line somewhere in the Upper Agenais.

of a large number of forts in this region which were either built or strengthened by Justinian but which have not been identified.[16] It may be that the mudbrick walls of such forts are no longer visible from the air and that only the ones at Thannouris, Tell Brak and Serjihan were built – at least partly - of stone. The locations of some of the forts mentioned by Procopius were discussed by Dillemann (1962: 108-9) but none are identified as lying on the Khabur or Jaghjagh; the other names shown in the Barrington Atlas of the Classical World (Maps 89 and 91) do not appear to correspond to any of these.[17]

The line of the frontier has been most cogently displayed in the series of maps produced by TAVO (Tübinger Atlas des Vorderen Orients). In particular, map B VI 4 (*Eastern Mediterranean and Mesopotamia- Late Roman Period 337-527 AD*), published in 1984 with Professor Erich Kettenhofen as author follows the same line as that accepted in this book.

It shows in particular that the Roman frontier reached the Tigris at Eski Mosul and not Mosul itself. This writer differs from Professor Kettenhofen however in regard to the line of the frontier to the north and east of Nisibis. Map 4 below shows the frontier as leaving the frontier post at or near Serjihan, circumventing Nisibis and then following the crest of the Tur Abdin eastwards to a point near the confluence of the Cehennem Dere with the Tigris near Hiaspis and some 10km west of Bezabde (Eski Hendek). The justification for this difference of appreciation lies in the doctrinal differences between monasteries along this crest, the especially important role of the monastery at Qartmin and the continued existence into the seventh century CE of the major Roman fortification at Rhabdion (Hatem Tai Kalesi). This part of the frontier is discussed in Comfort 2017: 185-188.[18]

[16] Procopius, *On buildings*, II;6. See the list provided in the discussion of Tell Brak above.

[17] In addition to the forts mentioned by Procopius and listed under the discussion of Tell Brak above, George of Cyprus (ed. Gelzer1890) who wrote his *Descriptio Orbis Romani* in the early seventh century mentions at least four places still unlocated in Osrhoene (p.45: Nea Valentia, Monithilla, Therimachon and Moniauga) and about 14 in Mesopotamia (pp.46-7). Some are discussed by Dillemann 1962: 108. This writer believes that the Khabur frontier after 363 was then still considered as part of Osrhoene, while that along the Jaghjagh would have been in Mesopotamia. Surprisingly Thannouris and Serjihan (Sargathon) are not mentioned under these names but could be among the unlocated toponyms. See also Honigmann 1939: 63 65.

[18] It should be noted that the TAVO maps B VI 5 (1988; *Eastern Mediterranean - The early Byzantine Empire*; author Thomas Riplinger) and B VI 6 (1988; *Caucasus and Mesopotamia 581-628 AD*) while apparently agreeing with this writer in regard to the line north of Nisibis disagree in regard to the frontier below Nisibis which, according to Riplinger, did not follow the Jaghjagh but a north-south line some 30kms to the west. The maps also show, for reasons unknown to this writer, that the land east of the Khabur around Circesium belonged to the Romans.

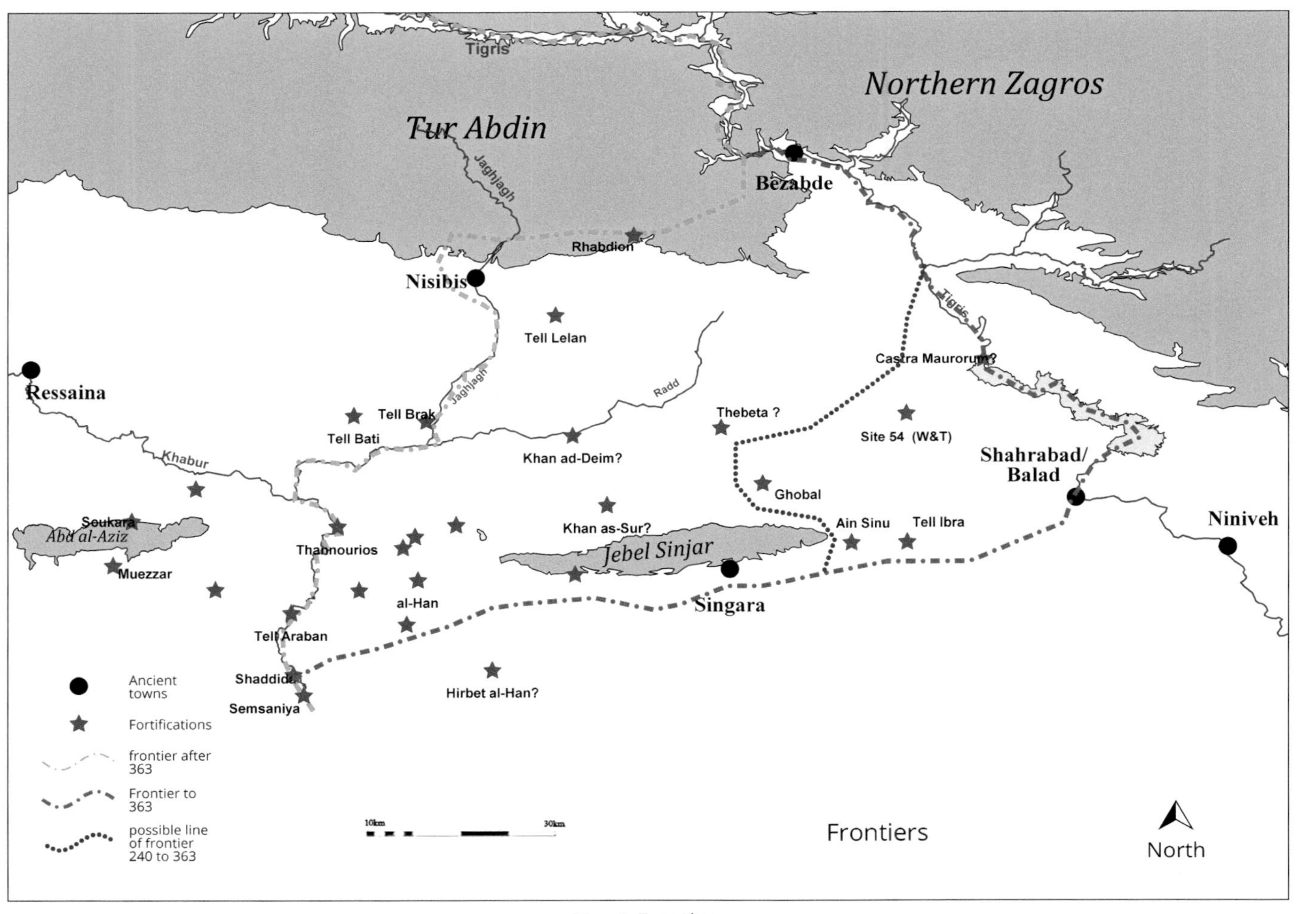

Map 4. Frontiers

Chapter 6

Conclusions

The fortresses and roads studied for this book confirm the importance of Singara as a fortified town at the south-east corner of the Roman frontier with Persia. Possibly the town first became notable for commercial reasons as a station on the roads to Hatra and to Nineveh, but Singara was clearly a military base for the period from the second century CE to 363 and the roads were probably more important for the logistic needs of the army than for traders during this period. Especially those roads between the Khabur valley and Singara seem likely to have been used during the period of Roman occupation rather as military highways intended for communications with the west and for supplying the Roman garrisons than as commercial highways.

Aerial photography and then the study of satellite imagery of the area between the Khabur and Mount Sinjar have revealed many fortified sites, as well as roads. It is unlikely that all of the fortifications are Roman or Sasanian, dating to the period between 200 and 650 CE, and much further research is needed. Corona imagery has been of special assistance in the identification of Sasanian fortresses, but it has also permitted the rediscovery and pinpointing of other sites mentioned by Poidebard and Stein in their reports of aerial surveys conducted in the 1920s and 1930s.

This book constitutes an early step in the study of north-east Mesopotamia or the Jazira during this period; it reveals a rather dense network of roads and fortified sites which provides a new basis for study of the frontier region between Rome and Persia. In particular, the location of the 'camp' at Qohbol and that discovered by Wilkinson and Tucker (their site 54) tend to support the view that the Sasanian Persians sought to fortify the frontier between Nisibis and to protect the Tigris crossings at Sharabadh and Nineveh in a way comparable to the forts along the Lower Euphrates encountered by Julian in 363, even if there was no 'line' defended by either side in the third and fourth centuries CE.

So, in conclusion, this study supports the idea that in north-east Mesopotamia both Romans and Sassanian Persians did seek to protect their frontiers and even – in the case of the Sasanians to push them back towards Nisibis – but they did not try to defend a line, relying rather on strongpoints both to hold back enemy invasions and to act as campaign bases from which to launch attacks. At some periods where a relative stability was possible, it seems probable that taxes were levied on cultivated land and that everyone knew where the frontier should be.

The use of aerial photos and satellite imagery can only take the analysis of the region so far. It is evident that the roads and forts discussed here will need to be investigated thoroughly on the ground when archaeological research becomes possible once again in this region.

Bibliography

Altaweel, M. and Hauser, S. 2004: 'Trade routes to Hatra according to evidence from ancient sources and modern satellite imagery' *Baghdader Mitteilungen,* 35: 59-86

Arce, I. 2015: 'Severan Castra, Tetrarchic Quadriburgua, Justinian Coenobia, and Ghassanid Diyarat. Patterns of transformation of Limes Arabicus forts during Late Antiquity' in R. Collins, M. Symonds and M. Weber (ed.), *Roman Military Architecture on the Frontiers. Armises and their architecture in Late Antiquity*. Oxford, Oxbow: 98-122

Aylward, W. 2013 *Excavations at Zeugma : conducted by Oxford Archaeology* Los Altos, California The Packard Humanities Institute

Ball, W. 1989: 'Soundings at Seh Qubba, a Roman frontier station on the Tigris in Iraq' in D. H. French and C. S. Lightfoot (ed.), *The eastern frontier of the Roman Empire*. Oxford, BAR International Series: 7-18

Ball, W. 1990: 'The Tell al-Hawa project. The second and third season of excavations at Tell al-Hawa, 1987-88' *Mediterranean Archaeology,* 3: 75-92

Ball, W. 1996: 'The upper Tigris area. New evidence from the Eski Mosul and North Jazira projects' in K. Bartl and S. Hauser (ed.), *Continuity and change in northern Mesopotamia from the Hellenistic to the early Islamic period*. Berlin, Reimer: 415-427

Ball, W. 2003 *Ancient settlement in the Zammar region* Oxford British School of Archaeology in Iraq

Ball, W., Tucker, D., et al. 1989: 'The Tell al-Hawa Project: Archaeological Investigations in the North Jazira 1986-87' *Iraq,* 51: 1-66

Barnes, T. 1980: 'Imperial Chronology, A. D. 337-350' *Phoenix,* 34: 160-166

Barnes, T. 1985: 'Constantine and the Christians of Persia' *Journal of Roman Studies,* 75: 126-136

Benjamin of Tudela, t. a. e. b. M. S. 1983 *The Itinerary of benjamin of Tudela; Travels in the Middle Ages* Malibu Joseph Simon, Italica Press

Bivar, A. 1983: ' The Seleucid, Parthian and Sasanian Periods' in E. Yarshater (ed.), *Cambridge History of Iran, Volume 3.1*. Cambridge, Cambridge University Press:

Bounni, A. 1990: 'The Khabur and Haseke dam projects and the protection of threatened antiquities in the region' *Orbis biblicus et orientalis Series archaeologica Tall Al-Ḥamīdīya 2: Symposion:,* 6: 19-29

Buckingham, J. S. 1827 *Travels in Mesopotamia including a journey from Aleppo, across the Euphrates, to Orfah* London Colburn, (repr.1971)

Cagnat, R. 1927: 'Inscription romaine du Sindjar au nom de Trajan' *Syria,* 8: 53-54

Cahen, C. 1937: 'La Djazira au milieu du treizième siècle' *Revue des Etudes islamiques,* 8: 119-128

Cameron, H. 2018 *Making Mesopotamia: Geography and Empire in a Romano-Iranian Borderland* Brill

Chapot, V. 1907 *La frontière de l'Euphrate de Pompée à la Conquete arabe* Rome Erma de Bretschneider (reprinted 1967)

Comfort, A. 2009 *Roads on the frontier between Rome and Persia.* PhD thesis, Exeter University, Exeter http://hdl.handle.net/10036/68213

Comfort, A. 2011 'Roman bridges of South-East Anatolia' in H. Bru and G. Labarre (ed) *L'Anatolie des peuples, des cités et des cultures (IIe millénaire av. J.-C. - Ve siècle ap. J.C.)* Conference 2013 Besançon 315-349

Comfort, A. 2017: 'Fortresses of the Tur Abdin and the confrontation between Rome and Persia' *Anatolian Studies,* 67: 181-229

Comfort, A. 2018: 'Travelling from the Euphrates to the Tigris in Late Antiquity' in A. Kolb (ed.), *Roman roads: new evidence - new perspectives* Berlin, De Gruyter:

Comfort, A. 2021: 'The rivers of Mesopotamia in Herodotus' *Histories*' *Orbis Terrarum,* 19: 47-64

Comfort, A., Abadie-Reynal, C., et al. 2000: 'Crossing the Euphrates in antiquity: Zeugma seen from space' *Anatolian Studies,* 50: 99-126

Comfort, A. and Ergeç, R. 2001: 'Following the Euphrates in antiquity: north-south routes around Zeugma' *Anatolian Studies,* 51: 19-50

Comfort, A. and Marciak, M. 2018 *How did the Persian king of kings get his wine? The upper Tigris in antiquity (c.700 BCE to 636 CE)* Oxford Archaeopress

Dark, K. 2001 *Byzantine Pottery* Stroud Tempus

Diehl, C. 1896 *L'Afrique byzantine : histoire de la domination byzantine en Afrique (533-709)* Paris Leroux

Dillemann, L. 1962 *Haute Mésopotamie orientale et pays adjacents* Paris Geuthner

Dmitriev, V. 2015: 'The 'Night battle' of Singara: Whose victory?' *Historia I Swiat,* 4: 65-70

Dodgeon, M. H. and Lieu, S. N. 1991 *The Roman eastern frontier and the Persian wars (AD226-363)* London Routledge

Dussaud, R. 1927 *Topographie historique de la Syrie antique et médiévale* Paris Geuthner

Edwell, P. 2008 *Between Rome and Persia. The middle Euphrates, Mesopotamia and Palmyra under Roman control.* Abingdon Routledge

Eichler, S., Wäfler, M., et al. 1990: 'Tall al-Hamidiya - Vorbericht 1985-1987' *Orbis biblicus et orientalis Series archaeologica Tall Al-Ḥamīdīya 2: Symposion:,* 6: 233-317

Elton, H. 1996 *Frontiers of the Roman empire* London Batsford

Farrokh, K. 2017 *The armies of ancient Persia: the Sassanians* Barnsley Pen and Sword

Feissel, D. and Gascou, J. 1989: 'Documents d'Archives romains inédits du Moyen Euphrate (IIIe siècle après J.-C.)' *Comptes Rendus, Académie des Inscriptions et Belles-Lettres*: 535-560

Fiey, J. 1964a: 'Balad et Beth 'Arbaye' *Orient syrien,* 10: 189-232

Fiey, J. 1964b: 'The Iraqi section of the Abbassid road Mosul-Nisibin' *Iraq,* 26: 106-117

Fiey, J. 1977 *Nisibe: métropole syriaque orientale et ses suffragants des origines à nos jours* Louvain CSCO

Fiey, J. and Conrad, L. e. 2004 *Saints syriaques* Princeton, NJ Darwin Press

Foietta, E. 2018 *Hatra: Il territorio e l'urbanistica* Oxford Archaeopress

Forbes, F. 1839: 'A Visit to the Sinjár Hills in 1838, with Some Account of the Sect of Yezídís, and of Various Places in the Mesopotamian Desert, between the Rivers Tigris and Khábúr ' *Journal of the Royal Geographical Society,* 9: 409-430

Fowden, G. 1994: 'The Last Days of Constantine: Oppositional Versions and Their Influence' *Journal of Roman Studies,* 84: 146-170

Fuller, M. and Fuller, N. 1998: 'Archaeological Discoveries at Tell Tuneinir, Syria' *Journal of Assyrian Academic Studies,* 12:

Gaborit, J. 2007 *Géographie historique du Moyen-Euphrate de la conquête d'Alexandre à l'Islam* PhD thesis, 3ème cycle, Université Paris 1,

Gaube, H. 1974 *Ein Arabischer Palast in Sudsyrien. Hirbet el-Baida* Beirut Orient-Institut des Deutschen Morgenländ Gesellschaft

Greatrex, G. 2007: 'Roman Frontiers and Foreign Policy in the East' in R. Alston and S. Lieu (ed.), *Aspects of the Roman East. Papers in honour of Professor Fergus Millar FBA.* Turnhout, Brepols: 103-173

Greatrex, G. 2011 *The chronicle of PseudoZachariah Rhetor. Church and war in Late Antiquity* Liverpool Liverpool University Press

Gregory, S. 1989 'Not 'Why not playing cards? 'but 'why playing cards in the first place?'' in D. French and C. Lightfoot (ed) *The Eastern Frontier of The Roman Empire (Proceedings of a colloquium held at Ankara in Sept. 1988)* Conference 169-175

Gregory, S. 1995 *Roman military architecture on the eastern frontier* Amsterdam Hakkert

Gregory, S. 1996: 'Was there an eastern origin for the design of late Roman fortifications? Some problems for research on forts of Rome's eastern frointier' in D. Kennedy (ed.), *The Roman army in the east.* Ann Arbor, Journal of Roman Archaeology Supplementary Series: 170-209

Gregory, S. and Kennedy, D. 1985 *Sir Aurel Stein's Limes Report* Oxford BAR International Series

Hammond, D. 1987 *Byzantine Northern Syria, AD 298-610: integration and disintegration.* PhD thesis, UCLA, Los Angeles

Harrel, J. 2016 *The Nisibis War: the defence of the Roman East AD 337-363* Barnsley Pen and Sword

Hauser, S. 1995: 'Die mesopotamische Handelswege nach der Tabula Peutingeriana' in U. Finkbeiner, R. Dittman and H. H (ed.), *Beitrâge zur Kulturgeschichte Vorderasiens. Festschrift fûr R.M. Boehmer.* Mainz: 225-235

Hauser, S. 2009: 'Where is the man of Hadr, who once built it and taxed the land by the Tigris and Chaboras? On the significance of the final siege of Hatra' in L. Dirven (ed.), *Hatra. Politics, Culture and Religion between Partthia and Rome.* Amsterdam, Steiner 119-139 and 315-118

Hauser, S. and Tucker, D. 2009: 'The final onslaught: The Sasanian siege of Hatra' *Zeitschrift für Orientarchäologie,* 2: 106-139

Herzfeld, E., Sarre, F., et al. 1911-1920 *Archäologische Reise im Euphrat- und Tigris-Gebiet* Berlin Reimer

Honigmann, E. 1929: 'Note sur deux localités de la Syrie' *Syria,* X: 283

Honigmann, E. 1934: 'Review of Poidebard, La trace de Rome dans le désert de Syrie' *Byzantion,* XI: 473-480

Honigmann, E. 1935 *Die Ostgrenze des Byzantinischen Reiches von 363 bis 1071* Brussels Institut de Philologie et d'Histoire Orientales

Honigmann, E. 1939 *Le Synekdèmos d'Hiéroklès et l'opuscule géographique de Georges de Chypre* Brussels Institut de Philologie et d'Histoire orientales et slaves

Howard-Johnson, J. 2001/2008: 'The destruction of the Late Antique World Order'. Durham

Howard-Johnston, J. 2012: 'The late Sassanian army' in B. Bernheimer and A. Silverstein (ed.), *Late antiquity: eastern perspectives.* Exeter, Gibb Memorial Trust: 87-127

Ibrahim, J. 1986 *Pre-Islamic settlement in the Jazira* Baghdad

Isaac, B. 1992 *The limits of empire: the Roman army in the East* Oxford Clarendon 2

Kennedy, D. 1988: 'A lost Latin inscription from the banks of the Tigris' *Zeitschrift für Papyrologie und Epigraphik,* 73: 101-103

Kennedy, D. 1998 *The twin towns of Zeugma on the Euphrates: rescue work and historical studies* Ann Arbor

Kennedy, D. and Bewley, R. 2004 *Ancient Jordan from the air* London Council for British Reasearch in the Levant, British Academy

Kennedy, D. and Riley, D. 1990 *Rome's Desert Frontier from the air* Austin University of Texas

Kennedy, H. 1994 *Crusader castles* Cambridge

Kennedy, H. 2000: 'Syria, Palestine and Mesopotamia' in A. Cameron (ed.), *Cambridge Ancient History.* Cambridge, CUP: 588-611

Keser-Kayaalp, E. and Erdoğan, N. 2017: 'Recent research at Dara/Anastasiopolis' in E. Rizos (ed.), *New cities in Late Antiquity. Documents and archaeology.* Turnhout, Belgium, Brepols/ Association pour l'Antiquité tardive: 153-175

Konrad, M. 2001 *Der spätrömische Limes in Syrien* Mainz Deutsches Archäologisches Institut; Philipp von Zabern

Kühne, H. 1977: 'Zur historische Geographie am unteren Habur' *Archiv für Orientforschung*, 25: 249-255

Kühne, H. 1978: 'Zur historische Geographie am unteren Habur. Zweiter, vorlaûfiger Bericht über eine archäologische Geländebegehung ' *Archiv fûr Orientforsching*, 26: 181-195

Labourt, J. 1904 *Le christianisme dans l'empire perse sous la dynastie sassanide, 224-632* Paris

Layard, A. 1853 *Discoveries in the ruins of Nineveh and Babylon, with travels in Armenia, Kurdistan and the desert* London John Murray reprinted by Gorgias Press 2002

Le Strange, G. 1905 *Lands of the Eastern Caliphate: Mesopotamia, Persia and Central Asia from the Moslem conquest to the time of Timur* Cambridge CUP, reprinted by Elibron Press, 2006

Lescot, R. 1938 *Enquête sur les Yézidis de Syrie et du Djebel Sindjar* Beyrouth Librairie du Liban

Lightfoot, C. S. 1988: 'Facts and fiction - the third siege of Nisibis (AD350)' *Historia*, 37: 105-125

Lloyd, S. 1938: 'Some ancient sites in the Sinjar district' *Iraq*, V: 123-142

Lyonnet, B. 1996: 'Settlement pattern in the Upper Khabur ' in Bartl and Hause (ed.), *Continuity and change in northern Mesopotamia.* Berlin: 349-361

Mahmound, A., Bernbeck, R., et al. 1988: 'Die Ausgrabung zuf dem Tell Agaga/Saikanni 1982' *Damaszener Mitteilungen*, 3: 141-184

Mallowan, M. 1936a: 'The Excavations at Tall Chagar Bazar, and an Archaeological Survey of the Habur Region, 1934-5' *Iraq*, III: 1-85

Mallowan, M. 1936b: 'Report on the archaeological survey of the Habur and Jaghjagh regions'. British Museum : unpublished report available in Sackler Library, Oxford

Maunsell, F. 1890 *Reconnaissances in Mesopotamia, Kurdistan, North-West Persia and Luristan from April to October 1888* Simla

Meijer, D. 1986 *A survey in Northeastern Syria* Leiden Nederlands Historisch-archaeologisch Inistuut te Istanbul

Miller, K. 1916 *Itineraria Romana* Stuttgart Strecker und Schröder

Mitford, T. 2018 *East of Asia Minor. Rome's hidden frontier* Oxford OUP

Morony, M. G. 1982: 'Continuity and change in the administrative geography of late Sassanian and early Islamic Al-Iraq' *Iran*, XX: 1-50

Mosig-Walburg, K. 1999: 'Zur Schlacht bei Singara' *Historia: Zeitschrift für Alte Geschichte*: 330-384

Musil, A. 1927 *The Middle Euphrates* New York American Geographical Society

Napoli, J. 1997 *Recherches sur les fortifications linéaires romaines* Rome

Nemati, M., Mousavinia, M., et al. 2019: 'Largest ancient fortress of south-west Asia and the western world? Recent fieldwork at Sasanian Qaleh Iraq at Pishna; Iran' *Iran*: online DOI: 10.1080/05786967.05782019.01586449

Niebuhr, C. 1778 and c.1992 *Reisebeschreibung nach Arabien und andern umliegenden Ländern (Travels through Arabia and other countries in the East - trans. into English 1968 by Robert Heron)* Copenhagen, Beirut Manesse Verlag, Librairie du Liban

Nokandeh, J., Rekavandi Omrani, H., et al. 2012 *Persia's Imperial Power in Late Antiquity: The Great Wall of Gorgan and the Frontier Landscapes of Sasanian Iran* Oxford Oxbow

Oates, D. 1955: 'A note on three Latin inscriptions from Hatra' *Sumer*, 1: 39-43

Oates, D. 1956: 'The Roman frontier in northern Iraq' *Geographical Journal*, 122: 190-199

Oates, D. 1968 *Studies in the ancient history of Northern Iraq* Cambridge British School of Archaeology in Iraq

Oates, D. 1985: 'Excavations at Tell Brak, 1983-4' *Iraq*, 47: 159-173

Oates, D. and Oates, J. 1959: 'Ain Sinu: a Roman frontier post in northern Iraq' *Iraq*, 21/2: 207-242

Oates, D. and Oates, J. 1990: 'Aspects of Hellenistic and Roman settlement in the Khabur basin' in P. Matthiae, M. Van Loon and H. Weiss (ed.), *Resurrecting the past: a joint tribute to Adnan Bounni*. Istanbul, Nederlands Historical Institute: 227-248

Oppenheim, M., von 1899, 1900 *Vom Mittelmeer zum Persischen Golf durch den Hauran, die syrische Wüste und Mesopotamien* Berlin

Otter, J. 1748 *Voyage en Turquie et en Perse* Paris (republished 2010)

Palermo, R. 2011-2012 *Settlement patterns and cultural interactions in Northern Mesopotamia between the second and fourth century CE*. PhD thesis, Università desgli studi di Napoli Federico II, Naples

Palermo, R. 2018: 'Pots on the border: Ceramics, identity and mobility in Northern Mesopotamia between Rome and the East' in (ed.), *Migration and Migrant Identities in the Near East from Antiquity to the Middle Ages*. Routledge: 197-221

Palermo, R. 2019 *On the edge of empires. North Mesopotamia in the Roman period (2nd to 4th C. CE)* Abingdon and New York Routlege

Palmisano, A. 2018 *The geography of trade. Landscapes of competition and long-distance contacts in Mesopotamia and Anatolia in the Old Assyrian Colony period*. Oxford Archaeopress

Panaino, A. 2016: 'Kirder and the re-organisation of Persian Mazdeism' in V. e. a. Sarkhosh Curits (ed.), *The Parthian and early Sasanian empores: adaptation ajnd expansion*. Oxford, Ixbow: 53-58

Peeters, P. 1926: 'La passion arabe de S. 'Abd al-Masih' *Analecta Bollandiana*, xliv: 270-341

Pierobon Benoit, R. 2008: 'Tell Barri: sito di frontiera?' in (ed.), *Tell Barri. Storia di un insediamento antico tra Oriente e Occidente*. Naples, Macchiaroli: 169-202

Poidebard, A. 1934 *La trace de Rome dans le désert de Syrie : le limes de Trajan à la conquête arabe* Paris Geuthner

Pollard, N. 2000 *Soldiers, cities and civilians in Roman Syria* Ann Arbor University of Michigan

Raphael, K. 2011 *Muslim fortresses in the Levant* London/New York Routledge

Reitlinger, G. 1938: 'Medieval Antiquities West of Mosul' *Iraq*, 5 143-156

Riley, D. N. 1986: 'Archaeological air photography and the eastern Limes' in P. Freeman and D. Kennedy (ed.), *The defence of the Roman and Byzantine East*. Oxford, BAR, International Series 661-695

Ritter, K. 1854 *Allgemeine Erdkunde* Berlin

Röllig, W. and Kuhne, H. 1977: 'The lower Habur. A preliminary report on a survey conducted by the Tübinger Atlas des Vorderen Orients in 1975' *Annales archéologiques arabes syriennes*, 27-3: 115-140

Sachau, E. 1883 *Reise in Syrien und Mesopotamien* Leipzig Brockhaus

Sarre, F. and Herzfeld, E. 1911-1920 *Archäologische Reise in Euphrat und Tigris gebiet* Berlin Reimer

Sauer, E. 2017: 'Sasanian Persia: Between Rome and the steppes of Eurasia'. Edinburgh

Sauer, E., Nokandeh, J., et al. 2017 'Innovation and stagnation: military infrastructure and the shifting balance of power between Rome and Persia' in E. Sauer (ed.), *Sasanian Persia: betweeen Rome and the steppes of Eurasia*. Edinburgh, Edinburgh University Press: 241-267

Sauer, E., Omrani Rekavandi, H., et al. 2013 *Persia's imperial power in late antiquity: the great wall of Gorgan and frontier landscapes of Sasanian Iran* Oxford Brtish Institute of Persian Studies, Oxbow

Simpson, S. 2017: 'Sasanian Cities: Archaeological perspectives on the urban economy and built environment of an empire' in E. Sauer (ed.), *Sasanian Persia. Between Rome and the steppes of Eurasia*. Edinburgh, Edinburgh University Press: 21-50

Simpson, S. J. 1996: 'From Tekrit to the Jaghjagh: Sasanian sites, settlement patterns and material culture in northern Mesopotamia' in K. Bartl and S. R. Hauser (ed.), *Continuity and change in northern Mesopotamia from the Hellenistic to the early Islamic period*. Berlin, Reimer: 87-126

Sinclair, T. A. 1989 *Eastern Turkey: an architectural and archaeological survey* London Pindar Press

Sommer, M. 2004: 'The desert and the sown: imperial supremacy and local culture in Partho-Roman Mesopotamia' *Parthica, incontri di cultura nel mondo antico,* 6: 235-246

Stein, A. 1938: 'Note on remains of the Roman Limes in north-western Iraq' *Geographical Journal,* 92: 62-66

Stückelberger, A. and Grasshoff, G. 2006: 'Klaudios Ptolemaios. Handbuch der Geographie 1. Teilband: Einleitung und Buch 1-4 2. Teilband: Buch 5-8 und Indices'. Basel

Trombley, F. and Watt, J. 2000 *The Chronicle attributed to Pseudo-Joshua the Stylite* Liverpool Liverpool University Press

Tuba Ökse, A., Erdoğan, N., et al. 2018: 'Ilısu Barajı İnşaat Sahası Kurtarma Kazıları III: Roma Dönemi / Salvage Excavations of the Construction Area of the Ilısu Dam III: Roman Empire Period and Middle-New Ages sites. '. Mardin

Ur, J. 2003: 'Corona satellite photography and ancient road networks: a northern Mesopotamian case study' *Antiquity,* 77: 102-115

Wagner, J. 1976 *Seleukeia am Euphrat/Zeugma* Wiesbaden Ludwig Reichert

Weiss, H. 1983: '. Excavations at Tell Leilan and the origins of north Mesopotamian cities in the third millennium BC' *Paléorient,,* 9(2) 39-52.

Whitby, M. 1988 *The emperor Maurice and his historian* Oxford OUP

Whittaker, C. R. 1994 *Frontiers of the Roman Empire* Baltimore Johns Hopkins University Press pb 1997

Wilkinson, T. and Tucker, D. 1995 *Settlement development in the North Jazira, Iraq* Baghdad, London British School of Archaeology in Iraq

Wilkinson, T. J. 2003 *Archaeological landscapes of the Near East* Tucson University of Arizona

Wilkinson, T. J., Tucker, D.J. 1995 *Settlement development in the North Jazira, Iraq* Baghdad, London British School of Archaeology in Iraq

Wood, G. 2004: 'The Roman fort at Qubur al Bid, Mesopotamia' *Journal of Roman Archaeology,* 17: 397-404

Zachariah 1899 *The Syriac Chronicle known as that of Zachariah of Mitylene. Transl. by F. J. Hamilton & E. W. Brooks. London. Author also known as Zacharias Rhetor or Scolasticus* London

Placename Index